CHINA AND INDIA
ECONOMIC PERFORMANCE AND BUSINESS
STRATEGIES OF FIRMS IN THE MID-1990s

Also by Sam Dzever

AN APPRAISAL OF THE ROLE OF FOREIGN FIRMS IN THE
NIGERIAN TIN INDUSTRY

INDUSTRIAL BUYING BEHAVIOUR

*PERSPECTIVES ON ECONOMIC INTEGRATION AND BUSINESS
STRATEGY IN THE ASIA–PACIFIC REGION (*editor with*
Jacques Jaussaud)

Also by Jacques Jaussaud

*PERSPECTIVES ON ECONOMIC INTEGRATION AND BUSINESS
STRATEGY IN THE ASIA–PACIFIC REGION (*editor with*
Sam Dzever)

* *from the same publishers*

China and India Economic Performance and Business Strategies of Firms in the Mid-1990s

Edited by

Sam Dzever
Professor of Marketing and International Business
Université de Poitiers
France

and

Jacques Jaussaud
Associate Professor in Management
Université de Poitiers
France

First published in Great Britain 1999 by
MACMILLAN PRESS LTD
Houndmills, Basingstoke, Hampshire RG21 6XS and London
Companies and representatives throughout the world

A catalogue record for this book is available from the British Library.

ISBN 0–333–72974–9

First published in the United States of America 1999 by
ST. MARTIN'S PRESS, INC.,
Scholarly and Reference Division,
175 Fifth Avenue, New York, N.Y. 10010

ISBN 0–312–21556–8

Library of Congress Cataloging-in-Publication Data
China and India : economic performance and business strategies of
firms in the mid-1990s / edited by Sam Dzever and Jacques Jaussaud.
p.   cm.
Includes bibliographical references and index.
ISBN 0–312–21556–8 (alk. paper)
1. Investments, Foreign—China.   2. Investments, Foreign—India.
3. International business enterprises—China.   4. International
business enterprises—India.   5. Business planning—China.
6. Business planning—India.   I. Dzever, Sam, 1956–   .
II. Jaussaud, Jacques, 1957–   .
HG5782.C443   1998
332.67'3'0954—DC21   98–15612
                                                           CIP

This book is printed on paper suitable for recycling and made from fully managed and
sustained forest sources.

10   9   8   7   6   5   4   3   2   1
08   07   06   05   04   03   02   01   00   99

Printed and bound in Great Britain by
Antony Rowe Ltd, Chippenham, Wiltshire

Contents

List of figures and tables

FIGURES

TABLES

Notes on the contributors

Indru T. Advani, a French national, was born and raised in that part of undivided British India which is now called Pakistan. After graduating from Imperial College, London, Advani spent several years in Asia (the last 15 in the People's Republic of China) as the senior executive of a European conglomerate. He has retired from active service and now occupies the post of Honorary Délegué Géneral of Comité France–Chine in Paris, where he lives.

Bernadette Andréosso-O'Callaghan is Senior Lecturer and Vice-Dean (Research) at the University of Limerick, Ireland.

Jean-Pascal Bassino is Associate Professor of Economics at Paul Valéry University (Vauban campus), Nîmes, France. He is also Research Fellow at the Centre d'Economie et de Finances Internationales, a CNRS associated research unit. Dr Bassino has published widely in the areas of economic and financial analysis of Asian countries.

Pascale Boureille is a Researcher at the Université Pierre Mendès Grenoble II, France.

Charles R. Chittle is Professor of Economics at Bowling Green State University, Ohio, USA.

Michel Delapierre is a CNRS Research Fellow at the Centre de Recherche sur l'Entreprise Multinationale (FORUM), located at the University of Paris X, Nanterre. He has published widely in the area of Asian economies, including *Les Firmes Multinationales* (with Christian Milelli) (Paris: Vuibert, 1995).

Sam Dzever is Professor of Marketing and International Business at IAE, the University of Poitiers, France. His research focuses on industrial marketing and business strategy in the Asia-Pacific region. His most recent publications include: *Le Comportement d'Achat industriel* (Industrial Buying Behaviour) (Paris: Economica, 1996) and *Perspectives on Economic Integration and Business Strategy in the Asia-Pacific Region* (with Jacques Jaussaud (eds), Macmillan, 1997).

Jacques Jaussaud is Associate Professor of Management at IAE, the University of Poitiers, France. His research interests are in the areas of business strategy and human resources management (with a particular focus on Japan and Asian countries). He has published widely in these areas, including *Perspectives on Economic Integration and Business Strategy in the Asia-Pacific Region* (with Sam Dzever (eds), Macmillan, 1997). He is the editor of the French management journal, *Japon in Extenso*.

Kyoo H. Kim is Professor of Economics at Bowling Green State University, Ohio, USA.

Christian Milelli is a CNRS Research Fellow at the Centre de Recherche sur l'Entreprise Multinationale (FORUM), located at the University of Paris X, Nanterre. His research focuses on the strategy of multinational enterprises and the globalization of manufacturing operations. He has several publications in these fields, including *Les Firmes Multinationales* (with Michel Delapierre) (Paris: Vuibert, 1995).

Shyama V. Ramani is a Researcher at Institut National de la Recherche Agronomique (INRA), Grenoble, France.

Robert Taylor is Director of Chinese Studies at the University of Sheffield. He has taught at universities in Britain and overseas, and is the author of a number of studies of East Asia, including *Greater China in Japan* (Routledge, 1996).

Rene Teboul is Professor of Economics at Paul Valéry University, France.

Aline van Beveren is with the Chambre de Commerce et d'Industrie Franco-Chine, Paris.

M.S. Venkataramani is with the International Affairs Research Group, New Delhi, India.

Wang Zhengyi is an Associate Professor at Nankai University, the People's Republic of China.

Wei Qian is a PhD candidate at the University of Limerick, Ireland.

Editors' introduction

As we approach the twenty-first century, China and India are bound to rank among the world's most important economies. They are already regarded as important potential markets that neither mutinational firms nor smaller-sized companies can afford to ignore. Both economies are in the process of opening up to the outside world, production and incomes are growing, and foreign direct investment (FDI) is being encouraged. China has a population of 1.3 billion and India 930 million. Both countries are experiencing growth in per capita incomes, as well as increased consumer demand (the latter being especially the case in China). With these indicators, the two countries may be looked upon as the new El dorado for business. A list compiled by the United Nations (UN) in 1994 placed China in seventh position out of a total of 230 countries in terms of GNP growth, just behind the United Kingdom and ahead of Canada. India was ranked sixteenth on that list.[1]

This said, it must be added that both countries still have relatively low GNP per capita growth. On this point they were ranked 176th and 197th positions respectively on the UN list. Large parts of the population in both countries still have very low incomes. Inequalities in income distribution and geographical development still persists in both countries. It is important to bear this in mind when considering these markets.

Growth is clearly present in both countries, however. Average GDP growth rates reached 10.3 per cent per annum between 1981 and 1990 in China, and 5.6 per cent in India. As Table 1 shows, growth rates were at their highest from 1992 through 1995 in China, and 1993 through 1995 in India. Demands for infrastructural projects, industrial equipment, and consumer goods are growing at a rapid rate in both countries.

China and India have a lot in common: long histories, advanced civilizations, huge populations, and significant natural resources. Both countries have experienced colonialism, and experimented with planned economic systems (although, admittedly, in different ways). And both are now in the process of liberalizing their economies as they open up to foreign investment.

But the countries also have significant differences: India has never

xi

Table 1   China and India: selected indicators

	1991	1992	1993	1994	1995	1996	1997 (*)
China							
Growth rate of GDP (%)	9.3	14.2	13.5	11.8	10.2	9.7	9.0
Balance of trade (million US$)	8,743	5,183	–10,654	7,290	18,050	14,359	10,011
Foreign direct investment (million US$)	4,366	11,156	27,515	33,787	37,500	42,300	—
Debt service ratio (% of exports)	11.9	10.2	11.1	8.9	9.9	10.1	9.8
Overall deficit of central government (% of GDP)	–1.1	–1.0	–0.8	–1.2	–1.0	–0.2	—
India							
Growth rate of GDP (%)	0.8	5.1	6.2	7.2	7.1	6.8	7.0
Balance of trade (million US$)	–2,798	–4,368	–2,386	–4,990	–8,943	–8,094	–8,806
Foreign direct investment (million US$)	141	151	273	620	1,750		
Debt service ratio (% of exports)	30.2	28.6	26.9	27.5	25.7	27.1	28.1
Overall deficit of central government (% of GDP)	–5.9	–5.7	–7.4	–6.1	–5.8	–5.0	—

Source: Asian Development Outlook, 1997 & 1998, Asian Development Bank, Oxford University Press, 1997

(*) Data for 1997 are estimates.

experienced collectivism (neither in agriculture nor in other sectors), even though state-owned enterprises have dominated industry since the 1960s. Economic planning in India has never reached the level of centralization experienced in China. While China is a socialist state, India is the largest democracy in the world. Last but not least, the opening-up process for foreign investment is not at the same stage in the two countries. This is a very important issue and we shall take a closer look at it below.

Table 2 is a summary of the reforms undertaken in China and India from the late 1970s up to the present.

Starting with China, in 1978 Deng Xiaoping succeeded in persuading the Communist Party to accord economic growth its highest

Table 2   Economic reforms in China and India: an overview

China	India
1976 Mao ZeDong's death. End of the Cultural Revolution (1966–76).	*1984* Prime Minister Indira Gandhi assasinated (31/10). Her son Rajiv Gandhi takes over power.
1978 Deng Xiaoping starts the Economic Reforms. He launches the "four modernizations" programme (in agriculture, industry, sciences & techniques, national defence). Decollectivization of agriculture. Private enterprises authorized.	*1985* The government admits the failure of the Nehru (Prime Minister 1947–1964, father of Indira Gandhi) inspired model of "self-sufficient socialism". First attempt to lessen state control over production, and to open up the economy to the outside world: liberalization of import of certain industrial equipment.
1980 China enters the IMF. Special Economic Zones for foreign investment set up in Xiamen, Shenzen, Shantou, and Zhuhai provinces.	*1991* India faces a balance-of-payments crisis. IMF grants an emergency loan of US$150 million, and asks for further liberalization of the economy. Narashima Rao becomes Prime Minister. Economic Reform programme intensifies, including customs tariffs reductions, dismantling of import licence procedures, import of capital goods possible (even if same could be produced locally), opening up of several sectors of the economy to private investment (electricity generation, coal mining, telecommuncations, etc.).
1984 The Central Committee of the Communist Party decides to implement the reform of the economic system. 22 cities authorized to set up Technological and Economical Development Zones open to foreign investment.	
1986 Promulgation of law encouraging foreign direct investment.	
1989 Tiananmen repression. Li Peng becomes Prime Minister.	
1992 Deng Xiaoping visits south China, revamping the reform. Looking for a "socialist market economy".	
1993–94 Restrictive economic policy in order to lessen inflationnary tensions.	
1994 Fiscal and financial system reforms.	
1996 IXth Plan: reform of state owned enterprises.	
1997 Deng Xiaoping's death (19/02). Hong Kong reverts to China (01/07).	

priority. In the same year (two years after the death of Mao) the Cultural Revolution was largely acknowledged as unfortunate and a waste for the country. The reform introduced in the economy consisted primarily in the decollectivization of the agricultural sector, authorization of the participation of private enterprises in the economy, and the creation of "Special Economic Zones" for foreign investment. The first results being positive, the Central Committee of the Communist Party decided in 1984 to go ahead with further implementation of the reform policy in other sectors of the economy. Twenty-two "open coastal cities", stretching from Dalian in the north to Beihai in the south, were allowed to set up "technical and economic development zones" with special tax incentives for foreign investment. In the following year, new zones were further created in the Pearl and the Yangtze River deltas.

In this context of experimentation, FDI grew slowly during the 1980s. Political friction resulting from the Tienanmen repression also delayed some projects. But from 1991, FDI grew at a very rapid pace (US$3.49 billions in 1991, 42.3 billion in 1996). China was in 1996 the second most important FDI recepient country on a global scale, coming only after the United States.

Economic reform and the opening-up process have led to sustained growth, as can bee seen in Table 1. It is clear that growth of this nature benefits an increasing percentage of the populace. However, it is also clear that it does little to bridge the ever-widening gap between the rich and the poor in the country. Balance of trade has shown a healthy growth, thanks largely to the significant contributions to exports by foreign firms now established in the country. The major challenges facing the authorities, however, still remain in the areas of infrastructural development, the problem of geographical disparities, and the question of how to restructure the state enterprises without creating adverse social consequences.

In India, economic reform and the opening-up process have largely been accelerated by external pressures, and particularly so during the 1991 financial crisis. This is perhaps one of the major differences compared to the situation in China, where the process was largely driven by internal forces. Some observers expressed concern that economic reform in India could be slowed down because of social and political difficulties which might occur due to the liberalization process. But so far this has not proved to be the case. This is despite the fact that a new coalition government has been put into place following the general elections of 1996. We shall below take a closer look at the economic liberalization process in this country.

Rajiv Gandhi became the Prime Minister of India in 1985 following the assassination of his mother, Indira Gandhi. He immediately recognized the shortcomings of the Nehru-inspired model of "self-sufficient socialism" for India. The model was considered to be more or less responsible for the low growth of approximately 4 per cent – the so-called "Hindu rate of growth" – in an economy that needed much, much more. The new government tried to lessen excessive state control over production, and allowed higher imports of industrial equipment. As a result, there was a marked increase in imports, but at the same time exports plummeted, leading to significant balance-of-trade problems, growing external debts, and finally, the balance-of-payments crisis of 1991.

In the end, India turned to the IMF requesting an emergency loan of US$2.5 billion – it received US$150 million under the condition that it significantly restructure its economy and open it up to foreign investment.[2] Soon after, a 23 per cent devaluation of the rupee was implemented. The IMF demanded an additional liberalization programme (e.g., the easing-up of trade barriers, promotion of exports, and so on) as a condition for further financial support. Such demands were seen throughout India as unnecessary pressure, particularly in the light of the fact that the government had already decided, on its own initiative (and in full consultation with the business community), that such a programme was necessary given the country's economic situation. Narashima Rao, the new Prime Minister, thus had enough support to implement the programme.

The main measures undertaken in respect to the programme were the following: reduction of import duties (primarily on capital goods: maximum rate decreased from 400 per cent in 1990–1991 to 65 per cent in 1996, and average rate decreased from 33 per cent to 25 per cent), dismantling of the complicated import licensing system from April 1992, incentives to FDI, dismantling of the system of authorization for investment and new production decisions, tax reform (introduction of VAT), opening up to private investors sectors of the economy which were previously reserved for public companies (e.g. electricity generation, coal mining, telecommuncations), and the restructuring of state-owned enterprises. Today some positive results are already evident from these incentives. FDI is fast growing, and there has been a slowing down of the trade deficit (see

Table 1). Exports have been rising almost at the same pace as imports, the latter of which have been liberalized primarily for capital goods. Growth rates could reach higher levels compared to the previous decades.

India still faces a lot of difficulties, however. Public deficits are still high, both at the central and states levels. Successful restructuring of the state-owned enterprises is proving an arduous task as workers are heavily protected by labour laws and trade unions' vigilance. There is also the question of whether FDI will grow as quickly in India as it has done in China since there still exist some important constraints in the economy.

As already mentionned, observers fear that political willingness to strengthen economic reform in India may be lacking due to the so-called "true game of democracy". Where social unrest exists (which is the case regarding, for example, the restructuring of state-owned enterprises), ruling parties may prefer to delay implementation of unpopular programmes. This explains to some extent why economic reform and its consequences was very much a hot political issue during the general elections of April 96 which brought a new majority to power. The new government has already promised to press ahead with the liberalization programme already started.

Such is the general picture regarding economic restructuring and liberalization programmes undertaken in both countries. In order to obtain a more detailed picture of these issues and their impact on business strategy of firms in these markets, the reader is referred to the individual contributions that follow.

The present volume represents a selection of the contributions presented at the Third International Euro-Asia Research Conference held in Nantes, France, in November 1996. The conference was organized jointly by IAE – Université de Poitiers, and Groupe ESC Nantes Atlantique. The contributions are among the latest research findings concerned with the analysis of economic performance and business strategies of firms operating in these markets. They were each selected on the basis of two blind reviews, and each has been thoroughly revised and updated for the purpose of this volume.

The volume is divided into three parts. The first part is concerned with a comparative analysis of the economic performance and business strategies of firms operating in the two markets; while the second and third parts are country-specific and analyze the problem of economic performance and business strategies of firms operating in the respective countries.

THE PAPERS

Part I China and India: A Comparative Analysis of Economic Performance and Business Strategies of Firms

Charles R. Chittle and Kyoo H. Kim's contribution explores the impact of the economic environment in China and India on European, Japanese, and American businesses in these markets during the last two decades. The analysis is specifically concerned with FDIs. The authors examine specific environmental factors such as recent trade balances, the rates of inflation, economic growth rates, budget balances, exchange rates, political stability, economic policy orientation, government regulations, quality of the labour force, infrastructure facilities, possibilities of integrating production, and the legal systems. They conclude that the policies of economic liberalization recently introduced in both countries have considerably opened up these markets for foreign investors, and that most of the environmental factors mentioned above are no longer a major constraint to business. A challenge that still remains in both countries, however, is that which relates to how to increase overall productivity of resources, in the face of an expanding labour and capital market.

Bernadette Andréosso-O'Callaghan and Wei Qian compare European Union (EU) investments in China and India. With a relatively low share of FDI in China, the EU holds a large (but nevertheless decreasing) part of FDI in India. The authors compare sector orientation of EU FDIs in both countries, pointing out similarities and differences. They wonder whether differences between the two countries are primarily a result of the time lag in the implementation of economic reforms, or whether they are due to differences in the countries' industrial policies, or farther, due to the differences in incentives and priorities in the two recipient countries.

The authors conclude that infrastructural shortages are among the major challenges facing most rapidly developing economies, and that China and India are no exception to this problem. Infrastructural development requires significant capital commitment, and private investors have a lot to contribute in this area for both countries.

Indru T. Adavani analyzes Build-Operate-Transfer (BOT) projects in both China and India. He explains why inviting private capital (through BOT projects) is relevant for thermal power plants and telecommunications projects, but not for hydro-electric plants or mass-transit projects. China and India have both experienced significant private capital in infrastructural projects with positive results. The author points out, however, that there are limitations as to how much BOTs can be used as the basis for developing a country's infrastructure, citing the case of electricity generation in India as an example.

Part II Country-based Analysis – China

Michel Delapierre and Christian Milleli analyze the nature of economic relations between Japan and China. Using their empirical investigation, as well as data from the Japan Eximbank, the authors examine the main objectives of Japanese firms in the Chinese market, and the obstacles they face in operating in this environment. With regard to joint-venture enterprises, the authors find that the main difficulties relate to the Chinese partners (in most cases local authorities), who often are more concerned with the social ramifications of projects than simply their economic value. The deficiency of the legal framework is also a matter of major concern, although significant improvements have been introduced in the system since the last ten years.

Jean-Pascal Bassino and René Teboul investigate Japanese investment in China during the last two decades. They point out discrepancies between Japanese and Chinese statistical sources and undertake detailed analysis of the causes. They then provide an overall assesment of Japanese business strategies towards China. Japanese investors are very sensitive to risk, particularly the risk of excessive technology transfers. This explains why in some industries (for example, car manufacturing and electronics), Japanese companies do not carry out major investments even though they enjoy large market shares and growing consumer demand. The authors study both sectoral and geographical distribution of Japanese investments in China. They provide a useful insight into the question of the determinants of spatial dynamics of FDI in China.

Jacques Jaussaud analyzes the effects of horizontal *keiretsu* group relations on the strategies of the nine Japanese General Trading Companies (known *sôgô shôsha*) in the Chinese market. The research is based on an investigation of subsidiaries which have been set up in China by the general trading companies in joint ventureship with other Japanese firms. The following questions were central in the investigation: do Japanese partners in this market belong to the same multisectoral industrial grouping as the trading company? If so, does the joint-venture enterprise compete directly with members of the group to which the trading company belongs? Jaussaud finds that, contrary to the opinion of many commentators, group relations still matter a lot to Japanese firms when considering strategies towards the Chinese market.

Sam Dzever and Wang Zhengyi analyze the changes that have recently been introduced in the distribution channels for industrial products in the Chinese market and assess their overall impact on organizational buyer–seller relationships in this market. Data for the study were collected during the months of May through July 1996 and comprise 72 distributors (both private and government-owned) currently doing business in this market. The study addressed itself to the following specific issues: the nature and degree of competition between private distributors and state-owned purchasing agencies; the extent to which private distributors have equal access to foreign exchange (lack of foreign exchange is one of the major problems facing companies in this market) compared to the state-owned distributors (all foreign exchange requests are subject to government approval); the extent to which industrial distribution channels are now more efficiently run compared to the situation before the reform; import licences; the degree of freedom foreign suppliers have in choosing distributors in the market place; and the degree of government control over the running of the channels following the reform.

Taiwan has been a major investor in mainland China for a number of years now, although statistics show that only a part of the total flow as investments from this country are often officially recorded as coming from Hong Kong. Economic relations between Taiwan and the People's Republic of China (the PRC) have been strained in recent years for a number of reasons, among which should be mentioned the complex regulations (from both sides) regarding business relations, the absence of diplomatic relations, and many outstanding political issues.

Robert Taylor analyzes strategies of Taiwanese firms towards the Chinese market, particularly in relation to the economic and politic risks involved. The author studies the shift in strategy during the 1990s, from geographical concentration (Fujian and Guandong provinces) to more widely spread distribution, and from labour-intensive industries to capital-intensive ones. There is growing anxiety in Taiwan that close economic integration may strengthen the PRC's resolve to unify the two countries on its terms. On the assumption that this becomes a reality, Taylor maintains, Taiwan's industry may be hollowed out as its technological expertise and employments are transferred to the mainland.

Part III Country-based Analysis – India

Pascale Boureille studies the economic liberalization process in India, and its effects on FDI and external trade. The author introduces the reader to the major deregulation measures undertaken since the reform, and a breakdown of FDI by industrial sector. Boureille maintains that due to insufficient liberalization of the financial sector (and in the absence of sufficient public funds), foreign suppliers of heavy industrial equipment have gained considerable competitive advantage since they have their own sources of financing. This, however, leads to higher costs and import ratios, even though in some cases (such as electricity generation equipment) local producers offer higher quality products. This question was particularly topical during the general elections of 1996. The biggest foreign investment contract (signed between the Maharashtra State Electricity Board and the American Enron company) had to be renegotiated following the elections, in order to reduce the total cost of the project. Boureille maintains that liberalization of the financial sector will lessen the problem of unfair competition against local producers.

India is a country of cultural diversity and with a rich history. But it is very often percieved through stereotypes abroad, particularly in some European countries. Aline Van Beveren puts into perspective the economic liberalization process and points out which kinds of opportunities exist for foreign companies. The author then provides an appraisal of the current situation in major industrial sectors such as transportation, telecommunications, agriculture, and finance.

Shyama V. Ramani and M.S. Venkataramani analyze the possibilities of integrating biotechnology in the Indian pharmaceutical industry. They present the evolution of the Indian pharmaceutical industry since 1945 and the underlying domination of foreign multinational companies in this sector until the 1970s. The government enacted the Indian Patent Law in 1972, which protects production process but not the product itself. The authors emphasize the specificities of requested resources in the field of biotechnology (organization, finance, human resources), which very few Indian companies already have. On the basis of interviews with the executives of major Indian pharmaceutical firms, the authors distinguish six different types of strategies regarding innovation, and conclude that at the moment, very few companies can afford to adopt innovative strategies in the field of biotechnology in India.

Sam Dzever
Jacques Jaussaud

NOTES

[1] *AtlaSeco, 1997* (Paris: Les Editions O.C.) 1996.
[2] *Inde, un marché*, CFCE (Centre Français du Commerce Extérieur), Paris, 1995.

REFERENCES

Asian Development Bank, *Asian Development Outlook, 1997 & 1998*, Oxford University Press (China), 1997.
CFCE (Centre Français du Commerce Extérieur), *Chine, un marché*, Paris, 1997.
CFCE (Centre Français du Commerce Extérieur), *Inde, un marché*, Paris, 1995.
Dzever, Sam and Jaussaud, Jacques, *Perspectives on Economic Integration and Business Strategy in the Asia-Pacific Region* (Basingstoke: Macmillan, 1997).
The Economist, "India, a Survey", 1997 February 22–28.
Les Editions O.C., *AtlaSeco 1997*, Paris, 1996.
Martin, Jean-Louis, "Chine et Inde: quelles perspectives de croissance?" in "Risque Pays 1997", *Le MOCI* (Paris: CFCE, 1997).
Marie-Chantal Picques, *L'Art des affaires en Chine* (Arles (France): Editions Philippe Picquier, 1996).
Gao Shangquan and Chi Fulin, *Theory and Reality of Transition to a Market Economy* (Beijing: Foreign Language Press, 1995).

Part I

China and India: A Comparative Analysis of Economic Performance and Business Strategies of Firms

1 Foreign direct investment in China and India
The economic environment
Charles R. Chittle and Kyoo H. Kim

The increasing globalization of the world economy has stimulated the appetite of multinational enterprises for investing abroad, while at the same time it has forced host countries to create a more favorable environment for foreign direct investment (FDI). Net FDI in the developing countries was almost three times as large in 1991 as it was during all of the 1980s, while it increased by about 30 per cent in 1992 and 40 per cent in 1993.[1] FDI rose from 4 per cent of total net resource flows to developing countries in 1970 to 15 per cent in 1986 and 27 per cent in 1992.[2] World gross FDI inflows reached $315 billion in 1995, an increase of 40 per cent over the previous year. Inflows of FDI in the developing countries amounted to $100 billion in 1995, an increase of 15 per cent over the 1994 total. Of global FDI inflows in 1995, the industrialized countries received 65 per cent, the developing countries 32 per cent, and Central and Eastern Europe 4 per cent. FDI flows have a high degree of country concentration. About two-thirds of the outflow in 1995 came from five countries (the US, Germany, the UK, Japan, and France). The ten largest recipients of FDI inflows in 1995 also received about two-thirds of the total. China, the developing country with the largest inflow, accounted for 38 per cent of the total inflow to developing countries in 1995, while South, East, and Southeast Asia accounted for 65 per cent. Only the US received a larger inflow of FDI than China in 1995.[3]

In this chapter we explore the economic environment facing potential European Union, Japanese, and American foreign direct investors in China and India. These countries, from the standpoint of population, represent the world's largest country and the largest democracy, respectively. The analogies between the Chinese and Indian economies draw obvious comparison. Over the last two decades, both countries have experienced a dramatic change in economic policies. Each has moved from an economy with a pervasive government role to a more market-orientated economy in terms of openness, outward orientation, economic deregulation and liberalization.

We examine recent trade balances as well as other variables such as Chinese and Indian rates of inflation, economic growth rates, budget balances, and exchange rates. We also look at China and India from the standpoint of political stability, macro and micro economic policy orientation, as well as government regulations that may directly affect foreign direct investors. Further considerations important to foreign investors include the quality of the labor force, infrastructure facilities, possibilities for integrating production, and the legal system. While the motive for FDI was at one time primarily to serve the host country's domestic market, this investment has increasingly become an integral part of the overall scheme of multinational companies of minimizing overall costs of serving their various markets.

The policies of China and India regarding FDI have become significantly more liberal during the past several years. We compare the success of the two countries in attracting foreign investment, indicate reasons for the differences in inflows of FDI, suggest how the countries might improve their investment climate, and consider how Western firms and host countries might benefit from such investment.

CHINA: ECONOMIC ENVIRONMENT

The reform in China since the death of Mao has been truly spectacular. The first decade of reform (1978–1988) produced a two-and-one-half-fold multiplication of China's GDP, and a quintupling of foreign trade. The second decade (1988–1996) was also spectacular despite a brief pause caused by the Tiananmen event. The economic reforms led to a compound annual growth of national income of 10 per cent during the 1980s. Double-digit growth has continued during the first half of the present decade. During the first nine months of 1996 the GDP was up 9.6 per cent. China has also become a major world trader; it ranks among the top ten world exporters. It has had a balance of trade surplus during each year from 1990 to 1995. The trade surplus reached a record US$17 billion in 1995. Earlier fears that the trade surplus would vanish in 1996 are proving to be unfounded. Through the first nine months of 1996, the trade surplus amounted to $8.1 billion. Its large and growing trade surplus with the US has become a matter of concern in America.[4]

INDIA: ECONOMIC ENVIRONMENT

Post-World-War II economic growth in India was stagnant until the 1980s. This was mainly due to the protectionist and regulatory economic policies of the Indian government. India's industrial and economic policy relied on import substitution rather than export promotion and global trade. The overall effect of large-scale protectionism of Indian industries from foreign competition generated inefficiency of resource allocation. The result has been products of low quality and high cost. Also the government relied heavily on foreign aid, especially from the former Soviet Union, fatally mimicking its failed, centrally planned economy as the role model for India.

Following Rajiv Gandhi's assassination in 1991, India adopted a policy of economic liberalization, reversing the protectionist strategy. Industries under state monopoly have been opened to the private sector, while import and foreign investment controls have been significantly relaxed. A large area of the economy was opened to foreign investment. As a result, capital inflows have risen steadily since 1991. GDP growth in the 1990s is averaging more than 4 per cent. This is less than in the Far Eastern economic super-performers but is an improvement over the previous three decades. The collapse of the former Soviet Union has contributed to an improvement in relations with the West. Corruption continues to have a retarding effect on economic performance and contributed to a recent change in government. The new prime minister, H.D. Deve Gowda, has put reduction of the nation's large budget deficit high on its list of economic policy objectives. Although tax rates are being reduced and government spending increased, an objective is to reduce the budget deficit from 5.9 per cent of GDP in 1996 to 5.0 per cent in 1997. This implies that the government is optimistic regarding the pace of economic expansion.

FOREIGN DIRECT INVESTMENT POLICIES OF CHINA AND INDIA

Our focus is on inward FDI for both China and India. In India's case, the government has regulated the inflow of FDI through a highly selective policy. The Industrial Policy Statements of 1980 and 1982, for example, announced a liberalization of industrial licensing (approval) rules, a host of incentives, and exemption from foreign equity restrictions under the Foreign Exchange Regulation Act to 100 per cent export-orientated units. The trade policies in this period gradually liberalized the imports of raw materials and capital goods by expanding the list of items on Open General License. Tariffs on imported capital goods were also slashed. Exemptions from the general ceiling of 40 per cent on foreign equity were allowed based on the merits of individual investment proposals. Approvals for opening liaison offices by foreign companies were liberalized and procedures for the outward remittance of royalties and technical fees were streamlined. A "fast channel" was set up in 1988 for expediting the clearance of FDI proposals from Japan, Germany, the US and the UK. Bhagwati (1993) has termed these policy changes as neither "credible" nor "momentum-giving" reforms because they were not comprehensive in their scope and did not go far enough to make a significant impact.

The election of the Rao government in India led to reforms in 1991–1993 that are dramatically different from the earlier reforms. The FDI investment climate has considerably improved. The policies initiated by Rao are starting to pay off with a sharp increase in FDI. India has taken steps to open power and telecommunications projects to foreigners, speeded approval of manufacturing investments by foreign and domestic investors, and reduced import barriers on everything from garments to computers. In 1994, FDI reached $620 million, up from $151 million in 1992. In 1995, the inflow of FDI more than doubled to $1.75 billion. As a share of GDP, the stock of FDI was 0.7 per cent in 1980, 0.5 in 1985 and 1990, and 0.9 in 1994.[5] Multinationals now see India as a good bet in spite of political uncertainties. The general election in April 1996 produced a new prime minister, H.D. Deve Gowda, supported by a 13-party coalition. His finance minister, P. Chidambaram, recently announced that foreign institutions are permitted to raise their portfolio holdings in a single Indian company to 10 per cent of its equity, up from the current 5 per cent. Foreign investors will also be allowed for the first time to buy shares in unlisted Indian companies. In an effort to boost private investment in infrastructure, Mr Chidambaram revealed a plan to offer long-term government loans to domestic and foreign investors. The finance minister has pledged to attract $10 billion in FDI in 1996, up from $1.75 billion on 1995 (*Wall Street Journal*, various issues). Whether or not his pledge will succeed depends on various uncertain political and economic conditions, including the pace of reforms. But the point is that the reforms that began in the early 1990s are continuing. The government has issued a list of 36 industries for which automatic approval for foreign technical agreement and for 51 per cent foreign equity is permitted.[6]

Unlike India, China has not experienced democracy, which may make for greater instability as it faces the challenges of reform. However, China has gained much ground against rival India. After decades of isolation, China decided to open up to FDI in 1979 by creating special economic zones (SEZs) in coastal provinces. The advantages of SEZs for foreign investors come from both their geographic proximity to Hong Kong and their lower labor costs compared to neighboring Asian countries. Since then China has gradually adopted a number of policies to improve its investment climate and its attractiveness to foreign investors. The competitiveness of domestic enterprises has been systematically upgraded because of a decentralization of economic decision making and the introduction and extension of the market mechanism. The stock of FDI amounted to more than $60 billion at the end of 1993, while China has ranked second in the world since 1993 as a recipient of FDI annually, being exceeded only by the United States. The ratio of the stock of inward FDI to China's GDP increased from 1.2 per cent in 1985 and 3.8 per cent in 1990 to 17.9 per cent in 1994.[7] FDI became the single most important source of external capital for China, although up to one-fourth of the recorded flows of FDI may have consisted of recycled funds of Chinese firms. Of developing countries, China has received the largest amount of FDI since 1992.[8]

IMPLICATIONS

With a decrease in the rate of fiscal deficit to GDP from over 7 per cent in 1994 to below 6 per cent in 1996, the Indian government displayed a crucial plank in its drive to liberalize the economy, signaling to foreign investors that Indian market reform will continue. With larger outlays for agricultural subsidies, infrastructure, and education, total spending will increase 13 per cent for the fiscal year ending March 1997 from the previous fiscal year. But thanks to economic growth and a wider tax base, government revenues are projected to grow by 16 per cent, resulting in a drop in the fiscal deficit in 1996 and a further decline to 5 per cent of GDP in 1997.

Both India and China have attracted massive FDI in recent years and offer an immense market. But domestic markets need to be supplemented with foreign markets. International markets are vitally important; they determine the size of the future domestic market as well. Both countries' effective shift to globalization, with the removal of the inward-orientated bias of the pre-reform economic policies, should create the framework for substantial and continued inflows of investments. Japan, the EU and the US can play an important role for both China and India, as major sources of FDI and technology. India's foreign trade has followed a pattern of chronic deficits, as did China's until 1990 (see Tables 1.1 and 1.2). Unlike Japan, which runs on average a trade surplus, China and India cannot finance more imports by simply eliminating trade barriers from their liberalization policies. Their domestic savings, given the level of domestic investment, are not sufficient. Importing more would require additional capital inflows – for example, through greater inward FDI. Each country has attracted more FDI in the past five years than ever before. But some adjustments in the direction of FDI in both China and India are called for.

Japan might be more attractive to India than to China, first, because Japan does not have any past historical animosity with India through World War II, and second, because Japan wants increasingly to play an international role in Asia, as the United States is doing in South America and the EU in Africa. On the other hand, China is more interested in the EU than in Japan, precisely because of its bad memories with Japan that would cause the Chinese to worry about Japanese dominance. So FDI from the EU is likely to be seen as an important countervailing or balancing measure by China.

Do China and India receive a fair share of the FDI from the EU, Japan, and the United States? Perhaps surprisingly, there is empirical evidence that China receives less FDI from the EU and

Table 1.1 Selected economic indicators for India (1978–1993)

Year	Per capita GNP (US$)	GDP (billions of 1987 Indian rupees)	GDP deflator (1987 = 100)	Budget deficit (−) or surplus (billions of Indian rupees)	Exports (billions of US$)	Imports (billions of US$)	Foreign exchange rate (Indian rupees per US dollar)	Labor force participation rate (%)	Secondary school enroll. ratio
1978	190	2,314	45	−51	8.9	10.4	8.2	38.7	28.0
1979	210	2,192	52	−63	10.8	13.6	8.1	38.7	30.0
1980	250	2,337	58	−89	12.3	18.1	7.9	38.5	32.0
1981	280	2,490	64	−87	12.3	18.1	8.9	38.5	34.0
1982	270	2,585	69	−107	11.8	17.5	9.6	38.4	35.0
1983	270	2,776	75	−133	12.8	18.5	10.3	38.5	35.0
1984	270	2,879	80	−176	13.7	19.7	11.9	38.4	37.0
1985	280	3,034	86	−226	13.3	21.5	12.2	38.4	38.0
1986	290	3,181	92	−272	14.1	22.5	12.8	38.4	39.0
1987	330	3,332	100	−278	16.7	25.8	13.0	38.4	38.0
1988	380	3,664	108	−321	18.6	29.9	14.5	38.3	41.0
1989	370	3,905	117	−362	21.6	31.8	16.7	38.3	43.0
1990	370	4,108	130	−435	24.1	37.0	17.9	38.2	43.0
1991	330	4,139	149	−358	24.1	29.9	24.5	38.2	43.0
1992	330	4,328	163	−366	25.3	32.2	26.4	38.1	43.0
1993	300	4,450	177	−372	29.5	34.0	31.4	38.0	43.0

Source: The World Bank, World Tables, Johns Hopkins University Press, 1995

Table 1.2 Selected economic indicators for China (1978–1993)

Year	Per capita GNP (US$)	GDP (billions of 1987 Chinese yuan)	GDP deflator (1987= 100)	Government budge (billions of Chinese yuan)	Exports (billions of US$)	Imports (billions of US$)	Foreign exchange rate (yuan per dollar)	Labor force participation rate (%)	Secondary schl. enroll. ratio
1978	..	501	72	..	10.4	12.4	2.5	54.4	63.0
1979	..	539	74	..	15.4	18.5	2.3	55.0	56.0
1980	280	586	76	..	20.9	24.8	2.2	55.8	46.0
1981	290	610	78	..	25.1	24.4	2.5	56.4	..
1982	280	659	79	..	24.7	19.5	2.6	56.9	36.0
1983	280	726	80	..	24.7	21.0	2.6	57.6	35.0
1984	310	831	83	..	28.7	27.1	2.8	58.1	37.0
1985	350	938	91	..	29.6	41.3	2.9	58.8	39.0
1986	380	1,018	95	..	30.7	38.1	3.5	59.0	42.0
1987	390	1,131	100	..	40.2	40.0	4.5	59.2	43.0
1988	400	1,259	112	..	47.4	51.6	4.9	59.3	45.0
1989	390	1,311	122	..	49.7	54.4	4.9	59.6	46.0
1990	410	1,363	136	-36	60.4	48.7	5.2	59.9	48.0
1991	440	1,478	147	-49	69.6	57.2	5.7	59.9	51.0
1992	470	1,690	158	..	84.4	79.2	6.4	59.9	..
1993	490	1,927	177	..	91.2	104.0	8.0	60.0	53.0

Note .. = no data

Source: The World Bank, World Tables, Johns Hopkins University Press, 1995

the US than might be expected based on certain characteristics of host countries, including economic size, level of development, level of human capital, and geographic location. However, the inflow of FDI from Japan exceeds the "normal" amount. We have constructed a deviation table (see Table 1.3) of actual FDI from the predicted FDI for India and China in 1990, which is based on Shang-Jin Wei's regression results.[9] For example, China received 88 per cent less investment by Germany than expected in 1990, based on its economic characteristics. On the other hand, FDI in China by Japan was 25 per cent greater than predicted. A similar pattern exists with respect to Japan's share of the stock of FDI. In so far as the stock of FDI is concerned, additional data available for the US and France indicate that FDI by the US was close to 90 per cent less than expected, while that by France fell short of expectations by 3 per cent. FDI flows to India from Germany and Japan were, respectively, 73 per cent and 71 per cent less than predicted. In contrast, the flow of FDI from the US was 76 per cent greater than expected, while that from the UK exceeded expectations by 35 per cent. The pattern of the stock of FDI presents a somewhat different picture, especially concerning the US. The stock of FDI by the US was 50 per cent less than the predicted amount.

The absence of reliable legal and secure property rights and vast differences in culture help to explain China's below par performance in attracting FDI from Western countries. The UK's long involvement in India is a factor in its strong FDI inflow in India. America's less than expected stock of FDI in India may reflect India's friendly relations with the USSR during the Cold War. As the Cold War wound down and US–Indian relations became more cordial, the flow of FDI from the US exceeded the predicted level. India's long history of private property, democracy, and freedom for creative activities, and a skilled labor force, should prove attractive for foreign investors in India as the benefits of economic liberalization continue to expand. India's labor force is also relatively attractive to foreign investors. According to the results of a survey of 223 expatriate managers based in Asia, India's workforce scored highest among 16 Asian and Western countries in terms of quality, cost, availability, and turnover.[10]

Table 1.3 Deviation of actual from predicted foreign direct investment (percentages)

Source country	China Flow	China Stock	India Flow	India Stock
France	—	–3	—	—
Germany	–88	–74	–73	–4
UK	—	—	35	17
Japan	25	62	–71	–60
US	—	–89	76	–50

Source: Calculated from data in Shang-Jin Wei, "Attracting Foreign Investment: Has China Reached its Potential?" *China Economic Review*, 6, 2 (1995)

CONCLUSIONS

China and India are two giants on the world stage. Their populations, areas, labor forces, international capital flows, and national outputs are immense. Their rates of economic growth are impressive. They have relatively stable political environments. They have a vast potential to attract foreign investment to serve the local market and to become a more important part of the global integration that is taking place.

Foreign direct investment has become more important to China and India, as well as to other countries, in recent years. Global FDI increased rapidly during the 1990s. Policies of economic liberalization, including foreign trade and investment policies, macroeconomic stabilization, economic growth, and infrastructure improvement in China and India have encouraged the inflow of foreign capital, especially foreign direct investment. A challenge for these Asian giants is to increase the overall productivity of their resources in addition to the expansion of labor and capital. The share of European firms in the FDI in these two countries appears to have been less than its potential. This in turn implies that firms in Europe may be missing out on some good opportunities to increase their own wealth and contribute to an increase in welfare outside of Europe as well. European firms may make up for lost ground in the future as a result of a number of programs the EU has designed to encourage FDI in Asia. These programs include the following:

- *The Asia-Investment Program,* which consists of instruments to promote business contacts between EU and Asian companies;
- *The European Community Investment Partners,* which supports the formation of joint ventures between EU and Asian partners; and
- *Financing Facilities of the European Investment Bank,* through which the bank engages in investment projects in Asia involving EU and Asian firms.[11]

APPENDIX I

Table 1.4 Inward foreign direct investment for China and India (1979–1993) (millions of US$)

Year	Contracted	Actual	Contracted	Actual inflow
	(China)		(India)	(*millions of SDRs)
1979–1982 (Cumulative)	6,999	1,767		
1983	1,917	916		60*
1984	2,875	1,419		62*
1985	6,333	1,959		152*
1986	3,330	2,244		172*
1987	4,319	2,647		
1988	6,191	3,739		
1989	6,294	3,773		
1984–89 Annual average	4,890	2,282		133
1990	6.987	3,487		162
1991	12,422	4,366		141
1992	58,736	11,156		151
1993	110,850	25,515		273
1979–1993 (Cumulative)	220,630	60,210		
1994		33,787	4,500	620
1995		37,500	10,000	1,750

Sources: Lardy, *China in the World Economy,* Institute for International Economics, 1994; United Nations, *Foreign Direct Investment and Technology Transfer in India,* United Nations, 1992; United Nations, *World Investment Report 1996,* 1996

NOTES

[1] Joel Bergsman and Xiafang Shen, "Foreign Direct Investment in Developing Countries: Progress and Problems," *Finance and Development*, 32(4) (December 1995) pp. 6–8.
[2] Malcom Gillis, Dwight H. Perkins, Michael Roemer, and Donald R. Snodgrass, *Economics of Development*, 4th edn (New York: W.W. Norton & Co., 1996).
[3] United Nations, *World Investment Report 1996* (New York and Geneva, 1996) p. xiv.
[4] Sophie Roell, "China: Urban Residents Growing Poorer," *Financial Times*, electronic edn (24 October 1996).
[5] United Nations, *op. cit.* p. 270.
[6] Wordservice International, "India: Poised for Growth," *World Trade*, 9(10) (October 1996) p. 75.
[7] United Nations, *op. cit.* p. 270.
[8] Nicholas R. Lardy, "Economic Engine?" *The Brookings Review*, 14(1) (Winter 1996) pp. 10–15.
[9] Shang-Jin Wei, "Attracting Foreign Direct Investment: Has China Reached its Potential?" *China Economic Review*, 6(2) (1995) pp. 187–199.
[10] "Asia's Costly Labour Problems," *The Economist* (21 September 1996) p. 62.
[11] United Nations, *op cit.* p. 53.

BIBLIOGRAPHY

Bergsman, Joel and Xiafang Shen, "Foreign Direct Investment in Developing Countries: Progress and Problems," *Finance and Development*, 32(4) (December 1995): 6–8.
Bhagwati, Jagdish, *India in Transition: Freeing the Economy*, Oxford: Clarendon Press, 1993.
The Economist, various issues.
Gillis, Malcolm, Dwight H. Perkins, Michael Roemer, and Donald R. Snodgrass, *Economics of Development*, 4th edn (New York: W.W. Norton & Co., 1996).
Lardy, Nicholas R., *China in the World Economy*, Institute for International Economics (Washington, DC: 1994).
Lardy, Nicholas R., "Economic Engine?" *The Brookings Review*, 14(1) (winter 1996): 10–15.
Roell, Sophie, "China: Urban Residents Growing Poorer," *Financial Times*, electronic edn (24 October 1996).
United Nations, *Foreign Direct Investment and Technology Transfer in India* (New York: United Nations, 1992).
United Nations, *World Investment Report 1996* (New York and Geneva: United Nations, 1996).

The Wall Street Journal, various issues.
Wei, Shang-Jin, "Attracting Foreign Direct Investment: Has China Reached its Potential?" *China Economic Review*, 6(2) (1995): 187–199.
World Bank, *World Tables* (Baltimore: Johns Hopkins University Press, 1995).
Worldservice International, "India: Poised for Growth," *World Trade*, 9(10) (October 1996): 74–76.

2 EU foreign direct investment and technology transfer in Asia
China and India compared

B. Andréosso-O'Callaghan and Wei Qian[1]

With 40 per cent of the world's population, India and China are potentially both the world's largest markets and the biggest host countries for EU foreign direct investment (FDI). Investment from abroad has been a major driving force in the attainment of high growth rates in these countries.[2] The attraction of inward investment has occurred as a result of unprecedented programmes of economic reforms, which were facilitated by the phenomenon of trade liberalization and globalization of both production and investment. It became clear to both the Chinese and Indian governments that their economic take-off could only be achieved by attracting technology-embodied foreign investment. Given their size and their level of development,[3] China and India are apparently direct competitors for FDI.

In 1995, of the $2 billion FDI flows to the South Asian region,[4] nearly two-thirds went to India (Haniffa, 1996a). However, in spite of its being well positioned in the South Asian region, India compares rather weakly in relation to other East and South-east Asian countries. Indeed, despite the fact that foreign investment in India nearly doubled to $2 billion in the year to 31 March 1996, this amount corresponds approximately to what China gets every three weeks. Beyond the large disparities that contrast China and India in their roles and strategies related to FDI, one is compelled to highlight the many interesting characteristics shared by these countries. The aim of this chapter is to analyse similarities and differences between the two countries, in the context of their technological and investment relations with the European Union.

The poor performance of EU direct investment in Asia has been widely noted and decried. Already small compared with overseas Chinese,[5] Japanese and US investments in Asia as a whole, EU foreign investment in the two countries selected appears even more marginal. Between 1990 and 1994, EU firms invested a total of 7.5 billion ECU in Asia. Of that, Malaysia, the Philippines, and Thailand absorbed 44 per cent. In 1993, China received less than 7 per cent of total EU investment, but 14.4 per cent of all US investment in Asia.[6] India absorbs less than 0.5 per cent of all EU investment (one of the lowest shares) and Malaysia, with 19.6 of the EU total, represents the major destination for EU FDI in Asia (European Report, 1996).

The EU lag in terms of FDI must be assessed in the reality of the immense potential represented by the two biggest economies in the world in the long term. We will first analyse the flows and patterns of EU FDI over a given number of years, as well as the major elements of the enabling policies in the two countries. Whenever possible, a particular emphasis will be placed on technology-embodied FDI, or technology transfer.

FDI AND TECHNOLOGY TRANSFER TRENDS IN CHINA AND INDIA – CONTRASTS AND SIMILARITIES

FDI is distinct from portfolio investment and refers in this chapter to a foreign firm's equity participation in an Indian or in a Chinese company. Technology transfer refers to the spatial diffusion of technology. It encompasses licensing agreements, patents, know-how, design, trade marks, models, and different services (such as technical studies, technical assistance), and R&D.

This section will look at FDI flows in the two countries under review and will identify the major investors. It will then briefly review the major aspects of the policies put in place by the two governments to attract FDI, and then appraise the major entry barriers facing would-be investors into the two markets.

The magnitude of FDI flows and the significance of the EU as an investor

India's opening up to FDI, an integral part of its economic liberalization process, has produced dramatic results. Prior to the economic reforms introduced in July 1991, FDI flows into India were

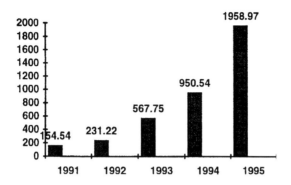

Source: Reserve Bank of India

Figure 2.1 Total FDI in India (inflows) (US$ million)

barely US$100–$200 million a year. But since 1991 there has been a significant increase in FDI, with both approvals and actual inflows recording phenomenal growth, as Figure 2.1 shows.

Actual FDI in India has increased 13-fold between 1991 and 1995, when it reached nearly US$2 billion. However, in spite of this spectacular increase, India lags well behind China as a host country in terms of FDI. In 1995, realized FDI in China totalled $38 billion, a figure up 11.65 per cent on the 1994 figure (EIU, 1996). This is 16 times more than what India got in that year. Adjusting for the size of the countries, China received $31.6 of direct investment per capita of the population, whereas India received only $2.5. As we will see later, the delayed opening-up of the Indian economy to foreign investors only partly explains this first major difference between the two countries.

Types of investors

The "FDI gap" between the EU and its Japanese and US competitors, on the Asian market as a whole, has been widely acknowledged (CEC, 1994; CEC, 1995).[7] Being the smallest investor of the three, the EU is only marginally involved in Asia. According to EU sources,[8] less than 4 per cent of the EU's total FDI stock is in Asia and the Pacific area, against 7.2 and 11.7 per cent for the US and Japan respectively. Is this lack of dynamism valid for the two individual countries under review here?

In terms of investors' categories, China and India combine a

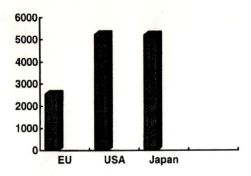

Source: Adapted from CEC (1995)

Figure 2.2 FDI in China by investing country (1979–1993) (used capital in US$ million)

Table 2.1 FDI flows in China from the triad (US$ millions and percentages)

Country	1980 Value	Share of total	1985 Value	Share of total	1993 Value	Share of total
EU	300	13.6	584	8.3	2,018	3.5
USA	128	5.8	502	7.2	4,288	7.5
Japan	372	16.9	1,106	15.8	4,680	8.2
Total triad	800	36.3	2,192	31.2	10,986	19.2
All countries	2,202	100.0	7,015	100.0	57,172	100.0

Source: European Report, 20 March 1996, no. 2117, pp. 9–10

common characteristic, which is the relative importance of overseas Chinese and Indian investment flows. Non-resident Indians (NRIs) are a distinct category of investors in India. This group has accounted for a third of total capital inflows since 1993. The share of overseas Chinese investing in China is very large, reaching more than three-quarters of total direct investment. When these two categories of investors are excluded, the major investors, by country of origin, are shown in Figures 2.2–2.4 and Tables 2.1–2.2.

Although investment *flows* in East and South-east Asia[9] over the 1990/93 period show that EU firms compare quite well in relation to their US and Japanese counterparts, the very small involvement of EU firms on the Chinese market, and moreover their declining

Table 2.2 FDI flows in India from the triad (1991–1995)

% of total	1991	1992	1993	1994	1995
EU-15	39.8	30.5	26.8	33.2	11.6
USA	9.3	17.4	26.8	11.3	10.3
Japan	2.2	10.7	3.8	9.2	3.4
NRIs	45.6	22.2	32.5	38.9	30.9
Others	3.1	19.2	10.1	7.4	43.8
Total	100.0	100.0	100.0	100.0	100.0

Source: Authors' calculations based on SIA Newsletter, Ministry of Industry, Government of India, various issues

share of total investment in China since the beginning of the economic reforms, is a subject for increasing concern (Table 2.1). EU investment in China is less than half that of either US or Japanese investment in the region. These figures point to the increasing lethargy of European firms on the Chinese market, especially when one takes into account the increasing role of US firms which have succeeded in establishing a strong foothold in the region.

However, figures on FDI approvals and flows in India would tend to portray a more nuanced picture (Table 2.2 and Figures 2.3 and 2.4). Given that India is a former British dominion, European FDI (essentially British) was the single most important source of foreign investment in India up until the beginning of the economic reforms. However, the share of the EU in the total FDI flows declined from 39.8 per cent in 1991 to 11.6 per cent in 1995 (Table 2.2). Although FDI flows from both the US and Japan have fluctuated during the period under review, both countries have managed to consolidate the share they held at the beginning of the period. What is noticeable in the case of the EU-15 is a continuous declining trend, with a slight and short-term upsurge in 1994. With more than 30 per cent of all investment flows in the country, the NRIs are by far the biggest category of investors in India.

If, at the beginning of the period (1991–1993), FDI tends to originate from a few selected sources (UK-EU, USA, and NRIs), the latter part of the period shows a diversification of investing countries, with the entry of new firms from other Asian countries (Malaysia, the Philippines, Thailand, Taiwan), from Eastern Europe (Estonia, Ukraine, Hungary, and Russia), from Israel, and from a myriad of islands (Cyprus, the Channel Islands, the Bahamas, Bermuda, British Virgin Islands, and Mauritius). FDI from this latter

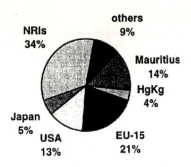

Source: Author's calculations based on *Secretariat of Industry Approvals (SIA) Newsletter*, India, January 1996

Figure 2.3 Cumulated FDI inflows in India, by country of origin (1991–1995)

group of countries is explained to a large extent by the special tax regimes implemented by these islands.

In particular, the relatively high share of Mauritius, representing 14 per cent of FDI flows in India during the period 1991–1995, should be interpreted with care. India has signed a favourable tax treaty with Mauritius, enabling the country to be used as a tax haven by foreign companies investing in India (see Appendix).[10] High tax costs can thus be reduced by opting for an offshore investment structure involving countries that have favourable tax treaties with India.

With nearly 3.7 per cent of all FDI flows during the period 1991–1995, Hong Kong is another important investor in India (Figure 2.3).

Leaving Mauritius and the NRIs aside, the EU-15 as a whole still precariously holds its predominant role as a major investor in India.

Among the EU countries, the UK still has the lion's share in terms of European investment in India (Figure 2.4). FDI from the UK represented 37.7 per cent of EU investment in India during the 1991–1995 period (and 7.9 per cent of the total). The other most active EU investors in India are: Germany (20.5 per cent of the EU total), the Netherlands (16.9), Sweden (4.4 per cent) and Denmark (with 3.6 per cent).

In recent years, German firms, such as the car manufacturer Mercedes-Benz, have been the most dynamic EU investors in India. In October 1995, the first Indian manufactured Mercedes-Benz

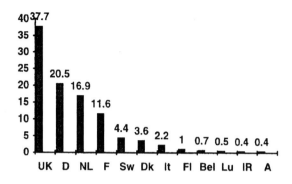

Source: SIA based calculations – *SIA Newsletter*, January 1996

Figure 2.4 FDI flows in India, relative share of each EU country in the EU total, 1991–1995, cumulated

E-220 was produced as a result of a milestone agreement between two corporate giants in India and Germany. The deepening economic relationship between India and Germany is reflected by the rising number of German banks operating in India. Apart from Deutsche Bank – Germany's largest bank, which has increased its branches in India to five from three – the Dresdner Bank and the Commerzbank are also increasing their presence in India. In addition, the B.H. Bank and the Bayerische Vereinsbank have opened offices in Bombay. The Kreditanstalt für Wiederaufbau, a "soft-loan" bank, has also started an operation in Delhi. In April 1996, the Anglo-Dutch consumer goods group Unilever announced a merger of its two main Indian subsidiaries, Hindustan Lever (soap maker) and Brooke Bond Lipton India (Food-drinks). This would create India's second largest private company, in terms of sales, second to the Indian Reliance Industries (*Far Eastern Economic Review*, 1996).

The shares of France and Italy, at 11.6 per cent and 2.2 per cent respectively, are quite deceiving for two among the four largest EU economies. The share of France is less than that of the Netherlands in absolute terms, and less than that of Denmark and Sweden in relative terms. French investment in India has been sluggish, as summarised by the following quotation: "French companies have been losing the race in India's burgeoning infrastructure market to the US, Japan and other European companies due to their wait and watch policy" (*India News Network Digest*, 1996).

Industrial sectors

In 1994, more than 42 per cent of EU total investment in Asia was in mining and quarrying (ECU 1,210 million), with another 29 per cent in the manufacturing sector (ECU 824 million).[11] Given their relatively similar levels of economic development, one would expect that China and India would both predominantly be host to investment in the primary (extractive) and secondary sectors, if we follow the logical "investment development paths" put forward by Dunning (1981) and Ozawa (1992).[12]

Although the EU is still the biggest investor in India (exclusion being made of the NRIs), its presence is essentially confined to the traditional sectors (fuels, metallurgical industries, fertilizers and chemicals) and is much less high-tech-orientated than US investment. Despite the upsurge of German banking activities, the services sector (including consultancy) is still primarily in the hands of US firms. The same can be said about the computer software industry, where the US share is close to 38 per cent of the total invested from abroad. In the "hotel and tourism" sub-sector, more than 50 per cent of investment originates from Thailand, Hong Kong, and Singapore, in spite of the Irish breakthrough at 8.6 per cent of the total. The exception to the rule above is mechanical engineering, a sector where the reputation of German firms translates into a well-established leadership.

The EU is conspicuous by its absence in the industrial sector that attracted the bulk of FDI since the reforms: the EU (and especially France) have definitely missed the telecommunications race up to now, leaving most of the sector to Israel, the USA, and other Asian countries (Table 2.3).

Statistics on the sectoral breakdown of FDI in China do not unfortunately display the same level of detail. However, basic information gathered on the relative performance of the industries in terms of FDI shows that China has progressed quite smoothly on the FDI path, moving from natural-based to innovation-driven industries. Up to now, the largest amount of overseas investment has been in the energy sector, and the real estate sector accounted for the next largest amount of foreign investment. The 1990s initiated a complete change in the FDI patterns, with a definite commitment to deploy the technology-orientated industries (see below).

Table 2.3 Sectoral breakdown of FDI approvals[13] in India (August 1991 to January 1996)

Industrial sector	Share in total FDI (in %)	Major investing countries (ranked by order of importance)
Telecommunications	30.4	Israel, USA, Thailand, Malaysia
Fuels	19.5	USA, UK, Switzerland, Oman
Metallurgical industries	6.8	Australia, Germany, UAE, Italy
Chemicals*	6.1	USA, UK, Japan, Switzerland
Services**	5.5	USA, NL, UK, Hong Kong
Transport	5.0	USA, Germany, Japan, France
Electrical equipment & computer software, etc.	4.8	USA, Germany, Japan, UK
Food processing	3.9	USA, Thailand, Italy, NL
Hotel & tourism	3.2	Thailand, Hong Kong, Singapore, Ireland
Mechanical engineering***	3.2	Germany, USA, Switzerland, NL
Textiles	2.6	USA, Italy, Switzerland, S. Korea
Others	9.0	

Note: * Other than fertilizers. ** Other than Hotel & tourism and consultancy services. *** Essentially industrial machinery.

Source: *SIA Newsletter*, Ministry of Industry, India, February 1996

Summary

Although India is a "first-phase FDI recipient", in that most investors concentrate on selling on the expanding domestic market, the country seems to be moving very fast along the FDI developmental path. Total FDI in the traditional sectors – fuels, metallurgical, textiles, and some segments of the chemicals industry – represent today only 35 per cent of the total. Telecommunications, electrical equipment, and mechanical engineering capture 38.4 per cent of the total invested. The share of the services sector increases smoothly with the expansion of India's financial base and the development of the tourism industry. Less than a third of FDI is in other non-high-tech (but not necessarily traditional) industries (food-processing for example). In spite of the British historical dominance in India in terms of FDI, EU investment is essentially concentrated in the traditional sectors, and is almost absent from the telecommunications sector.

China, as a more mature FDI recipient, attracts more investment in the sunrise sectors. Totally in opposition to the Indian situation, the EU, a relatively small investor in China, tends to invest more in the high-tech sectors than its Japanese or American counterparts.

It is useful to understand the causes of the different degrees of openness to foreign investment in the various industries of the two countries, as well as the qualitative difference in EU investment in both countries. Are these differences due to a perception of different international specializations, to the time lag in the implementation of the economic reforms, to different industrial policies, or to different types of incentives or priorities? This is the theme of the next paragraph.

Policies in place: an attractive package for investors?

Both countries have been able to offer interesting packages aimed at attracting FDI.

Reform and policies in India

In India, it is customary to distinguish between four phases relating to the Indian government's attitude in terms of FDI (Kumar, 1995). First, the period spanning independence (1947) to the late 1960s corresponds to a transition phase with a receptive attitude towards FDI. The industrialization strategy of India, as embodied in the Five Year Plan, and based upon the principle of import-substitution, focused "on the development of local capability in heavy industries" (Kumar, 1995: 3228). However, given the insufficient technological base, any FDI that was fostering scientific, technical and industrial knowledge was welcome. Major Western Multinational Enterprises (MNE's) started to show interest in India and more than 50 per cent of FDI was in chemicals, metals products, food and drinks, and pharmaceuticals.

Second, during the late 1960s through to the 1970s, a restrictive policy towards FDI was put in place. Much technological and management expertise had been accumulated locally during the previous period, and large outflows of profits, royalties, and technical fees started to become a large part of foreign exchange requirement. The foreign stake in the equity of an Indian subsidiary had to be less than 40 per cent, and all projects with foreign equity above that threshold had to be dealt with within the newly created Foreign Investment Board (FIB). Some minor exceptions were accorded to industries that required highly sophisticated technology, and FDI was really welcome only when it made a contribution in terms of technical know-how and skills (OECD, 1982). Consequently, the activities of foreign companies were restricted to a very selected group of high-priority industries. Inflows of direct investment were becoming concentrated on technology-intensive sectors, such as electrical goods, machinery, and chemicals. Small, perceptible policy changes occurred in 1978, when imports of technology were made possible in 22 industries in which such activity had previously been banned. Overall, as FDI was severely restricted, the local indigenous industry was shielded from international competitive pressures.

Third, the 1980s initiated a more liberalized trade and industrial policy, aimed at improving the competitiveness of the Indian economy.

Technological obsolescence, poor product quality, appalling export performances, a capital-intensive industrial structure, and high costs were the characteristics of the Indian manufacturing sector.[14] In its quest to expose the domestic productive system to a more global competitive framework, the government removed tariff protection, liberalized capital goods and technology imports, and put in place some incentives to encourage MNEs to set up export-orientated units (EOU) of production. Consequently, four more export processing zones (EPZs) were created, bringing the total number to six. In addition, the stringent rules and guidelines streamlining FDI were relaxed (Kumar, 1995). This more outward-orientated policy culminated with the 1991 "liberal economic reforms".

Fourth, from July 1991 onwards, a further and radical liberalization of the Indian economy was introduced by the then Prime Minister Narasimha Rao as part of wide-ranging economic reforms undertaken in order to solve the severe fiscal and foreign exchange crisis.[15] The New Industrial Policy placed a large emphasis on the encouragement of inward investment, acknowledged as the key route to success.[16] The small-scale sector and the agricultural sector, which account for 14 per cent and 31 per cent of GDP respectively, have been excluded from this reform process (Haniffa, 1996b). New sectors have been opened to FDI – in particular, telecommunications, banking, mining, and highways construction (Kumar, 1995).

As a "first-phase FDI recipient', India would ideally need to be developed into an export platform for other countries – a feature that is expected to characterize FDI in the next century – in order for FDI to have a beneficial impact on the current account (Haniffa, 1996b).

The "New Industrial Policy" of the Indian government, centred on the attraction of FDI, can be summarized as follows:[17]

Fiscal policy: tax holidays and tax incentives   Although corporate tax rates remain high, at 46 per cent for local subsidiaries and 55 per cent for branches, many tax concessions and tax incentives (such as accelerated depreciation, tax exemptions on profits from exports) are available. Investment projects in the power sector, in infrastructure, or in economically less developed states, are liable to 100 per cent tax relief for the first five years, followed by a 50 per cent relief for the next five years. Also, India applies a 20 per cent withholding tax rate to dividends and interest payments. These tax costs can be reduced by using offshore investment vehicles in locations that have favourable tax treaties with India, such as Mauritius (see Appendix). The status of Mauritius as a gateway for direct and portfolio investment explains to an appreciable extent the attraction exercised by India on foreign investors since the beginning of the reforms.

Foreign ownership   Approval for 100 per cent foreign ownership is given on a case-by-case basis. For example, in the power generation sector, 100 per cent foreign equity is permitted (Kumar, 1995). Automatic approval is now given for up to 51 per cent foreign ownership in 36 high-priority industries, including mining, power, telecommunications, and highways, airports, and seaports. Companies already established in India can raise their equity holding above the 51 per cent mark as part of an expansion programme (*India Newsletter*, March 1996). However, foreign companies are restricted to 49 per cent equity in some segments of the telecommunications industry. The electronics and software industry is subject to special provisions. In short, India welcomes direct foreign investment in virtually every sector of the economy (after having restricted it), except those of strategic concern such as defence and atomic energy.

Promotion of exports through export-orientated units (EOU) and free trade zone units   Additional advantages and facilities are available for EOU and for units of production located in designated Export Processing Zones (EPZ). The objective of an EPZ is to promote the exports of labour-intensive goods in the light manufacturing, garments, and electrical industries. The policy incentives and facilities that attract indigenous firms and foreign collaboration in the EPZs include: a five-year complete tax holiday for any 100 per cent export-orientated undertaking set up in an EPZ (UN, 1992); duty-free imports and exports; easy repatriation of profits; single "window" clearance for all bureaucratic dealings with the government; excise duties exemptions and subsidies on rent, power, and water. There are six operational EPZs, and the SEEPZ (Santa Cruz Electronics Exports Processing Zone) near Bombay's international airport, the New Delhi- and the Madras-based zones account for most exports in electronics and software.

Because of their location, it can be argued that the setting-up and revival of the EPZs may lead in the long term to a multi-tier economy, with the relatively wealthier or more dynamic states being able to attract the bulk of FDI. For example, the EPZ in dynamic Madhya Pradesh (a state that registered the highest per capita income growth during the 1961–1991 period) offers 100 per cent equity ownership in ventures, adequate infrastructure support, and long-term lease of land at very low costs. In contrast, other states, such as Bihar, the poorest state in the country, are developing at a very slow pace and are struggling to attract investment.[18] In order to offset the risk of peripheralization of poorer states, the government initiated in 1991 an ambitious scheme for the development of 68 "growth centres" to be developed across the country between 1992 and 1997. In particular, the "model industrial towns" are a magnet for attracting foreign, essentially Japanese, direct investment (Kar, 1992).

In addition to these specific elements of industrial policy, a broad macroeconomic framework has facilitated inward investment over the period under review.

Reforms and policies in China

As in the Indian case, four different phases can be identified in the reform process in China (CEC, 1995). From the first phase of economic reforms, December 1978 to September 1984, placed a great emphasis on the modernization of the agricultural sector. However, during that time the first SEZs (Special Economic Zones) were created with a view to boosting foreign investment in the coastal areas. China announced that it would seek cooperative partnerships with foreign investors in the following industries and sectors: electric power; energy resource development; communications and transportation; raw materials; chemical fibres; construction materials;

precision machinery and electronics; iron, steel and ferrous metals industries.

In the second phase, October 1984 to September 1988 the reform of state enterprises was given a new impetus, and prices were being liberalized. In particular, efforts were made to separate government functions from enterprise management, and this second period in the reform process culminated with the promulgation in April 1988 of the Law on Industrial Enterprises Owned by the Whole People. This law defined for the first time the legal status of state-owned enterprises (*Beijing Review*, 1995).

The decentralization process, with the devolution of increased powers to the provinces, became somewhat jeopardized by different policies taken by the provinces themselves. On the one hand, the further liberalization of FDI and foreign trade resulted in a dynamic economic climate; the volume of foreign trade and FDI increased markedly during this period of time. On the other hand, local authorities were competing one against another in importing luxury goods, a policy that drained the already limited foreign exchange resources. As a result, further decentralization was suspended for a while.

The third phase (October 1988 to December 1991) corresponded to a period of "retrenchment", with the need to regain control of an overheated economy by slowing down the reform process and by slashing investment. The impact of the Tiananmen Square occurrences on China's open door policy was a cost to its economy. The Chinese economy fell into a low cycle of development.

In the fourth phase – since January 1992 – reforms have accelerated, have been applied to the services sector, and have enabled the inland areas (Nanjing, Wuhan, and Chongqing) to open up to foreign trade and investment. The new targeted industries are: automobile, telecommunications, computers and microelectronics, household electrical appliances, machinery and electrical products, instruments and meters, medicine, food processing, garments, new building materials, new types of chemicals and special purpose metal materials. In short, the emphasis in the 1990s is on the development of high-tech industries with the full support of state banks.

The Five Year Plan is a crucial benchmark in terms of industrial policy in China. It delineates the evolving priority industries, and it calls for the investment structure in fixed assets to conform with the adjustments of the industrial structure. FDI that meets the requirements of the national industrial policy can be conducted smoothly and in turn is granted favourable treatment (*Beijing Review*, 1994). A bias towards technologically advanced investment, embodied in a broad, "wholesale" technology import programme, is an essential feature of the current policy. The objective is to infuse a high-technological and scientific level in the industrial structure in order to meet the new emerging consumption patterns (that is, new, durable consumer goods). The major elements of today's Chinese industrial policy include:

1 tax exemptions available to technologically advanced foreign investments;
2 the gradual establishment of a legal framework that protects, governs, and encourages FDI;
3 the upgrading of technical skills; and
4 the inclusion of a regional policy dimension, with the absorption of surplus rural labour into the secondary and tertiary sectors of the economy.[19]

A relatively high level of education and skills in the receiving country is paramount to the successful application and absorption of foreign technology into the domestic industrial system. Successful technology transfer strategies in China are supported by active training programmes.

The industrial policy is very sophisticated in the SEZs and in the Pudong Development Zone of Shanghai, where tax and import-duty privileges have been the major incentives for location. It should be noted that the special fiscal status of the SEZs, which was necessary in their infant stage, is gradually being harmonized and integrated into China's domestic economic system (*People's Daily*, 1995). In 1988, half of the SEZs custom duties as well as the industrial and commercial taxes were retained by the SEZs. In 1994, the state adjusted the SEZs' foreign exchange retention policy and unified it into a state uniform tax system. Also, tax privileges on imports of capital goods were phased out in December 1995. At present, the major remaining incentives in the SEZs are as follows: (1) low corporate tax rate (at 15 per cent against 30 per cent nation-wide); (2) the SEZs still retain their decision-making power for the approval of projects that are less than US$30 million; (3) Shenzen, Xiamen, and Hainan are free to promulgate their own laws (*People's Daily*, 1995).

It is expected that the Ninth Five Year Plan (1996–2000) will alter further some of the privileges enjoyed by the SEZs. The zones will be used as test fields for FDI in banking, insurance, and legal services.

At a more macroeconomic level, the recent changes in China's monetary policy are an additional incentive for foreign investors. The Renminbi has been partially convertible since the end of 1996. This partial convertibility covers current account transactions, and enables foreign investors to convert profits made in local currency into foreign currencies at local banks, and transfer them abroad.[20] As a result of the Chinese Industrial Policy, it is expected that approximately $30 billion of foreign investment will flow into China in 1996 (EIU, 1996).

An analysis

Both experiences have striking similarities, as if some elements of an optimal model were immutable, but they offer at the same time very marked contrasts.

Similarities   In both cases, the approach is a multi-stage approach; reforms proceed by a series of steps that are constantly under review. The use of a Five Year Plan in both countries as a synthetic framework of economic policy helps in designing the reforms. There are many common instruments of the economic reforms in the two countries: outward-looking policies; attraction of FDI through fiscal incentives; creation of free trade zones (SEZs in China, and export processing zones in India); emphasis on technology-embodied FDI; willingness to tackle the regional problem.

Major differences   The first dividing factor is the different positioning of the two countries on the learning curve. Since China initiated its new policy 12 years before India, it is well able to fine-tune its incentive package, whereas India, as a "first-phase FDI recipient", is primarily concerned with the revival of its growth rates.

The approach has been gradual in both cases indeed, but in the Chinese case, there is a continuum, a logical and chronological flow of policies and events, whereas in the Indian case, there is a series of spurts followed by contractions. The Chinese Five Year Plan is well thought of and is aimed at designing and implementing *coherent* strategic choices, whereas in India the decisions to accept new foreign investors are taken on a case-by-case basis, a practice that leads to arbitrariness, and that militates against a coherent view. There are no clear policy guidelines for investment in different sectors, there are no clear strategic choices, and the threat to reverse some freshly born policies is all too vivid.[21]

Another major difference between the two countries is the role played by technology in the growth and development process. Technology imports and technology transfer (TT) are strongly encouraged in China. TT has become a *sine qua non* condition for a successful investment strategy in China. In an effort to foster industrial upgrading and restructuring, China has been spending heavily on imports of technology, advanced machinery, and equipment. Trade figures with the EU, for example, reveal that China imported 1,985 different kinds of large-scale technology and equipment worth US$18.4 billion during the period 1979–1994 (*People's Daily*, 1996).

In theory, technology plays a vital role for India's developmental path. The official view is that "Foreign investment is considered as a vehicle for the introduction of technology" and that "technological upgrading and modernization is being pursued vigorously through private and government initiatives" (UN, 1992: 17 and 19). Already, one of the goals of the timid reforms of the 1980s was invariably to accompany FDI with TT, although two notable exceptions were allowed to this theoretical rule: imports from oil exporting developing countries, and imports from the NRIs (UN, 1992: 87). Ironically, these two exceptions were representing more than a third of total FDI. The emphasis on technology was not echoed in the 1991 reforms. Indeed, since 1991, the government has been so eager to accept inward investment that it relaxed its policy to a considerable degree. As recalled by Kumar: "FDI proposals do not necessarily have to be accompanied by technology transfer agreements" (Kumar, 1995: 3236). Thus, India's policy in relation to technology-embodied FDI has been fluctuating from aspirational stringencies to self-imposed laxity.[22]

Another major difference is that the objective of "national interest" is much stronger in China than in India. In China, Sino-foreign JVs and cooperative enterprises are required to abide strictly by the principle of sharing the *common interest;* both Chinese and foreign partners have to bear equal risks. In attracting FDI, China wants to maximize its own national interest by "accepting beneficial inputs, while restricting and eliminating those which may have an unfavourable impact" (*Beijing Review*, 1994, p. 13). Those activities with an "unfavourable impact" are those that have resulted in the monopolization of the market, in obstructions to the development of national industry, and that have created environmental pollution. In restricting foreign ownership to 51 per cent in some industries, India is also dedicated to the principle of "national interest", but the country allows foreign firms to gain quick returns on their investment, regardless of the economic externalities.

In its quest to increase FDI flows, the Indian government has not (yet) been able to discriminate between the beneficial and unfavourable activities. Some first steps in this direction are perceptible: the Environment Ministry will make it mandatory for all thermal power stations to switch over to washed coal by 2000. The notoriously high ash content in Indian coal, and the resulting carbon dioxide emissions from them, make them one of the most polluting industries.

Finally, the reforms are borne on the premises of two different political systems. As a result, the democratic system in India led to "liberal economic reforms", whereas central planning with a single party system gave birth to "socialist economic reforms" in China.[23]

In spite of the major attractive package included in the industrial and macroeconomic policies of both countries, many entry barriers have played (and still play) a deterring role for foreign investment.

Barriers to entry

Although the industrial economics literature focuses essentially on economic, business, and, to some extent, legal barriers to entry into a market, obstacles encountered by would-be (European) investors in countries such as China and India are much more numerous and diverse. For a comprehensive analysis of entry barriers in China and India, the cultural, institutional, and political barriers need to be taken into account as well. Although the entry barriers vary to a large degree between China and India, the two countries combine some common features.

In purely economic terms, the major entry barriers in China are the local content rule applied to the automotive, machine-tools as well as electronics industries, and the bias towards technology transfer. In India, the limits to foreign ownership substantially block entry of foreign investors. Also, it appears that the first movers in the markets have the ability to secure large market shares in blocking entry to latecomers. For example, Volkswagen, Daihatsu, Peugeot, and Citroën have all been first movers in the Chinese motor vehicles market. In the early 1990s, China shut down its doors to any new foreign car manufacturer who was attempting to form a joint venture with a Chinese counterpart. Among the losers of the "first mover strategy" were some large companies such as Toyota, Nissan, Honda of Japan, and Ford and Chrysler of the United States.

Also, since FDI took place in industries previously dominated by state-run and inefficient enterprises, risks have been very high. For example, the first round of private power projects with major overseas investment stakes in India required counterguarantees from the central government. These counterguarantees backed the purchase agreements made with India's state electricity boards in order to arrange financing (Moore, 1995). Finally, rigidities in the Chinese and Indian labour markets, compared with those of the four Asian "Tigers" and of Japan, have also been blamed for demotivating foreign investment in these countries (Lal, 1988).

Legal and institutional barriers include the lack of transparency of the legal framework, bureaucracy, and delays (as shown by the statistical discrepancy between "approved" and "realized" FDI projects in both countries). In China, the fact that more than 150 laws and regulations apply to foreign trade and investment creates ambiguity and confusion. Also of crucial importance to foreign investors is the issue of Intellectual Property Rights (IPR), which are not efficiently enforced in both countries, but especially in China.[24]

Finally, the political upheavals that have shaken the Indian democratic system, as well as the political opacity prevalent in China,[25] represent additional entry barriers. The elections in spring 1996 in India were animated, with lengthy debates over the need to curb inward direct investment. The free market reforms and the policy of attracting MNEs were strongly contested. MNEs are accused of "thinking short term, offering outmoded technology, hiring expatriate managers, . . . and breaking partnerships with local firms" (*Far Eastern Economic Review*, May 1996, p. 78). Anti-FDI feelings also arose because of high interest rates (between 15 and 20 per cent) created by the anti inflationary monetary policy of the government. Industrialists in India would like to lower the ceiling on foreign ownership (below the 50 per cent threshold). In spite of the resurgence of nationalist feelings in India and of the reluctance of the Indian people to sell their industry to foreigners, further liberalization of the economy will continue, as has been recently claimed by the new Prime Minister Deve Gowda.[26] It appears clearly now that India is committed to raising at least US$200 billion over the years 1997 to 2001 to improve its infrastructure. A quarter of this amount would be sourced from overseas, which suggests that a minimum of US$10 billion a year in FDI is needed (*Business Times*, 1996).

With its black economy estimated at between 15 to 50 per cent of GDP (Lal, 1988), India is thought to be one of the most corrupt countries in the world. Corruption takes also the form of positive discrimination in favour of national businesses. For example, in China, bidding procedures are opaque, and foreign suppliers are routinely discriminated in favour of national firms.[27] In India, foreign firms are concerned about the *swadeshi* ("buy Indian") campaign propounded by certain political organizations (Nayar, 1995).

Risks and uncertainties are large for firms investing in countries with an infant legal system, such as that of China. Legal, institutional, political as well as cultural barriers epitomize entry barriers in China and India alike. In China, probably the most insurmountable entry barrier is the industrial policy biased towards the quick acquisition of technology, and which takes the form of coerced joint ventures and local content ratios. India restricts foreign ownership in every industry, with the exception of the high-tech sectors.

Risks can be minimized with the appropriate strategy. A meaningful and pragmatic entry strategy is needed which may embrace the need to forge trustworthy partnerships with local interests (Andréosso-O'Callaghan and Qian, 1996).

CONCLUSIONS

The EU share of FDI is abysmally low in China, but is still relatively high in India, a "first phase FDI recipient", receiving 17 times less FDI than China. However, as India opens up further, the EU share recedes, leaving opportunities to new investors from Asia and Eastern Europe. Among the EU countries, the UK still holds a predominant position in terms of FDI in India, followed by Germany, the Netherlands, and Denmark. In spite of its size, France has not shown any serious interest in the Indian market.

Although both countries are moving very fast along the FDI developmental path, India still concentrates to a large extent on the primary sector (one-third of FDI), whereas China has moved faster in emphasizing technology and innovation-driven FDI. China's

FDI activities lie at a higher level of technological sophistication. Technology transfer is a "must" for any foreign firm wanting to enter the Chinese market, and to sustain a successful position there. In encouraging the accumulation of technological capability – in a coercive manner (through the requirement of local content ratios) – China lies today at a more advanced stage on the FDI path. Technology transfer is vigorously pursued in India, albeit in theoretical terms only. In its search for more FDI, the country is all too concerned about the maximization of inward investment flows; this factor militates against the type and quality of investment.

These contrasts are reflected in the structure of EU FDI in both countries. In India, EU investment tends to be clustered in the primary sector and in the traditional manufacturing industries, whereas EU investment in China has clearly been a vehicle for technology transfer. Connected to this issue is the fact that the concept of "sustainable" development is more enshrined in the Chinese than in the Indian policy.

Finally, the unprecedented performance achieved by both countries in terms of inward investment-led growth is the result of the economic reforms, be they "liberal" or "socialist". As the major target of both types of reforms, FDI has been favoured by attractive packages sharing interesting similarities in both countries: fiscal incentives, creation of special economic or export zones, and a regional component in the policy. However, the Chinese economic reforms lie on a gradual and logical continuum, and form a coherent flow of rigorous policies. On the contrary, the policy of attracting FDI in India is more dispersed (in spite of the prioritization of recipient industries), and evolves by spurts. Even in the power generation sector, where 100 per cent foreign equity is permitted, the expected positive outcomes, arising partly from privatization programmes and inward investment, have been hampered by the lack of a policy framework under which public utilities must operate. The mandatory nature of TT with regard to inward investment in India evolves back and forth and is another factor jeopardizing the attainment of a coherent approach.

APPENDIX

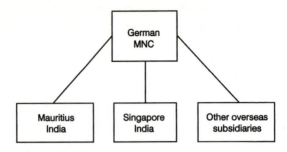

Note: In this structure, the withholding tax is reduced from the standard 20 per cent rate for dividends paid to both Mauritius and Singapore, and the Indian capital gains tax can be entirely eliminated where the disposal is made from Mauritius.

Source: *India Newsletter (1996)*, available through Indiaserver

Figure 2.5   An offshore investment structure

NOTES

1 The authors gratefully acknowledge the help of the Indian Embassy, Washington, and of the European Commission, Brussels, in providing statistical data.
2 The Chinese economy growth rate is forecast at around 9% for 1996, whereas in India the rate was recorded at 6.2% during the 1995/96 fiscal year.
3 GNP per capita was ECU 362 in China and ECU 214 in India in 1993 (EU Commission, "Europe, Partner of Asia", Jan. 1996).
4 It includes India, Pakistan, Sri Lanka, Nepal, Bangladesh, Maldives, Bhutan and Afghanistan.
5 I.e. originating from Hong Kong, Macau, Taiwan, Singapore, and other South-east Asian countries.
6 Asia is meant to include India but to exclude the other South Asian nations.
7 The lack of interest – or the extreme caution – of EU firms *vis-à-vis* the Asian markets has been a fundamental *raison d'être* of the first Euro-Asian Summit which took place in Bangkok in March 1996.
8 See EU Commission, cf. footnote 3.
9 For our purpose, this includes China, Indonesia, Malaysia, the Philippines, Thailand, Hong Kong, South Korea, and Singapore.
10 This has major statistical implications, since it distorts the figures appreciably.
11 Investment in financial intermediation represented 15% of the total (or 420 million ECU) and was essentially concentrated in Hong Kong,

Singapore, and Japan (all figures from *Bulletin of Economic Trends in Europe*, April 1996).

12 In particular Ozawa (1992) distinguishes four stages of FDI development: "factor driven", "investment driven", "innovation driven", and "wealth driven".

13 Real inflows represent only a small share of approvals. For example, in 1995, FDI approvals in India amounted to more than US$11 billion, compared with actual inflows of less than $2 billion.

14 Whereas the "four tigers" were becoming the new developing nations of the world, India, in spite of its many attributes (a well-diversified natural resource base, long experience with public administration, fairly elastic supplies of labour, the world's fourth-largest pool of skilled manpower, and a relatively stable political system), was unable to take off. Abysmally low growth rates of per capita incomes – when compared with those of other Asian countries – combined with the inability of successive governments to tackle the poverty issue have been noted and analysed by many economists (see in particular Lal, 1988; Bhagwati, 1993).

   Bhagwati (*op. cit.*, p. 47) puts forward three explanations for these phenomena: (1) "extensive bureaucratic control over production, investment and trade"; (2) inward-looking trade and foreign investment policies; (3) a substantial and inefficient public sector. The work of Weiner (1991) has demonstrated that the inability to raise literacy and educational levels has also contributed to stifling growth levels since Independence.

15 The initial impetus for the reforms came from a severe balance of payments crisis in 1990–91. That crisis led the government to adopt an adjustment programme that contained both immediate stabilization measures (centred on monetary tightening and fiscal rectitude) and ambitious structural reforms. These reforms concentrated on the industrial sector, and on foreign trade and investment.

16 The major objective of the reform process is to sustain a real growth rate of approximately 7 to 8% annually so as to eliminate the current account deficit. This growth rate can only be reached with a savings rate corresponding to 30% of GDP, a task totally unachievable given India's economic circumstances. The increase of FDI was thus the only way to boost high GDP growth, and the best-suited form of capital inflow to meet India's growth needs.

17 Most of the information given below is from *India Newsletter* (1996, various issues), available through *Indiaserver*.

18 In 1991, real per capita incomes were only Rs 2,655 in Bihar, against Rs 10,177 in Delhi, the richest state, compared with a national average of Rs 4,934 (IMF, 1996).

19 At the moment, it is estimated that China has a 120 million surplus labourers in the rural areas, and this figure is expected to reach 540 million by 2000 (*Beijing Review*, July 1994).

20 This also means that a foreign company can buy hard currencies in the swap centres as well as in some selected financial institutions at a given market rate.

21 The debate surrounding the April 1996 legislative elections provide one of the best examples in the country of a fluctuating economic philosophy. Although the Hindu nationalist Bharatiya Janata Party (BJP) – which came up as the winner of the elections (and which had a very short-lived first government) – and the Janata Dal, favour FDI, they want to restrict it to priority areas (infrastructure and technology), and to close the consumer non-durable goods to new FDI. For example, foreign companies will be able to set up wholly owned subsidiaries in high-technology areas. Takeovers of Indian companies will be made more difficult and disincentives should be provided in order to "dissuade firms from using India as a low-cost manufacturing and export base for foreign trade alone" (*Far Eastern Economic Review*, May 1996), a policy which would be totally opposed to the essence of the reforms.

22 There are nevertheless positive aspects to the relaxation of the policy, as large inflows of investment in the 1990s may be due to the fact that the Indian FDI policy is much less coercive than the Chinese one.

23 The latter expression is the official wording used by the media in China. We have borrowed it from the *Beijing Review*. It is not the intention of this chapter to draw any conclusions on the relationship between political system and economic efficiency. For an insight into this problem, see Kohli (1986).

24 India has signed the Uruguay Round Accord, which covers IPRs.

25 Perceived recently in Western countries through the "Taiwan" crisis, and fomented again with the preparation for the reintegration of Hong Kong.

26 His government aims at achieving a growth rate of 7–8% for the year 1996/97. Special efforts will be made to attract FDI in infrastructure and in areas where technology upgrading is critical.

27 For more on entry barriers in China, see Andréosso-O'Callaghan and Qian (1996).

BIBLIOGRAPHY

Andréosso-O'Callaghan, B. and Wei Qian, "Entry Barriers or Incentives? An Issue for FDI and Technology Transfer in China," *Proceedings of the Second South China International Business Symposium*, II (Macau: November 1996) pp. 1073–89.

Beijing Review, various issues.

Bhagwati, Jagdish, *India in Transition – Freeing the Economy* (Oxford: Clarendon Press, 1993).

Business Times. "India needs US$200 bn over 5 years to boost infrastructure", by Vikram Khanna (Singapore: 24 June 1996).

CEC, *Towards a New Asia Strategy*, Communication of the Commission to the Council, COM (94) 314 final (Brussels: July 1994).

CEC, *A Long-term Policy for China–Europe Relations*, Communication of the Commission to the Council, COM (95), 279 final (Brussels: July 1995).

Dunning, John, "Explaining the International Direct Investment Position of Countries: Towards a Dynamic or Developmental Approach", *Weltwirtschaftliches Archiv*, 117 (1981).

Economist Intelligence Unit, *EIU Country Report, China – 1st Quarter 1996* (London: 1996).

European Report. *Commission-Unctad Joint Report Highlights Lack of Investment*. No. 2117, (Brussels: March 1996) pp. 7–11.

Far Eastern Economic Review, various issues (1996).

Haniffa, Aziz, "Recorded Foreign Direct Investment Reported", *India Abroad*, an Indian American weekly newspaper on the website, Economy Section (Washington: 22 March 1996a).

Haniffa, Aziz, "Report Advises Increase in Foreign Direct Investment", *India Abroad*, Economy Section (Washington: 12 April 1996b).

IMF, *Internal Migration, Center–State Grants and Economic Growth in the States of India*, Report by the International Monetary Fund (Washington, 1996).

India Newsletter, an electronic monthly newsletter from the Government of India, Ministry of Industry, Department of Industrial Development, available through *Indiaserver*, various issues (1996).

India News Network Digest, "French Investors Upbeat on Long Term Potential in India" (20 March 1996).

Kar, Shampa, "Model Towns: Creating Infrastructure", *Business India*, no. 378 (31 August 1992) p. 21.

Kohli, A., "Democracy and Development", in John Lewis and Valeriana Kallab (eds) *Development Strategies Reconsidered* (Washington, DC: Overseas Development Council, 1986).

Kumar, Nagesh, "Industrialisation, Liberalisation and two Way Flows of FDI: Case of India", *Economic and Political Weekly* (16 December 1995) pp. 3228–37.

La Chine en Marche, Publication officielle des Ambassades de Chine en France, au Royaume-Uni, en Irlande et au Luxembourg (1993/94).

Lal, Deepak, "Ideology and Industrialization in India and East Asia", in Helen Hughes (ed.) *Achieving Industrialization in East Asia* (Cambridge: Cambridge University Press, 1988).

Moore, Taylor, "Developing Countries on a Power Drive", *Electric Power Research Institute Journal*, 20 (4) (July/August 1995).

Nayar, K.S., "NRIs Plan to Encourage Investment in India", *India Abroad* (New Delhi: 29 December 1995).

OECD, *North/South Technology Transfer – the Adjustments Ahead* (Paris: 1982).

Ozawa, Terumoto, "Foreign Direct Investment and Economic Development", *Transnational Corporations*, 1(1) (1992) pp. 27–54.

People's Daily, Overseas edn (in Chinese), 12 December 1995.

People's Daily, 1996, various issues.

United Nations, *Foreign Direct Investment and Technology Transfer in India* (New York: 1992).

Weiner, Myron, *The Child and the State in India* (Princeton, NJ: Princeton University Press, 1991).

3 Infrastructure projects public and/or private

I.T. Advani

For the last few years, seminars and colloquia have been held particularly in the developing world, regarding BOT – Build Operate Transfer projects. To a certain extent the term "BOT" holds a certain mystique. The object of this chapter is to demystify the subject to the uninitiated and to examine the status at the present date.

The Industrial Revolution started with industry built by private individuals. With the progress of industrialisation, society became more complex and called for extended infrastructure: railways, telecommunications, and power supply. In a similar manner as for other industries, the private sector stepped in to perform this entrepreneurial work. The state, whether in the form of a central administration or local communities, granted concessions to entrepreneurs extending over a span of several years to build projects to this effect. Not only the developed countries in the Western world but also countries which in those days were relatively less developed, such as China, Russia, Latin American countries and India, resorted to this practice.

The Shanghai telephone system was privately owned at the turn of the century. The supplier of the equipment of the Shanghai telephones was chosen 80 years later by the Chinese authorities to form a joint venture named Shanghai Bell for the manufacture and supply of telephone exchanges in China. Very probably the antecedents dating from the early twentieth century contributed to the choice of the foreign partner. Several railway lines in China and Russia were built and operated by private companies. The same applied to power supply systems, which more often than not were privately owned. In India the Tata group built the hydroelectric power stations near Bombay in the early 1920s despite protests from nationalist political parties opposed to the building of power stations on environmental and ideological grounds. There was a strain of thought in those days which was vehemently opposed to industrialization and wanted India to remain an agro-based society with reliance on cottage industry. It was alleged that large-scale industrialization dehumanizes society, increases disparities of wealth, and creates joblessness.

Immediately after the Second World War, a vast amount of capital was needed to ensure the rebuilding of infrastructure destroyed during the war and also to cater to the needs of emerging nations which had won freedom. Private capital was chronically short and could not answer the challenge and therefore infrastructure projects, being capital intensive, fell in several countries into the orbit of the state sector. Furthermore, on ideological grounds it was felt that the state should take over the responsibilities for projects of national interest. Not only the developing countries but also a large number of European countries such as the UK and France resorted to a large-scale nationalization of infrastructure projects, and development for the coming decades was taken over by the state sector. Multinational financial organizations such as the World Bank, IDA, ADB were structured to finance large-scale infrastructure projects in the developing world.

The terminology BOT, BOO, DBM or other combinations of initials were not used in those days, and we are in fact rediscovering the extensively applied practice of yesteryear.

BOT means Build, Operate, Transfer;
BOO means Build, Own, Operate;
DBM means Design, Build, Maintain.

Paradoxically, the tilt towards the private sector for infrastructure projects started in the early 1980s in China, a country which was supposed to be the inner sanctum of socialist orthodoxy. Guangdong Province was a fertile area in which to develop export-orientated industries for the manufacture of consumer products, but the shortage of electricity constituted a major bottleneck. The state did not have the means at short notice to provide the capital to add extra power plant capacity. With the pragmatism that has characterized the Deng era, when he declared that the cat may be black or white as long as it catches the mice, ways were found to circumvent the strait-jacketed doctrines of centralized planning. The building of small-sized power plants having an individual investment of less than US$30 million were authorized without the prior permission of the State Planning Commission. Tens of privately or semi-privately owned plants aggregating a capacity of nearly 1000 MW mushroomed in a span of four to five years, clearing the way for the manufacture of consumer goods which are now flooding the world and which are incidentally creating a trade imbalance with several countries in the Western world.

Against this backdrop, a well-known developer from Hong Kong by the name of Gordon Wu appeared on the scene. While building and operating a major hotel in the city of Canton in Guangdong Province, he experienced severe difficulties due to endemic brownouts and blackouts. He had to provide a back-up power plant at high cost. Profiting by the entrepreneurial spirit of Guangdong Province he proposed building a privately owned and operated power plant of major size which normally fell in the orbit of the state. Through excellent market research and the backing of some leading banking corporations based in Hong Kong, who were willing to take advantage of the emerging trends in privatization in South China, Gordon Wu proposed to put up a power plant within a time deemed by the state authorities to be unrealistically short. It was an offer which the authorities had difficulty in refusing. In return, Gordon asked for a handsome reward in case he redeemed the pledge. Gordon took the right options, was successful, and in the process he realized a handsome profit. Since this success story, the trend to call upon the private sector to take on infrastructure projects has been gathering momentum. In the beginning, it was a trickle, then a river, and now it has become a flood. Even multi-national institutions such as the World Bank and ADB (Asia Development Bank) in some cases are encouraging the private sector to step in here so that they can divert their attention to other areas of public welfare. We will try to examine in this chapter whether this method can have a generalized application.

ADAPTABILITY OF INFRASTRUCTURE PROJECTS TO THE PRIVATE SECTOR

It is now contemplated that the private sector might take over a very wide range of projects, such as telecommunications, rail links, roadways, and even airports. A uniform doctrine cannot be applied to all types of projects, and until now the accent has been on thermal power plants, which lend themselves well to privatization. This is mainly due to the fact that the unit size and the technology involved is fairly well standardized and that thermal plants have a relatively small element of civil works, the ratio of the cost of plant and machinery to civil works being in the order of 80:20. The pay-back period of the investment can range between 8 and 10 years, a duration acceptable to the investors. Power plants lend themselves well to project financing as they are subject to well-defined power purchase agreements and fuel supply agreements which diminish the imponderables.

On the other hand, hydro-electric projects have a heavy involvement of civil engineering with greater imponderables, and the ratio of plant and machinery to civil works is appropriately 20:80. Hydro-electric plants are non-standard and they have long lead times and even longer pay-back periods on investment. Despite these drawbacks, the Hub River project in Pakistan has been earmarked for the private sector and, according to information available, the contract is expected to be concluded shortly. However, there is no rush to undertake private plants as with thermal projects.

Mass transit projects such as metro systems are often public welfare services which enjoy subsidized rates of travel. Consequently, they lend themselves only with difficulty to private ownership. Even today, a century after the Paris Metro was built, the tariff is subsidized. Moreover there is uncertainty regarding the volume of traffic. The same applies to new developments in rail travel. The huge deficit of the French railways is a case in point. Nevertheless the British and the German rail systems have recently been privatized. On the other hand, the Eurotunnel project has been disastrous for private investors, who would be most reluctant to repeat a similar investment.

Telecommunications with the short lead times and pay-back periods lend themselves very well to privatization, but there are several political issues involved. China has so far been averse to privatization but India has already started introducing private control. Due to diversity and the size of the country, the task is not easy but several projects are proceeding ahead. British Telecom and Deutsche telecommunications have recently been privatized. Under pressure from the European Economic Community, France has to do likewise but it is doing so kicking and screaming.

For the last few years privatization in the form of BOT projects has in a vast majority of cases had an application to thermal power projects, and we shall explore this subject in the succeeding paragraphs.

BOO/BOT PROJECT FINANCE PLAN FOR THERMAL POWER PLANTS

We shall attempt to explain the basic principles involved in such projects.

The capital cost comprises:

- land purchase;
- mobilization cost;
- plant purchase costs;
- interest during construction; and
- consultancy charges.

They are funded by:

- shareholders' equity;
- bank loans.

In countries like India and China the authorities insist upon an equity of at least 25–30 per cent of the capital cost.

FINANCING STRUCTURES FOR BOT/BOO PROJECTS

Figure 3.1 explains one of the financial schemes adopted in China. In the early 1980s, the Chinese authorities showed a marked preference for projects in the form of a joint venture. For the projects in Guangdong Province, the ratio of equity of Party A to Party B was 60:40. One of the important features was that the Chinese financial institutions gave a guarantee to the joint venture company which greatly reassured the lenders and the foreign investor.

After their early experiences, the Chinese standardized the new procedures, which are more stringent than those shown in Figure 3.1. There is no insistence on participation of the Chinese entity in the project company. Moreover, the guarantee of the Chinese financial institutions is conspicuous by its absence, which is irksome both to the foreign investors and the lenders. The scheme is shown in Figure 3.2.

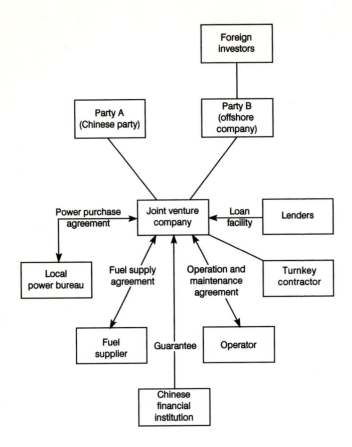

Figure 3.1 Typical structure of a joint-venture power project

SITUATION OF PRIVATELY FINANCED POWER PROJECTS IN CHINA AND IN INDIA

China has an installed capacity of electric power of nearly 200,000 MW and is adding power at the rate of 6–7 per cent per annum. China has to a large extent overcome the chronic shortages that were impeding growth in the 1980s. The capital for implementation of the extra capacity is raised by the traditional methods and there is only a marginal reliance on private participation.

India, which, on the other hand, started its opening to the exterior only in the early 1990s finds itself in the throes of chronic shortage of electricity, which are seriously impeding growth. The

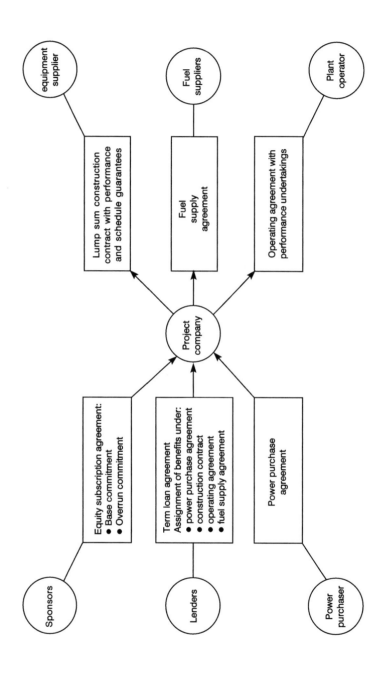

Figure 3.2 Power project: limited recourse financing structure

basic difficulty in India stems from the fact that the traditional producers of electricity are impoverished due to unrealistically low tariffs and widespread theft of electricity. This is aggravated by the fact that the railways are not able to supply coal at a steady rate and on schedule. The same applies to the coal mines, which have difficulty in ensuring a steady supply of coal in quality and in quantity. The cash-starved electricity boards are not able to generate the funds for further development. With this hiatus, the presence of privately operated power plants may appear to be a panacea, but the major problems will reappear unless the basic reasons underlying the shortage of power are solved. Private power plants may temporarily provide a breathing space, with electricity possibly at a somewhat higher cost, but the basic environment has to be altered to permit growth both in the private sector and the public sector.

CONCLUSIONS

It has not been my intention to dwell upon the intricacies of project financing and the actuarial calculations necessary for project appraisal. The object has been to examine the role of private ownership for infrastructure projects. Private ownership and public ownership have parallel roles to play and each has its terrain. Public ownership need not be completely discarded.

BIBLIOGRAPHY

Donoghu, Neil. Power Structures: Private Power projects in China. The article appeared in a symposium on Private Power Projects in emerging markets, held 18 May 1994 at JW Marriot Hotel, Hong Kong.
Jackson, R.W. "Private Sector Financing of Infrastructure Projects" (Internal document, GEC Alsthorm, 1994).

Part II

Country-based Analysis – China

4 Japanese direct investment in China

"One bed for two dreams"[1]

Michel Delapierre and Christian Milelli[2]

Since 1993 Japanese direct investment in China has been growing rapidly. But as in the previous periods there is no supporting commitment from the Japanese administration or government. However, this trend, led by a private business rationale, is encountering in China a national policy structured along public objectives, quite different from what is occurring in other Asian countries. The result is a set of constraints for the Japanese operations in China, whether Sino-Japanese joint ventures or wholly-owned subsidiaries. Therefore, Japanese investors have devised some responses to downgrade the constraints and keep risk exposure at sustainable level.

THE GENERAL FRAMEWORK: ECONOMIC RELATIONS BETWEEN CHINA AND JAPAN

Up to 1972, which featured the renewal of diplomatic ties between China and Japan, Japanese economic activities in mainland China were at a standstill. A further delay was still needed to formalize economic relations between the two countries after the signature of the China–Japan Long-term Agreement on 16 February 1978, which, however, made no mention of Japanese direct investment in China. Afterwards, bilateral trade exchanges were fostered and decisions on the institutional framework were further protracted to 1990.

Despite the opening of the Chinese economy initiated in 1979 by the so-called Open Door Policy, it was only in 1988 that an arrangement was reached to enhance Japanese investments in China, following the visit by a delegation composed of members of the

Ministry of Industry and International Trade and the Ministry of Foreign Affairs. Upon their return to Japan the delegates released a blueprint, stating that the time had come to back up Japanese investments in China. The Tiananmen Square slaughter of June 1989 delayed the formulation of a Japanese organization, which was eventually established in 1990 as the Japan–China Investment Promotion Organization. It was only a private association receiving grants from the Japanese government, whereas its counterpart was a first-rank Chinese governmental body, the Ministry of Foreign Trade and Economic Cooperation (MOFTEC).

During the 1960s the exporting small and medium-sized enterprises – mainly located in western Japan – promoted numerous private organizations which were focused on the gathering and dissemination of information and also on support for business in China. Japanese authorities did not favour the upholding of the economic relations between the two countries despite the improvement in the Chinese political and economic environment after 1979. During the early 1990s, there was no change in the actions of the Japanese authorities in giving stronger support to Japanese investment in China. Throughout that period Japanese investment flows towards China remained fundamentally driven by private rationale. Since 1993 China has become a major recipient of Japanese outward investments (see Table 4.1), following the bursting of the Japanese financial bubble, the renewal of Japanese foreign investments, and the Japanese focus on the Asian region.

According to Chinese statistics, in 1995 the inward direct investment from Japan in terms of agreements reached US$7.6 billion and $3.1 billion for realized investments (investments actually carried out). Japanese effective investments (investments earmarked) reached a third place, at a par with those of Taiwan, but still far behind those from Hong Kong.[3]

Japanese direct investments in China kept their upward momentum during the first quarter of 1996 owing to the repeal of tax and tariffs breaks on imports of capital equipment on 1 April which was part of a wider move by Chinese authorities than their previous all-out investment promotion policies. Hence, Toyota Motors decided to go ahead by establishing a joint venture despite the daily problems encountered by its local subsidiary, Daihatsu Motors. Forecasts carried out by Japanese organizations[4] stressed the unfaltering attractiveness of China for Japanese investors. Finally, despite several difficulties met by Japanese enterprises, it seemed

Table 4.1 FDI in China by main country of origin (1990–1995):
amount (US$ millions) and share (percentage)

Years	Hong Kong	Japan	USA	Taiwan
1990	1,880	503.4	456	222.4
	(54%)	(14.5%)	(13.1%)	(6.5%)
1991	2,405.3	532.5	323.2	466.4
	(55%)	(12.2%)	(7.4%)	(10.6%)
1992	7,507.1	709.8	511	1,050.5
	(68.2%)	(6.5%)	(4.6%)	(9.5%)
1993	17,274.7	1,324.1	2,063.1	3,138.6
	(58.2%)	(4.8%)	(7.5%)	(11.4%)
1994	19,665.4	2,075.3	2,490.8	3,391
	(58.2%)	(6.1%)	(7.4%)	(10%)
1995	20,060	3,108	3,083	3,162
	(53.2%)	(8.2%)	(8.2%)	(8.5%)

Source: Ministry of Foreign Trade and Economic Cooperation, Beijing

obvious that investment in mainland China would be the sole way in which to build a foothold in what should become the world's largest single market.

Empirical studies[5] have recently underlined the growth of worldwide intra-branch and intra-firm trade, showing the interdependence between foreign direct investment and international trade.[6] Trade between China and Japan was growing at a firm pace, with a 40 per cent increase for the 1990–1994 period, to reach 20 per cent of overall Chinese trade in 1994 (see Figure 4.1). This growth was fuelled by exports of capital equipment from Japan to affiliates in China, on the one hand, and the re-export of semi-finished or finished goods to Japan on the other,[7] resulting in a growing commercial surplus for China *vis-à-vis* Japan – from US$6 billion in 1990 to $14 billion in 1994.[8]

The last survey by the Export-Import Bank of Japan directed to the international investment strategies of Japanese manufacturing enterprises undoubtedly emphasized the attractiveness of China.[9] In 1995, the Asian zone, with 70 per cent of the projects, was the main recipient for the enterprises of this sample and China ranked first, with 25 per cent.

Table 4.2 highlights the motivations of Japanese investors. First, more than the attractiveness of the current market the foremost incentive is its future. Thus, the development of new markets is put forward by more than 50 per cent of the firms, a proportion

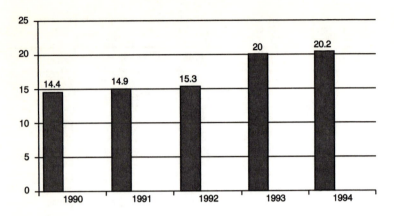

Source: *China Statistical Yearbooks*, Beijing

Figure 4.1 Japanese–Chinese trade related to the total of Chinese international trade, 1990–1994 (percentages)

which is slightly higher than those that focus on the maintenance or the extension of existing market shares. In the case of ASEAN countries and NIEs (Newly Industrialized Economies), the intentions are more centred on present, yet well-penetrated, markets, than on expected ones. As ASEAN countries emerge as manufacturing bases for global markets, through exports to third countries or parts-manufacturing locations for assembly manufacturers, these motives are less present in the investment projects to China. The local market is here the major incentive. A large domestic market open to consumer products, a tendency perceived as irreversible, is a particularly strong magnet.

Second, the access to cheap labour is also a motivation for Japanese investors. This is particularly obvious for small and medium-sized enterprises, mainly sub-contractors, coping with the sharp appreciation of the yen and the resulting constraints spurred by contractors. Hence, they were led to search outside Japan for cheap manufacturing bases. These firms were a substantial proportion of the new investors in China during the early 1990s. Nevertheless, the current skill level of the workforce and of the organization of manufacturing capacities up to now limits the prospects for the export of local manufacture of goods to sophisticated third markets.

Table 4.2 Investment motives of Japanese manufacturing enterprises by region (percentages)

Investment motives	China	ASEAN	NIEs	Other Asia
Development of new markets	54	31.5	23.5	55.5
Maintenance/expansion of market share	48	64.5	70	48
Export to Japan	36.5	36	22.5	16
Export to third countries	32	42.5	32	18.5
Spreading production bases overseas (horizontal division of labour)	31	31	22	16
Sourcing for inexpensive labour	59	40	11.5	37
Supply of parts to assembly manufacturers (including Japanese overseas affiliates)	21.5	32.5	23.5	17
Avoidance of exchange risk	13.5	22	20.5	7.5

Source: Questionnaire on Foreign Direct Investment in Fiscal 1995, Export-Import Bank of Japan, Tokyo

THE PERSISTENCE OF A STRONG POLITICAL RATIONALE IN CHINA

It is trivial to say that China is characterized by a strong political logic: it is still a socialist country where power and control remain to the party and the state. It is also a country which is undergoing a "gradual" transition from a centralized system to a market economy, which is in sharp contrast with the Big Bang option followed by the former Soviet Union and which is more in accordance with the Mao practice of the Great Leaps Forward. In 1979, on behalf of the patriarchal leader, Deng Xiaoping, Chinese authorities embarked on a smooth transition to a market economy. The orientation followed can be labelled a cognitive one as it is largely based on learning processes. Accordingly, it legitimates the lack of determination of the time schedule for the implementation and contents of the rules set for buttressing the new economic system, in parallel with the maintenance of the dispensations which used to serve as incentives for industrial development in experimental and limited areas, such as the special economic zones or the coastal cities. Nevertheless, there are two colliding forces presently at work: the economic reforms tend to enlarge the autonomous power of private actors, on the one hand, while the state reforms maintain the political supremacy of the party and preserve economic and social stability within the whole country on the other. The Chinese authorities obviously try to avoid harsh conflicts between such opposite strengths by keeping their respective effects to sustainable levels.

Industrial policies under the Mao regime were based on the promotion of heavy industry through a central planning system by channelling investments towards the large-scale state-owned enterprises. The decline of the position of those enterprises in the overall industrial output – from 76 per cent in 1980 to 34 per cent in 1994 – is mainly due to the entry and excellent performance of non-state-owned firms in sectors such as textiles, and truck and car parts. However, they still have a central place in terms of employment: in 1995 their cumulated workforce constituted two-thirds of urban employment.

Since 1984 the Chinese government promoted strenuous efforts to improve the management of the loss-making state-owned firms by giving it more autonomy (Perkins, 1994): indeed, the goal was not to sell these firms to private investors. Hence, managers were responsible for operating performance, freed from planning guidelines, and they often struck fiscal agreements with authorities stating the amount of taxes to be paid. Again in 1993–1994, in order to reverse continuous poor performance by state-owned firms, new reforms were initiated with an emphasis on management troubleshooting (Huchet and Xiangjun, 1996). Thus the decision was formally taken to release full management autonomy to state-owned enterprises: they can hire or lay off personnel, retain earnings, or decide on the amount of investments, but they also may go bankrupt.

At the same time, the Chinese government promoted a decentralization process which gave more autonomous power to various local entities, be they regional, provincial, or county authorities. Such an orientation obviously constitutes, on one hand, a risk of multiple and contradictory regulations for the activities of foreign firms, and, on the other hand, an opportunity stemming from the duplication of investment projects and fresh competition to attract new businesses. Besides, industrial policies focused on national programmes aimed at the transfer of foreign technologies and know-how and at the sheltering of national manufacturers are still being implemented. Thus the automotive industry, textile and garment industries, and electric/electronic assembly industry are kept under the control of central authorities.[10] The foreign firms that want to invest in these fields must get approval from Beijing, which will have previously determined the number and the size of the eligible enterprises. By contrast, the other sectors have been liberalized: here only local authorities authorization is required. The choice and implementation of investment location is thus particularly critical as the Chinese partner in equity joint venture is often a community body providing land and workforce and setting the ancillary charges and the pace of equipment amortization. Foreign investors are bound to negotiate with every local administration for their investment projects. Moreover, continuous changes introduced by local authorities to existing policy in order to cope with evolving local market and global division of labour conditions can disturb and severely affect prior agreements held in different circumstances.

China's economic regime is currently a "bureaucratic capitalism" (Chevrier, 1994): the local authorities are assuming social responsibilities in labour and housing fields, as in the financing of the infrastructure and the continuity of social security systems. The financing of their activities is increasingly based on equity joint-venture earnings where their partner is often a non-resident investor, due to the lack of profitability of state-owned enterprises.

The Chinese industrial system maintains a structure which is not exclusively profit-orientated. Enterprises must provide housing, health insurance, training, and even education to their employees. In this context a lay-off would deprive the people thus affected of housing and social security advantages. Thus, in joint ventures where local communities are generally associated with private investors, be they domestic or (increasingly) non-resident, local communities are promoting policies backed by strong spatial rationale, while private investors strengthen industrial rationale, which could produce further conflicts. Besides, local administration searching to maximize employment determine the workforce level that each investor must reach. Private partners would not generally be allowed to recruit their employees. The expenses for social security systems, housing, and health care are determined according to the overall local needs and not according to the fund-earning capacity of each enterprise.

Finally, there are two contradictory forces in the Chinese approach. First, due to the political supremacy of the party, the central authorities, still exerts significant influence even the many lower-level administrative bodies. Nevertheless, through decentralization the latter have acquired some autonomous power, primarily on industrial issues. In this way they can move away from central authorities' control. But there are limits to this shift. For example, the lack of economic sanction for management inefficiencies of state-owned firms led, in the early 1990s, to a rise of inflationary pressures as the losses of these firms were quasi-automatically covered by bank lending with bad recovery prospects. A drastic holding based on the tightening of credit allocation was initiated in July 1993 by central authorities, which successfully curbed inflation by 1995.

Second, there is an increasing contradiction between the spatial rationale of industrial policies formulated and implemented by local communities and the capitalist rationale endorsed by foreign investors as globalization develops. This strain is reinforced by the fact that local authorities mainly secure their autonomous power in the economic domain. Their limited resources come from enterprises: the fiscal system being embryonic, the majority of taxpayers is imposed on a contractual base rather than as a percentage of their earnings as is the usual practice in developed countries. Finally, the two areas – the general interest on one side and the private one on the other – are still largely mixed together and need in the future to be more separated.

However, what appeared to be more worrying for foreign enterprises was the deepening of economic inequality across regions: by the early years 1990, regional inequality was claimed by some scholars to be among the worst in the world (Wang, 1995; Pairault, 1996). To reverse this threatening trend the central authorities are currently turning attention away from the coastal regions in favour of the inland areas. Nevertheless, the cumulative process of industrial output in the former regions will, by self-sustaining growth, enlarge the present disparities. Furthermore, necessary infrastructure spending – US$1,000 billion are envisaged by central authorities up to the year 2010 – is aimed to overcome striking regional inequality by focusing on the impoverished hinterland. This general tendency will not be limited to economics by featuring relatively autonomous regional subgroups buttressed by large internal markets but could lead to political struggles to influence or even capture central power in Beijing. However, central authorities seem at present able to balance the power between regions and large cities, such as Shanghai or Guangdong. Furthermore, a growing economic gap between rich regions, mainly from southern China, and the medium or poor ones could induce sizeable migratory flows. Central authorities are trying to regulate capital movements across regions as well as population displacements in order to curb inequality.

HURDLES FOR JAPANESE INVESTORS RAISED BY THE CHINESE REGIME AND THEIR RESPONSES[11]

As with any kind of investment, Japanese direct investment in China faces three types of risks. First, there is the business risk encountered in any industrial and commercial activities. Second, economic risk such as exchange rate risk or inflationary pressures has to be met. The third is the political risk based on law, regulations, or central and local policies. According to Japanese enterprises, the business risk is not particularly high in China. On the contrary, China appears to be a good manufacturing base and an attractive market for Japanese output. The economic risk is also bearable, as central authorities have exhibited their capacity to curb inflation during the recent period. But the level of political risk seems quite significant, generally speaking and more specifically when considering the difficulties met by Japanese investors in setting up cordial relations with central and local administrations and in tailor the management of their businesses to the constraints of the public regulations framework.

Access to the domestic market

Japanese firms emphasize particularly the difficulties encountered in accessing the Chinese market. This situation has several causes. First, the administration keeps a tight control over the domestic market, with the exception of the supply of imported equipment (Dzever and Zhengyi, 1996). Indeed, public authorities are not much concerned by sales-promotion activities or customer satisfaction. Prices are often set by local powers for relatively long periods of time. Foreigners must deal with Chinese societies or partners in joint ventures for the sale of their products on the domestic market. Manufacturing units have been favoured by the authorities,[12] whereas foreign commercial enterprises can only operate through export. Second, the bulk of customers are state-owned enterprises which are not seen by the Japanese as well-suited to funnel their output, due to their general lack of management expertise and the on-going privatization of public assets.

Therefore these hindrances are clearly perceived by the Japanese as a major hurdle to their development in China. Moreover, there is a contradiction between the orientation of the current Chinese industrial policy, on the one side, which is trying to allure foreign investments in order to foster domestic manufacturing activities by import substitution, and the upholding of regulations that slow down appropriate commercial systems on the other. The control of commercial networks, which was justified when foreign investment was completely export-orientated, is henceforth obsolete.

The sharing of the value added

The majority of Japanese investments in China are joint ventures[13] with a local partner who is most often a public organization. This kind of association between capitalist actors and territorial entities generates conflicts, as the goals of each partner are not similar and perhaps even antagonistic. On the one hand, the local public entity tries to maximize the income coming from the running of the joint venture. The foreign partner, on the other hand, who is providing the capital, expects a return on its investment. Hence, in many cases, local authorities try to drag the foreign partner into activities which contribute to the development of local resources. An involvement in the infrastructure, particularly transportation, is a common request. In such a case the foreign investor is committed to disbursements that are not directly profitable; they are in fact a free contribution to the general welfare. Moreover, some local authorities are searching to upgrade the land yield by favouring the setting up of high value-added activities rather than labour-intensive ones with low qualification level, thus changing the rules and rents applied to already established companies.

Another crucial issue for foreign affiliates in China is the way wages are negotiated and settled with the local union, which is controlled by the party. Staff representatives have obvious links with local power, which has its delegates on the board of the joint venture in accordance with the legal statutes. Thus, the wages are not determined according to the turnover or, more generally, the firm's competitiveness. Again, the foreign partner is constrained to pay for the housing of the workers in proportion with the total payroll. While the level of this disbursement is fixed by law, the effective amount to be paid is negotiated at the local level. It is modulated to lure in foreign capital, but the wage-base calculation is obviously a handicap for labour-intensive projects. Currently, this system is becoming a major lever adopted by local governments to select foreign investment with high-value added prospects.

Globally, Japanese firms operating in China reckon that their profitability is not sufficient. The last Export-Import Bank of Japan survey specified the low rate of return for Japanese affiliates in China in comparison with their counterparts in the NIEs or ASEAN countries. This is quite puzzling when matched with the high prospects for Japanese investments in China as expressed by the firms. One reason behind this apparent paradox could be found in the gap between the expressed intention behaviour of Japanese managers that appears in the survey, as they do not want to show fear *vis-à-vis* China, and the effective behaviour which is more cautious. Another reason, as mentioned before, could be that the prospects for the Chinese market are more appealing than its current situation and contribute largely to explaining the upbeat trend.

The management of the workforce

The management of manpower is also a severe constraint for Japanese firms. Table 4.3 shows that "local managerial staff" and "the level of local workers' skills" appear high in the ranking of the difficulties encountered by Japanese affiliates in China. The level of Chinese workers' skills seems lower than in Thailand or India. This is partly due to the conditions of job regulations. Local bodies which are partnered with foreign firms in joint ventures determine on an arbitrary base the payroll for every plant. As we have mentioned before, this improves the taxes yield, which is based mainly on wages, and also secures jobs to the local population. Hence, foreigners are confronting two problems. First, they are not allowed to hire in accordance with their needs and job qualifications. Second, the lack of concern for hiring and laying off has adverse effects on workers' motivation. Besides, in the case of former state enterprises, a surplus of personnel is a common problem that foreign partners have to deal with. A case in point is the experience of a Japanese firm engaged in a joint venture with a local partner who decided to train all Chinese employees imposed on him by the public partner and who had no first-hand experience of the consumer-orientated strategies or the profit motive of the new business. After the training period the Japanese decided to give back the redundant workers. The local partner thus acquired a requalified workforce while the Japanese firm kept only the employees necessary for its operations. The excess manpower was transferred to jobs inside the Party or the local administration or even to other companies in the same industry.

Table 4.3 Problems associated with Japanese foreign investment in selected host countries (1995) (percentages)

Problems	China (153 companies)*	Thailand (92 companies)*	India (25 companies)*	USA (91 companies)*
Personnel qualified for overseas postings	49	37	60	44
Local infrastructure	64	27	84	0
Local legal system	53	13	24	3.5
Local tax system	49	7.5	20	13
Local procedures for investment approval, etc.	22	6.5	20	1
Local procurement of raw materials & parts	48.5	37	52	15.5
Local managerial staff	37	45.5	20	24
Level of local workers' skills	34	26	24	11
Cost of local labour	10	7.5	0	10
Domestic fund-raising	2.5	4.5	0	5.5
Local fund-raising	25.5	10	20	8
Others	2	2	0	2

Note: *The total number of the firms which have answered appears in parentheses.

Source: Questionnaire on Foreign Direct Investment in Fiscal 1995, Export-Import Bank of Japan, Tokyo

The unpredictability of the transformation of the legal system

During interviews carried out in Japan in April 1996, convergent remarks arose stating that Chinese authorities often alter the local legal system unilaterally and especially in an unexpected way. Particularly, our interlocutors outlined the lack of announcement of time schedules and of the legal content of the modifications. Our interlocutors' emphasis reveals the high sensitivity of this issue for Japanese firms, as unpredictability has severe and adverse effects on the business climate.

The unpredictability affecting the evolution of the legal system can be understood, as China is a country in transition which progressively enforces previously non-existent rules: commercial legislation, fiscal and exchange regulations are continually modified.

In parallel with this uncertainty, another topic is outlined: the deficiencies of the whole national legal system. For, despite an impressive work done by the Chinese lawmakers in the last ten years, there are still numerous drawbacks and questions left unanswered. By and large, the laws are seen as inaccurate in as much as there is no publication of an unified translation and fiats can wait several years to be released. Moreover, some rules, called *neibu* in Chinese language are inaccessible to foreigners as they have not been translated, but nevertheless do not serve their interests. In the case of commercial litigation, the arbitration procedures are lacking and the Ministry of Foreign Trade and Economic Cooperation, together with the Ministry of Finance, have not yet decided on their legal status. Again, the unpredictability of the extent and timing of the removal of fiscal exemptions is underlined. All activities are concerned: manufacturing enterprises, be they wholly-owned subsidiaries or joint ventures, and bank representatives or branches which are still under stringent regulation (they are not allowed to manage operations in local currency except, since 1996, on an experimental basis in a few places like Shanghai).

Unpredictability is also evident in the management of capital resources, as was shown by the example of a new regulation implemented in 1 March 1996: it introduced more stringent conditions for foreign firms established in China for the management of their foreign currencies.

The raising of capital

Paradoxically, access to sources of funding is not a major problem for Japanese investors in China, although indicators and some private statements indicate the importance of this constraint. The underlying reason for this apparent contradiction is that a substantial part of Japanese investment in China is still new. Indeed, at this stage, the foremost preoccupation is not to manage large amount of financial resources as soon as the question of the initial financing or its sharing in joint ventures has been resolved. What is required at this stage are rough instruments or institutions to secure the convertibility of domestic currency so that the non-resident partner will hedge its international activities particularly in relation with the parent company.

Moreover, the present situation is so constrained compared with usual practices elsewhere that it can only improve in near future, as some recent statements indicate. The striking feature is the decision to remove the non-convertibility of the Chinese currency at the end of 1997. Undoubtedly, this will constitute a crucial step for foreign investors operating in China.

Globally, the financing mechanisms are perceived by Japanese as primitive. Up to now the Shanghai and Shenzhen stock exchanges do not seem prominent financing sources. This point of view is shared by all foreign investors in China except those from Hong Kong, who are not considered as foreigners by Chinese authorities. In the medium term, the Shanghai rather than the Shenzhen bourse, owing to strong political support, would constitute a valuable financing source for Chinese enterprises deprived of funds and often associated with foreign investors.

Japanese responses

Due to the lack of direct political support to direct investment in China from the Japanese government, Japanese investors have implemented some adequate responses to cope with the specificities of the Chinese business environment. In order to curb the whole "Chinese risk" these enterprises can broadly count on the solidarity of the parent company, the understanding of their bankers, who have footholds in China, and also increasingly on the flexibility of the general trading companies, *sôgô shôsha*, such as Itochu or Marubeni, which are well established and particularly active in China. The Japanese government is always cautious towards China and has exhibited a certain inconsistency in its general policy *vis-à-vis* this large country. Nevertheless, several public bodies have recently expanded their awareness and some are even supporting Japanese firms more directly. Since 1979 the Overseas Economic Cooperation Fund has increased the official development assistance contribution towards China on a regular basis,[14] whereas the Export-Import Bank of Japan refocused its involvement towards Asian countries whereby China became the first recipient, and the Ministry of International Trade and Industrialization enlarged its China risk coverage at the request of Japanese enterprises. Besides, the involvement of numerous Japan–China economic associations is worth mentioning.

First, the *sôgô shôsha* activities in China are impressive: the leader, Itochu, with a 1996 turnover of 460 billions of yen, has representative offices in 23 cities and commitments in 170 activities ranging from beer manufacturing to highways in built-operate-transfer (BOT) mode.[15] Mitsui has representatives in 18 cities and is involved in 100 projects, and the same is true for Marubeni. This presence obviously contributes to the lessening of the strain of commercial risk exposure for Japanese manufacturers, particularly through trade intelligence gathering and the capacity to set up compensated agreements or provide support in various industrial projects, particularly in remote areas. Then they are improving China is market access for Japanese enterprises – as experienced lately by Kirin Breweries or the Ito-Yokado group, which aimed approval by Chinese authorities to establish department stores across China[16] – and they also take advantage of the different local rules, whether fiscal, legal, or monetary, to get access to scarce resources or build commercial capacities. In the severe environment of China undoubtedly this is an outstanding lever for Japanese investors. Nevertheless, this know-how is not solely accessible to these groups, as anecdotal evidence shows cases of support provided to overseas Chinese who are the prominent investors in mainland China. For example, Itochu is very close to the Thai conglomerate Charoen Pokphand, viewed as the more efficient company in China, as is Marubeni with the first Indonesian conglomerate Salim. These ties are beneficial for Japanese manufacturing enterprises willing to invest in China. Asahi Breweries rapidly gained a foothold in the lucrative beer market by acquiring in 1995 three Chinese beer manufacturers located in the southern coastal area.[17]

Second, the operation of discreet Japan–China economic associations is also a valuable contribution towards Japanese enterprises, particularly those which are willing to invest for the first time in China. There are around 100 such associations, and the Japan–China Investment Promotion Organization established in 1990 is the sole body receiving grants from the Ministry of International Trade and Industry, whereas the majority of the others are private bodies. The counterpart to this quasi-public organization is the Chinese Foreign Investment Promotion Committee, under the administrative supervision of the Ministry of Foreign Trade and Economic Cooperation.

The general goal of the Japan–China Investment Promotion Organization is to trigger Japanese investments in China, which are viewed by the Chinese authorities as too low. In conjunction with general promotion tasks, the organization is focusing on ongoing or anticipated problems facing Japanese investors. This goal is carried out by bilateral working groups in quarterly meetings. The current uncertainty of the legal system for Japanese investors explains the importance of the legal section inside the organization. Besides, during interviews conducted at the Tokyo office, staff representatives stated that the organization was even able to anticipate the evolution of the legal framework, hence contributing to lowering the uncertainty which, as mentioned earlier, is a major concern for Japanese enterprises in China. Moreover, an extensive survey carried out every two years with Japanese companies established in China gives an accurate assessment of the major impediments, and permits the giving of appropriate responses by means of periodical meetings.

Third, the presence of Japanese banks in China through representatives offices or branches is also a potential support for Japanese investors. Those footholds have not been held at the request of Japanese authorities but result from banks' decisions to follow their customers established in China.[18] The geographical closeness of Japanese bank affiliates with Japanese manufacturing plants in places as Shanghai, Dalian, or Shenzhen is not accidental. They support Japanese manufacturing subsidiaries through the provision of consulting and advisory services, and contribute to the financing of their requirements in foreign currency since at the beginning of 1996 they were forbidden to operate in China's domestic currency.[19]

CONCLUDING REMARKS: THE SLOW APPROACH OF CHINA'S ECONOMY TOWARDS THE WORLD ECONOMY

China has applied for membership of the World Trade Organization. Many reforms have been enacted and others are under way.[20] The adhesion of China to the WTO will spur the liberalization of international trade flows and the lowering of trade tariffs in accordance with international levels. The major constraint for the Chinese economy will be to manage the current account balance. The dilemma will be either to follow an import substitution policy, which will increase the attractiveness for foreign enterprises willing to provide the domestic market, or to promote the competitiveness of the Chinese industry to strengthen its export capabilities. In both cases, China will suffer from a growth of imports due to the supply of a huge amount of capital equipment for manufacturing tasks. Hence, the country will have to balance the subsequent trade gap by means of a rise in exports. The further integration of China into the global economy will automatically induce the enlarged presence of foreign investors to provide funds, technologies, and even markets.[21]

From the point of view of Japanese investors, Chinese authorities are facing a dilemma as regards the development of the manufacturing sector as well as for the economy as a whole. One path would be to follow the line set by the broadly liberal model; the other would be a "gradual" transition towards a sheltered system with several safeguarding fences. The first way is conform with the pervasive US model, while the second is more in accordance with the Japanese system experimented with in the post-World War II period. This choice is eminently a political one. Nevertheless, Japanese people think that Chinese authorities will finally choose the second, primarily to avoid severe social upheaval. A brutal liberalization of state-owned enterprises would generate a large number of bankruptcies, which would deprive numerous workers of their safety nets. Provincial inequality would bolster and trigger social instability. China will thus try to follow an industrialization path based on its own economic, social, and political specificities, particularly through the sheltering of infant domestic industries. This tendency will be quite familiar for Japanese enterprises.

These firms are then ready to consider China as a country requiring special treatment: the local environment is not amenable to general rules; hence the current ambivalence that characterizes the Japanese authorities, views of China. By contrast, Japanese enterprises do not share the same feelings. They are well aware that the implementation of the current Chinese policy aimed at the promotion of a domestic industry linked to the world economy will take some time. But in the long run China will constitute an attractive production base for a huge market. Consequently, it is time to invest as soon as possible in order to secure a foothold for what seems to be the world single market in the next millennium.

NOTES

[1] Prime Minister Zhou Enlai, regarding the international state of power.
[2] *Centre de Recherches et d'Etudes sur l'Entreprise Multinationale*, research department of FORUM, Université Paris-X and CNRS, Nanterre-France.

[3] Hong Kong investments are in fact composed of a bundle of investments from numerous countries with a marked share transiting from mainland China.

[4] Export-Import Bank of Japan, 1995; Japan External Trade Organization, 1995.

[5] OECD, UNCTAD.

[6] In 1993, for the first time, the Japanese ratio in overall Chinese trade exceeded the Hong Kong one ratio.

[7] During the fiscal year 1994, 40% of output from Chinese affiliates was directed to the Japanese market (last MITI survey on Japanese affiliates in Asia).

[8] Data provided by the Japanese Ministry of Finance.

[9] Questionnaires were sent to 718 manufacturing companies holding at less three overseas affiliates, with at least one in manufacturing; 422 firms, 60% of the whole sample, answered. For the 1995 survey, the sample was composed of 469 subsidiaries in China from a world-wide total of 6,496. This survey is directed to firms that have some experience in overseas operations. Nevertheless, owing to the relatively small amount of data gathered, it is not a representation of the situation of all Japanese industries operating in China. It only gives a valuable tendency and highlights the ongoing phenomenon.

[10] The maintenance of central government control over key sectors was stressed by the Third Plenum of the 14th Party Central Committee held in 1993.

[11] This section is mainly based on interviews carried out in Japan in April 1996 with a sample of economic actors dealing with China.

[12] Nevertheless, the large-scale Japanese retail chains are gaining approval to establish affiliates (Isetan in Shanghai, Seibu in Guangdong, and Ito-Yokado across China), because the Chinese still have much to learn in the supermarket management field (quick rotation of orders, immediate monitoring of changes in consumer needs, in-out-flows computerization, points of sale, etc.).

[13] Such a preference is still valid for the future. It gathered 70% of responses in 1995 Export-Import Bank of Japan survey.

[14] The first recipient country of Japanese Official Development Assistance in 1995 with US$1.4 billion. Indonesia was second with $892 million, Thailand third with $667 million (ODA Report 1995).

[15] *Far Eastern Economic Review,* 1 February 1996, p. 51.

[16] The resulting venture associated the following shareholders: Ito-Yokado, with 36%; Itochu, with 13%; and the China Sugar and Wine Corp., a public body, securing firm control of the project with 51%. It is widely known that Itochu has intimate ties with Chinese authorities which certainly contributed to bolstering the venture (*The Nikkei Weekly,* 29 April 1996).

[17] *Far Eastern Economic Review,* 1 February 1996, p. 47.

[18] Due to the tradition of cross-shareholding between Japanese companies and banks, in which banks provide generous backing in exchange for a say in management.

[19] The only derogation was consistent with the fact that they could buy

or sell Chinese currency for their foreign customers through swap centres.
[20] Sweeping liberalization of trade and foreign investment regulations in 1996, including a 30% cut in tariffs, steps towards currency convertibility, elimination of many imports quotas and controls, and easing of restrictions on operations by joint ventures with foreign shareholders (*Financial Times*, 20 November 1995).
[21] "Far less of an easy ride", *Financial Times*, 5 October 1996.

BIBLIOGRAPHY

Abo, T. (1994) "Sanyo's Overseas Production Activities: Seven Large Plants in the US, Mexico, the UK, Germany, Spain and China", in H. Schütte, (ed.) *The Global Competitiveness of the Asian Firms* (London and New York: Macmillan and St Martins Press).

Cantor, R. and Packer, F. (1996) "La Notation du risque souverain", *Problèmes économiques*, 2,453, 3 January.

Chevrier, R. (1994) "Chine: la relance des réformes", *Universalia 1994* (Paris: Encyclopaedia Universalis).

Dzever, S. and Zhengyi, W. (1996) "Industrial Distribution Channels in the People's Republic of China", Contribution to the Euro-Asia International Seminar, 7 November, Nantes (published as Chapter 7 in the present volume).

French Chamber of Commerce and Industry in Japan (1995) "Japon-Chine: les amants terribles", *France Japon éco.* (Winter).

Goodhart, C. and Xu, C. "The Rise of China as an Economic Power", *National Institute Economic Review*, February 1996.

Huchet, J.F. and Xiangjun, Y (1996) "Les entreprises d'Etat chinoises à la croisée des chemins", *Revue Tiers-Monde*, 147 (July–September).

Japan China Investment Promotion Organization (1996) "Third Survey on Japanese Enterprises Implemented in China", Tokyo (in Japanese).

Japan Economic Institute (1996) "Managing China: American and Japanese Policies and Prospects for Cooperation", *JEI Report*, Washington, DC.

Kinoshita, T. (1996) "Japan's Direct Investment in China and its Implications", Export-Import Bank of Japan, Research Institute for International Investment and Development, *Staff Paper Series*, Tokyo.

Kume, G. (1996) "Japan's Foreign Direct Investment in a Global Context", Export-Import Bank of Japan, Research Institute for International Investment and Development, *Staff Paper Series*, Tokyo.

Kwan, C.H. (1994) "Asia's New Wave of Foreign Investment", *Nomura Research Institute Quarterly* (winter).

Kwan, C.H. (1996) "The Impact of the Yen's Appreciation on the Asian Economies: The New Wave of Japanese FDI", Nomura Research Institute, *Working Paper*, March 1996.

Pairault, T. (1996) "Les Régions chinoises: industrialization inégale et développements divergents", *Revue Tiers-Monde*, 147 (July–September).

Perkins, D. (1994) "Completing China's Move to the Market", *Journal of Economic Perspectives*, 8 (2) (spring).

Sianesi, B. (1995) "Macroeconomic Determinants of Japanese Foreign Direct Investment in Southeast Asia", *Rivista Internazionale di Scienze Economiche e Commerciali*, 42 (12).

Tokunaga, S. (ed.) (1992) "Japan's Foreign Investment and Asian Economic Interdependence", University of Tokyo.

Wang, S. (1995) "Regional Disparities and Central Government Intervention", *Journal of Social Sciences*, Juyu, Hong Kong.

World Bank (1994) "China, Internal Market Development and Regulation", *Report* 12,291, Washington, DC.

Ysuf, S. (1994) "China's Macroeconomic Performance and Management during Transition", *Journal of Economic Perspectives*, 8 (2) (spring).

5 The dynamics and spatial distribution of Japanese investment in China

Jean-Pascal Bassino and René Teboul[1]

ABSTRACT

The dynamics and spatial distribution of Japanese investment in China have several specific patterns. In spite of this country being the main economic power in the area, Japan's direct foreign investment (DFI) flows represent a relatively small share of the total. Although it may be necessary to re-evaluate the amount of Japanese FDI, this state of affairs seems to result from a better understanding of the country's risks. A greater concern for the medium-term return rate on investment than other foreign investors has, in many cases, induced arbitrage flows in favour of other East Asian countries. The same kind of considerations, but also geographical, political and historical factors, explain why the regional allocation of Japanese FDI flows in China is rather different. Thus its impact is concentrated on a few provinces where its contribution to economic development appears significant.

INTRODUCTION

Between 1980 and 1990, Japanese investment in China only represented a relatively reduced share of the foreign capital in this country but the amount of this investment and its strategic significance have probably been underestimated by Chinese official sources. This study provides a re-evaluation and an analysis of the growth and distribution of Japanese investment flows. In particular, it takes account of the different statistical methods and examines what makes up the determinants of their volume and their regional and sectoral distribution. The aim of this study is both to measure the contribution

73

of these flows to Chinese economic development, with the possible dependence that implies *vis-à-vis* trade with Japan, and also to evaluate the extent of Japanese relocation of its manufacturing industry and the possible impact of this on the productive structure and employment in Japan. Furthermore, it facilitates a comparative analysis of the economic rationality of investing in China, by comparing Japan's choices with those of the other flows of FDI from other countries in Asia and also Europe and North America.

The study carried out resulted in two main observations:

(1) Flows of Japanese FDI have represented globally, in corrected data, especially since the beginning of the 1990s, part of the gross formation of fixed, productive capital, which varies widely according to sector, but is not negligible.
(2) Their geographical distribution differs appreciably from that of other flows, which implies a probably decisive impact for the recent economic development of some provinces.

In the work on the dynamics and determinants of flows of FDI to China, especially investment from Japan, two aspects have been focused on with particular attention: on the one hand, institutional constraints, notably the stages involved in the opening of special economic zones and the development of incentive policies; and, on the other hand, the microeconomic determinants, cost, and availability of factors of production, especially when the regulations framework allows part of the production to flow into the Chinese market.

Understanding the current dynamics of Japanese investments in China does, however, require a historical perspective. Moreover, the sheer size and variety of China's land mass means that local spatial features have to be taken into account. This chapter offers an analysis of the determinants in Japanese investment in China during the period 1985–1995, both on the national level, globally and by branch, and in spatial distribution.

For reasons linked to the nature of available sources, this chapter is presented in two parts. In the first part, the contrast between Japanese and Chinese sources leads us to identify and explain the divergence in data. A comparison of the growth in Japanese investment in China both with that of other countries in East Asia and with global investment in China enables us to evaluate to what extent Japanese firms have atypical behaviour *vis-à-vis* opportunities for investment in China. The dynamics of direct investment seem in fact to result in privileging some countries and some branches according to their comparative advantages and the uncertainty that could affect them. In the second part, the regional distribution of Japanese direct investment is contrasted with the total FDI. The study focuses on the period 1985–1995, as flows were small and difficult to measure at the beginning of the 1980s. The data used correspond to Chinese and Japanese official sources for investment flows on the national level and for the regional distribution of the total of FDI.[2]

THE DYNAMICS OF JAPANESE INVESTMENT IN CHINA

The dynamics of Japanese investment in China pose some evaluation and interpretation difficulties. There are, in fact, persistent and large disparities between the Chinese and Japanese sets of data of flows of Japanese FDI. These can be partly explained by Japanese loans to China to finance local subsidiaries of Japanese corporations, to reinvest in local subsidiaries, and by the existence of investment passing through Hong Kong or other countries in Asia. In these circumstances, adding the amount of Japanese flows going to Hong Kong to those going to China provides a more accurate figure. It appears, however, that in contrast to other investors, Asian or not, Japanese flows of FDI in East Asia are not concentrated on China but remain fairly dispersed. This is also the case from the sectoral point of view, especially from 1990 on, when flows increased sharply.

Analysis and interpretation of divergence in Chinese and Japanese sources on Japanese FDI

The interesting point of contrast between the Japanese and Chinese sources is that a marked break and a divergence appear at the moment when the growth in flows accelerated (Figure 5.1). Thus, up to 1991, Chinese and Japanese sets of data remain relatively close. We can observe a regular, slow growth in investment flows, at a pace which is comparable to that of the total amount of flows. Thereafter, the figures for the exponential growth in investment go from running parallel to diverging increasingly, so that there is a widening gap between these two sets of data. This appears to be linked to the sudden increase in Japanese loans to

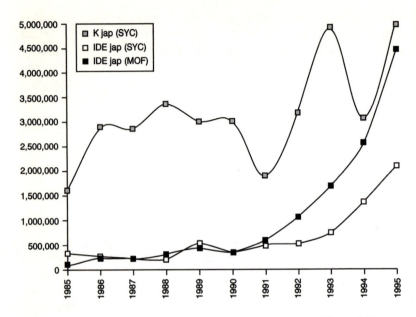

Notes: Kjap: annual total flow of capital from Japan to China; IDE jap: Foreign Direct Investments from Japan to China–SYC: *Statistical Yearbook of China*; MOF: Ministry of Finance of Japan.

Sources: *Statistical Yearbook of China*, Ministry of Finance of Japan

Figure 5.1 Japanese FDI flows and Japanese capital flows (in US$ '000s)

China. It seems indeed that the flows of FDI accounted for by the Japanese Ministry of Finance include loans agreed by Japanese banks or to Japanese companies in China, whereas the Chinese sets of data exclude this Japanese FDI capital, considering it to consist of loans to institutions which are Chinese or under Chinese law.

We can note, in fact, especially since the speculative bubble in Japan burst, that the Japanese banking system in Asia and its activity has strengthened, including within China. This covers not only investment flows to public and private Chinese agents but also to private Japanese agents. Taking loans into account for a revaluation of Japanese investment in China is justified by the fact that flows accounted for as direct investments, in the strict sense, by the Japanese authorities are essentially financed by loans from the Exim Bank, from other Japanese banks or other credit houses, including, in third countries, contributions in capital by controlling companies to their own funds, which represents only a negligible share.[3]

Whereas the level of Japanese loans to China remained largely higher than direct investments as measured by the Japanese authorities up to the end of the 1980s, this gap tended to become smaller from 1991 and even to disappear in 1994 and 1995. This phenomenon could have encouraged the authorities to relativize the apparent acceleration of Japanese investment growth in China in 1994 and 1995, as can be seen in both the Chinese and Japanese sets of data. Indeed, the number of new business set-ups went from 490 to 700 between 1992 and 1993, then to 636 and 770 in 1994 and 1995, according to data from the Japanese Ministry of Finance (respectively, 114, 231 378 and 360, as published in the *Toyo Keizai Yearbook*).

This rapid growth in investment flows, which took place at the same time as the number of new companies stabilized, can, however, be explained both by the existence of some large projects for production manufacturing which were relatively intensely capitalized, and by the increase in the capacity of already existing businesses.

The increasing preference of Japanese agents for financing in yen could be explained by a low rate of nominal interest and expectations of real depreciation of the yen to the dollar and even possibly to the yuan. Another explanation resides in relation to the country's risk and the relative security of this form of investment, in financial terms. Should political tension arise, China would certainly have more difficulty in cancelling private external debt than in freezing, in a more or less disguised form, private foreign assets in manufacturing industry and services.

Assessment of the Japanese share in direct investments in China

Only a small part of FDI to China comes from Japan, about 10 per cent on average, if we take the figures before correction from the Chinese sources. Furthermore, there are considerable fluctuations (Figure 5.2). If we measure the aggregation of loans and direct foreign investments, however, Japanese flows reach levels which are clearly higher, especially at the end of the 1980s, when they were distinctly dominant and generally exceeded 30 per cent of the total, coming down to approximately 15 per cent in the 1990s (see Figure 5.5 in the Appendix).

In the boom phase of investment flows to China from 1991 to

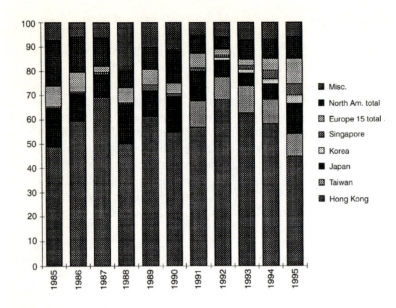

Source: *Statistical Yearbook of China, 1986–1996*

Figure 5.2   Sources of FDI in China (percentages)

1992, when total FDI exceeded 10 per cent of the gross fixed capital formation, Japan's share remained more stable and went from approximately 1 to nearly 2 per cent. This measurement, however, poses, the problem of using the yuan–US$ exchange rate at a time when the yuan was depreciating and in a price system of highly regulated land and capital goods.

Despite this apparent concentration of investment glows to China, if we compare it with the non-Japanese flows in East Asia, it can be seen that Japanese businesses have maintained a wide geographical variety for their FDI by strengthening their interests in Thailand, Indonesia, the Philippines, and even Malaysia, in spite of the comparative advantages in terms of labour costs, which have greatly diminished the attraction of Asian NICs (Newly Industrialized Countries) and ASEAN countries for other investors in the 1990s. The investment flows to China are, in fact, 60 per cent non-Japanese FDI in East Asia from 1992 to 1993.

Another explanation for the relatively low level of Japanese direct investments seems to be the existence of flows forwarded by Hong Kong and Macao. One indication is the growth in Japanese direct investments to the financial sector in Hong Kong between 1988 and 1990 and then since 1993. The increase in the yen's share in the liabilities and assets of banks in Hong Kong, rising from 5 per cent in 1983 to 57 per cent in 1991, tends to confirm this impression.[4] We can estimate from the results of a survey carried out in July 1996 on a number of Western and Japanese economists and financial experts that a volume of approximately 20 per cent of company investment in these two territories in China corresponds in fact to Japanese investments through the intermediary of subsidiaries, in contrast to approximately 30 per cent for Taiwan, approximately 15 per cent for Europe or North America, and probably less than 10 per cent for Hong Kong. In the 1990s, the transfers from this territory to China were practically completed, as the remaining share of manufacturing industries in the GDP shows (barely 10 per cent).

The justification for using Hong Kong as a relay for investments to China seems here again to correspond to a consideration of the country's risks. Taking commercial practices in China into account, it would appear less risky to adopt a territory where mercantile law is effectively respected according to international norms in operation as a base. Moreover, with political integration, subsidiaries of firms in Hong Kong have to aim at becoming Chinese businesses with the advantages that implies in some branches of industrial manufacturing, yet all the while keeping the advantages of a territory where international commitments made by China require the maintenance of familiar judicial frameworks.

In the 1990s, because of the level of Japanese capital stocks accumulated in East Asian countries, reinvestment represented a considerable part of investment by Japanese subsidiaries. The low level of capital flows, corresponding to the repatriation of profits to Japan, can be explained by the poor opportunities for investment in Japan, and the expected differential between the returns on manufacturing industries in Japan and in China.[5] The effect of capital stock accumulated in China in the course of the last few years explains why reinvesting represents the equivalent of approximately 50 per cent of Japanese direct investment in China in 1995, although it only reached a negligible amount up to 1990. These levels of reinvesting remain nevertheless, for the moment, much lower than those observed in Asian NICs and in ASEAN. In these countries they greatly exceed Japanese direct investment flows.[6]

Rather than being limited to recorded bilateral capital flows, the whole of the international organization for internal finance, group by group, should be taken into account in the reassessment of Japanese investment in China.

Jetro and MITI publications emphasize that, as well as subsidiaries in Hong Kong, there are also subsidiaries which are more than 50 per cent owned by Japanese companies in Singapore and other countries in South-east Asia, and these are also a source of Japanese investment in China.

The trends in the share of investment flows to China in terms of Japanese investment in East Asia.

The share of flows to China in the total Japanese investment in East Asia follows a trend which is comparable to that of the other countries but to a smaller extent. The very rapid growth of flows to China from 1984 made this country the main destination in Asia from 1987 on, practically on a par with Hong Kong, whose function as a filter for Japanese investment in China has already been underlined. If flows to this territory are included, Japanese FDI in China then remains at between 30 and 40 per cent.

The China–Hong Kong substitution is quite remarkable, the decline of flows to China between 1988 and 1990 being partly compensated by the increase of flows to Hong Kong. The trend was reversed from 1991, with China becoming, as such, the main destination. We can note in passing that there was practically no "Tiananmen effect"; this was moreover similar for the other sources of FDI.

Despite this appearance of investment flow concentration to China, by comparing it with non-Japanese flows in East Asia, we can observe that Japanese companies have maintained a fairly wide geographical dispersion of FDI by strengthening their interests in Thailand, Indonesia, the Philippines, and even in Malaysia, despite the existence of the comparative advantages of China, in terms of salary costs, which have greatly reduced the appeal of the NICs in Asia or ASEAN for other investors in the 1990s. Flows to China represent, in fact, more than 60 per cent of non-Japanese FDI in East Asia from 1992 to 1993.

Japanese companies thus seem to have adopted fairly atypical behaviour *vis-à-vis* expansion perspectives in China. Besides their sensitivity to the country's risk being greater than that of other external agents, they seem to have implemented choices which have

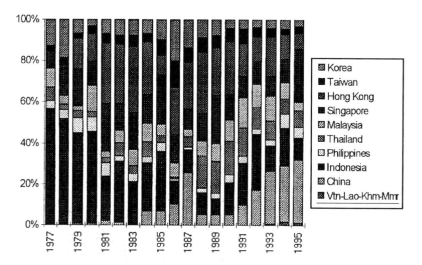

Source: Okurasho (Japanese Ministry of Finance)[7]

Figure 5.3 Distribution of Japanese FDI in East Asia

been determined by their forecasts concerning the position of foreign companies in the perspective of medium-term growth in the Chinese domestic market. In comparison with the situation in other countries in the region, Japanese groups do indeed seem to relativize, more than some of their competitors, the interest of a growth in productive capacity in China. The Japanese inclination for geographical dispersion of their investment is all the more manifest in that accumulated capital stocks, especially in relation to the population, still remain very low in China in comparison with other countries in South-east Asia.

Japanese producers thus appear reluctant to mass-produce automobiles and sophisticated consumer goods in the audio-visual and electronics sectors even though they dominate these markets on a fairly wide scale, as they do in the rest of East Asia. This does not mean that they doubt the existence of a durable and solvent demand, but rather that they fear the consequences of setting up in China in terms of technology appropriation by Chinese producers. In view of the Japanese experience concerning industrial development, they have in fact good reasons for doubting the possibility for foreign companies to carry out mass-production and on-the-spot marketing of sophisticated, strategic, or high-value goods. There is no doubt that, in the long run, the political authorities will reserve the essential elements of the market for national companies.

The sectoral dynamics of Japanese investment in China

Japanese direct investment in China has been characterized by a preponderant share in the manufacturing sector, at least since 1987, but especially since the wave of investment at the beginning of the 1990s. Similarly, China's share in Japanese manufacturing FDI, which increased sharply in the 1990s, reached 44.6 per cent of the Asian total in 1995 (19 per cent of the world total). We can interpret this trend by examining a succession of three stages.

In the first stage, it was the infrastructure of information networks, along with studies of the market place, financing, transport, and marketing, that was put in place with an increasingly fine mesh. An in-depth study could turn out to be very instructive, looking in particular at the setting-up in the different provinces of trading companies, banks, insurance companies, transport companies, and other services of each Japanese *keiretsu*, and also of some specialized groups. One could equally use sets of data on the opening of sales offices of industrial companies as a forward indicator of the manufacturing investment in the different sectors.

In the second stage, which began in 1988, we can see a thrust of investments in the manufacturing sectors that corresponds to production where Japanese firms had a technological advance, and also in sectors where Chinese comparative advantages of salary costs were unquestionable, and finally where local demand was growing strongly. This is the case for mechanical engineering, electrical machines, and precision equipment (included in other manufacturing industries). Here we encounter the traditional characteristics of Japanese investment abroad, fundamentally orientated to satisfying the local market rather than re-exporting to Japan and third countries, also with a large share of the activity relating to the production of plant and machinery, thus contributing to the national accumulation of capital. Moreover, this production was not substituted for production in the same sector in Japan, which was developing, however, towards top-of-the-range and more sophisticated goods.

A third stage has appeared in China from 1991 on with the growing importance of the textile industry, then, around 1992–1993, the growth in transport equipment including automobiles – industries, that is,

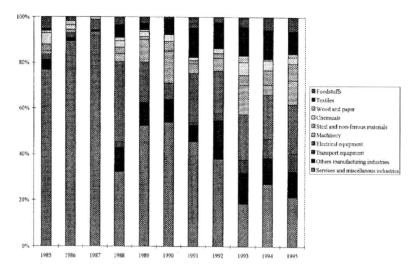

Source: Ministry of Finance, Japan

Figure 5.4 Distribution of Japanese investment by sector in China

which were close to or had reached maturity. This is an example of following a line of systematic relocation, relatively new for Japan, and which implies in the case of textiles the massive destruction of jobs in Japan, and in the case of automobiles the diminishing of exports. The same observation applies more and more to investments in electrical equipment even if Japanese relocation in this sector has benefited NICs and ASEAN.

Having examined the significance of the distribution by sector from the viewpoint of the development of the Japanese productive structure, we might consider the importance of companies with Japanese capital in different manufacturing sectors in China. In the absence of usable sets of data on the gross accumulation of fixed capital according to sector in manufacturing industries in China, the evaluation of the share of Japanese group subsidiaries in the different sectors can be undertaken based on the number of employees in these companies mentioned in the directory of Toyo Keizai, which describes approximately half of the subsidiaries and almost all large-sized companies.

We can thus compare the total Chinese working population and the working population of companies with Japanese capital in 1993 and 1995 (Table 5.4, in the Appendix). The choice of these two years is justified by the fact that the number of Japanese subsidiaries practically doubled in the course of this space of time. We find elsewhere this development in the working population employed in manufacturing industries, rising from 0.25 to 0.39 per cent. These very weak levels should not surprise us. They could, *mutatis mutandis*, be compared (for example) to the share of foreign companies in manufacturing employment in Japan. Moreover, the relocations incited by the search for lower salary costs, which corresponds to the logic of FDI from Hong Kong to China, is, for the moment, only partially that of Japanese groups that are equally active in sectors which are relatively high in capital intensity.

An analysis of sectors for which the ratio of people employed in Japanese capital companies to the total number employed in the sector differs clearly from the average, and enables us to distinguish two groups, other than those sectors close to the average level (textiles, foodstuffs, metallurgy, and so on). On the one hand, this is the case in the base or heavy industries sector where Japanese participation is low due to institutional constraints but also because prices are often regulated and sometimes lower than the world level (coal, among others). On the other hand, this is the case in the previously identified sectors seen as the strong points of Japanese business set-ups in China, with relative levels clearly higher than the average; for example, electrical machines (2 per cent), precision mechanical engineering (0.8 per cent) or even transport equipment (0.8 per cent).

THE SPATIAL DISTRIBUTION OF JAPANESE INVESTMENT IN CHINA

An analysis of the spatial distribution of Japanese FDI by province gives an indirect measure:

- of the efficiency of these investments, which can be perceived through the concentration in some provinces;
- of the image that the Japanese have of the differentiated spatial development of China. The distribution of flows reveals that they consider that Japan is at the centre of the Asian economic system, giving impetus to the whole area.

For the distribution by area of Japanese FDI in China, in the absence of available official sources, an extrapolation has been made using data from the Toyo Keizai Japanese directory numbering 1,425 Japanese company subsidiaries in China, and their founding date, out of a total of 3,698 companies listed in Japanese official data (Ministry of Finance) for the period 1980–1995.[8]

Specificity of the spatial distribution of Japanese investment in China

By examining the distribution by area of Japanese FDI in China in the period 1985–1995, we realize that it is concentrated on a small number of provinces, while the total FDI really only benefits just one province – Guangdong. There is therefore a specificity in the spatial distribution of Japanese investment in China, while flows from Europe and North America seem characterized by a certain tagging-along attitude in relation to flows of FDI from Hong Kong, Taiwan, or the Chinese diaspora. Indeed, because not all provinces have the same economic, demographic, and political weight, it would be desirable to sharpen the reasoning by relativizing the mass of capital according to these criteria. Nevertheless, these percentages enable us to measure the appeal that the different provinces might hold for foreign investors.

Over the period under consideration, five provinces received on average more than 10 per cent of Japanese flows – Beijing, Liaoning, Shanghai, Jiangsu, and Guangdong – and that represented in total approximately 75 per cent of Japanese FDI in China (Table 5.1). Outside the province of Guangdong the distribution of total FDI was more homogeneous since three provinces alone received approximately 10 per cent of the flows – Fujian, Jiangsu, and Shanghai (Table 5.2). Out of the 29 provinces corresponding to the official administrative constituencies, the ten principal provinces received significant Japanese FDI, in all, 93 per cent of flows. Japanese investment was nil in five provinces, and almost non-existent in five others. Conversely, the total FDI was more dispersed, so that the least attractive 19 provinces received nearly 16 per cent of the total and, with the exception of Tibet, all provinces received fairly regular flows. The trend seems, however, to be towards an increased dispersion in the course of the 1990s, both for Japanese and non-Japanese investors.

The logic of Japanese FDI in China thus differs appreciably from

Table 5.1 Estimation of the distribution of Japanese FDI in the main Chinese provinces (percentages)

Year	Beijing	Tianjin	Liao-ning	Shang-hai	Jiang-su	Zhe-jiang	Fujian	Shan-dong	Guang-dong	Si-chuan	Other areas
1985	22.86	14.29	11.43	11.43	5.71	0.00	5.71	2.86	22.86	0.00	2.86
1986	34.38	9.38	6.25	12.50	12.50	0.00	0.00	3.13	12.50	3.13	6.25
1987	35.48	12.90	6.45	16.13	3.23	0.00	6.45	9.68	3.23	0.00	6.45
1988	13.33	6.67	17.78	13.33	4.44	0.00	4.44	8.89	22.22	2.22	6.67
1989	15.52	8.62	17.24	15.52	13.79	3.45	5.17	5.17	13.79	0.00	1.72
1990	10.87	8.70	15.22	26.09	8.70	4.35	6.52	4.35	10.87	2.17	2.17
1991	7.79	2.60	20.78	16.88	7.79	1.30	6.49	3.90	20.78	1.30	10.39
1992	21.05	3.51	8.77	20.18	8.77	7.02	0.88	11.40	11.40	0.00	7.02
1993	8.23	4.33	14.29	26.84	16.45	2.16	2.60	6.06	12.55	0.43	6.06
1994	10.05	4.76	11.11	26.19	11.64	5.29	1.85	4.76	11.64	2.38	10.32
1995	8.89	5.28	8.33	24.72	19.17	5.00	1.11	6.39	11.67	2.78	6.67
1985–1995	13.42	5.88	10.75	22.91	13.45	3.91	2.55	6.51	11.76	1.70	7.16

Sources: 1996 Toyo Keizai Directory of new Japanese subsidiaries by province and by year; Ministry of Finance, Japan, annual flows of Japanese FDI to China

Table 5.2 Geographical distribution of total FDI in the main provinces (percentages)

Year	Beijing	Tianjin	Liao-ning	Shang-hai	Jiang-su	Zhe-jiang	Fujian	Shan-dong	Guang-dong	Si-chuan	Other areas
1985	6.74	4.24	1.86	8.16	2.54	2.02	9.00	2.70	49.42	2.18	11.14
1986	8.60	2.95	2.77	8.55	1.94	1.42	3.59	3.77	49.53	1.83	15.06
1987	6.58	8.79	4.45	14.74	3.21	1.61	3.54	1.64	41.60	1.46	12.38
1988	19.20	1.22	4.40	8.91	3.93	1.13	4.97	1.65	36.58	0.90	17.11
1989	10.19	0.90	6.03	13.50	2.99	1.66	10.52	4.20	36.99	0.26	12.77
1990	8.74	1.10	7.69	5.49	3.92	1.53	9.15	4.76	46.08	0.51	11.02
1991	5.93	3.20	8.46	3.52	5.15	2.22	11.30	4.35	44.18	0.59	11.09
1992	3.18	0.98	4.69	4.49	13.30	2.18	12.94	9.12	33.63	1.02	14.48
1993	2.44	2.24	4.68	11.56	10.40	3.77	10.51	6.85	27.63	2.09	17.81
1994	4.17	3.08	4.37	7.51	11.43	3.48	11.28	7.75	28.74	2.80	15.40
1985–1995	4.58	2.47	4.81	8.52	9.81	3.05	10.65	6.82	31.79	1.98	15.51

Source: China Statistical Yearbook[9]

that of the other FDIs. Non-Japanese investors do not grant the same interest to all the coastal zones, but rather turn most of their attention on Guangdong (nearly a third of total FDI), with relative neglect for Shanghai (less than 10 per cent), Beijing, Tianjin, and Liaoning (less than 5 per cent for each province). Conversely, the Japanese show relatively little interest in Canton and its province, privileging Shanghai, flows of Japanese FDI being twice as much to this province (more than 23 per cent on average over the period under consideration), than to Guangdong (approximately

12 per cent of the total on average). In the same way, the Japanese have invested massively in Beijing and Tianjin (more than 13 per cent for Beijing and nearly 20 per cent for the totality), while other investor countries seem to refer to a narrower economic logic which finds it difficult to integrate the political analysis of decision principles, but also the spatial dynamics of the cost of factors.

Many factors explain the differences in the destinations chosen by Japanese and other foreign investors in China, among which are obvious geographical considerations. For reasons linked both to institutional constraints and to the cost of internal transportation, foreign investors as a whole have, since the opening of China to external capital, been attracted by the coastal zones, which are also the most dynamic. However, Japanese FDI does not cover the whole of this area in a homogeneous way. More precisely, it is concentrated around the Yellow Sea; that is to say, on the coastal area that is situated closest to Japan, after Korea: Liaoning, Beijing, Tianjin but equally Shandong, Shanghai, and the neighbouring provinces.

Distance does not constitute the only determining factor, but it combines with other factors, notably historical ones. There would seem to be an inertia which is linked to a better knowledge by the Japanese of the physical and human environment, and this might partly explain the size of Japanese flows to the north-east of China and the area of Shanghai. After the setting-up of textile firms in the 1920s in Shanghai and Tianjin, in the 1930s and during the Second World War these provinces, along with that of Beijing and of course Liaoning (Dalian corresponds to the ancient Japanese colonial territory of Kwangtung) and the rest of Manchuria, but also Shandong, became a preferred destination for Japanese companies setting up abroad, including in heavy industry or high technology. Although it is not a question of comparable human affinities, this explanation has the same type of effect as that of the often-mentioned family links of the Chinese diaspora with provinces chosen to set up in, as happens very often in the provinces of Guangdong for Hong Kong, and Fujian for Taiwan, or again Shanghai for capitalists of the diaspora, who have become more or less distant heirs of groups which appeared in this city between the two world wars.

Thus in a similar way we might also analyze the political dimension of the choice of Beijing province as a zone to set up in or, more precisely, in the case of the large Japanese groups, one of their business set-ups. China remains, despite all the decentralization and economic liberalization reforms, a country where the decision-making process combines provincial or local levels with central powers, the representatives of companies and those from different hierarchical levels of the party – and if need be, those from unions and workforce organizations – with the problems of influence and corrupt trade that inevitably result from the accumulation of complementary and competitive levels of competence. The proximity of the central powers, independent of the microeconomic profitability of the establishment, gives rise to an advantage that can be analyzed in terms of a reduction in transaction costs and delays.

The spatial dispersion of Japanese investment in China

Nevertheless, the position is not a fixed one. It evolves with the economic development of China and its progression towards the interior of the country, in the same way as Japanese FDI has advanced into new provinces. They follow a dispersion logic which expresses itself in a relative reduction in the flow to Guangdong (the relative weight of FDI is divided by two in this province), and an acceleration of flows to Jiangsu, Zhejiang, and Hebei. Non-Japanese flows follow the same orientation, but it would seem with a certain delay which is due to the fact that Guangdong's share has only really declined since the 1990s and especially since 1992. We come to the paradoxical conclusion that Japanese FDI has a more pioneering behaviour than the other FDIs for which we presume that Chinese capital from overseas or from Hong Kong is dominant. In Shanghai, Manchuria, and Beijing, the percentage difference in distribution observed in the 1990s suggests that nearly half of the FDI in these provinces comes from Japan.

Institutional factors play an essential role here. Waves of foreign investment, but also especially Japanese investment in the different provinces, obviously follow closely the pace at which special economic zones are opened.[10] The logic of spatial concentration of FDI depends also, however, on direct economic determination. In this case, investors have to undertake an arbitration between the anticipated development of factor costs and those of the positive, Marshallian external factors affecting the areas, resulting from the rapid constitution of industrial districts, either *ex nihilo* in the case of some industrial parks (for example, in Jiangsu and Zhejiang) or by the continued specialization of local national companies.

However, similarly, and generally at a later time, negative external factors manifest themselves, which are linked to the rapid development of these specialized industrial districts. They appear in the form of a relative shortage of qualified workers and a very high increase in property or salary costs, which result partly from a deliberate desire of local authorities to reduce the proportion of labour-intensive manufacturing industry so as to facilitate the development of high-technology industries and the upper end of the services sector (for example, in Shanghai). Elsewhere, these negative external factors show up in the saturation of the transport systems and the deterioration of the environment (for example, in the provinces of Guangdong or Shenzhen).

From the viewpoint of the area's dynamics, we can distinguish within the period under review two quite distinct phases that correspond also to stages of the progressive opening-up of China. In the first phase, it is a question of getting a foothold, of establishing solid bridgeheads in the long term, especially in the case of Japanese companies, by putting in place marketing systems without necessarily producing on the spot (audio-visual products, automobiles, and so on). Concern for profitability, in the same way as political fears, incite Japanese investors first of all to locate their business around the big ports and close to the wheels of power (Beijing) which correspond equally to agglomerations where solvent demand is concentrated. FDI could possibly be directed towards provinces with a strong industrial tradition (Tianjin and Liaoning, for example), where Japanese companies have for a long time had preferential commercial partners and faithful clients for plant and machinery, especially in large public companies in the heavy industry or transformation sectors.

In the second phase, which corresponds to the opening of China to external capital and to the development of a large number of areas, a more flexible labour market is gradually being organized, also with a better quality labour force, especially where Chinese executive and management staff are concerned. The distribution of flows is made to neighbouring areas and to adjacent provinces. After Shanghai, FDIs go to Jiangsu and Zeijiang. In some ways it is a quick relocation movement. While non-Japanese FDIs progressed rapidly to Fujian, at the beginning of the 1990s, it was more the adjacent provinces of Shanghai, Zhejiang, and Jiangsu which attracted Japanese capital, which then spread to the inland provinces. The same thing happened starting from Beijing and Tianjin for Hebei, and from Liaoning to the north of Manchuria (Jilin and Heiliongjiang).

The imperative is to search for the lowest costs. It is especially noticeable in provinces where the manufacturing sector is already developed and where the growth of wages greatly exceeds inflation. As compared to Shanghai, the cost of labour is 30 per cent lower in Jiangsu and in Zheijiang, and 50 per cent lower in inland provinces (Anhui, Henan, Hubei). As a general rule, this search for the lowest cost of labour is also accelerated by the property speculation that is raging in the large coastal cities. The same determinants of these capital movements can be observed in Beijing, Tianjin, and Dalian (Liaoning). In the case of foreign investors in Guangdong province, Guangxi, and Hainan are directly concerned; however, these provinces hardly interest the Japanese.

This movement at first generally comes as part of a spatial continuity of investment projects, with industrial parks from the same province sometimes operating as one system so as to facilitate the devolution of business towards highly populated rural zones. Second, only neighbouring provinces are involved. We observe, however, a thrust of Japanese and non-Japanese investment towards inland provinces which are relatively cut off, especially Sichuan; however, it is a question of a trend which remains limited considering the large population of this province.

These movements express an area dynamic which in the end is quite understandable. If we consider that in Asia the economic development model has been given its momentum by Japan, then the penetration of Japanese FDI in China follows a logic of radial-concentric distribution based on hierarchical relationships between the centre and the periphery. The model spread first to NICs and then ASEAN, and it has now reached inland China and is continuing its pattern of spatial expansion. This contagion is brought about as much by the transfer of technologies as by the adoption of production and consumption norms by less developed countries.

CONCLUSION

The volume of Japanese capital invested in China seems to suffer from a certain misjudgement, and it could result in a tendency to neglect its specificity and efficiency. Modes of capital mobilization express, indeed, the account being taken of the country's risks and profitability in the medium term, giving rise to an arbitration in favour of other East Asian countries. By examining its distribution by sector and area, we are tempted to conclude that the economic rationality of Japanese firms concerning FDI in China is probably greater than that of other FDIs, except perhaps that of Hong Kong companies which do not really have a choice. In the provinces which are the preferential destinations of Japanese FDI, the impression of a decisive impact for the economic development of certain provinces does not exclude the fact that there are equally negative drifts. Taking into account estimated investment volumes, we should not exclude the fact that Japanese group subsidiaries have, for example, contributed to an aggravation of local speculative trends in the property market in Beijing and Shanghai. The estimation of FDI broken down by sector for the main provinces enables us better to understand Japanese group strategies and their place in the economic development of China.

APPENDIX

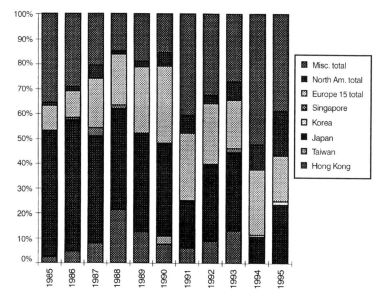

Figure 5.5   Origin of capital flows (loans and FDI) in China (percentages)

Source: *China Statistical Yearbook*, 1986–1996

Table 5.3 Total working population, and in Japanese subsidiaries by sector of manufacturing industry

	Total working population in 1993 (in 000s)	Japanese company employees in 1993*	Japanese company employees in 1995*	Japanese company employees in 1993 (as a %)	Japanese company employees in 1995 (as a %)
Total	614,700	142,564	232,739	0.0232	0.0379
Total manuf.	52,300	132,540	204,378	0.2534	0.3908
Agro-food	4,550	5,724	15,844	0.1258	0.3482
Textiles	8,480	26,235	41,502	0.3094	0.4894
Wood	2,320	615	974	0.0265	0.0420
Printing	930	493	939	0.0530	0.1010
Chemical products	5,230	8,819	9,826	0.1686	0.1879
Petroleum products	680	143	3,152	0.0210	0.4635
Rubber and leather	1,610	1,460	1,731	0.0907	0.1075
Building equipment	3,960	2,066	4,144	0.0522	0.1046
Iron & steel	3,410	857	2,367	0.0251	0.0694
Non-ferrous metals	920	681	1,380	0.0740	0.1500
Metal industries	1,920	3,401	6,078	0.1771	0.3166
Mechanical engineering	7,240	3,619	4,783	0.0500	0.0661
Electrical machinery	3,770	48,118	75,305	1.2763	1.9975
Transport equipment	3,380	4,550	19,657	0.1346	0.5816
Precision mechanical engineering	860	5,998	7,161	0.6974	0.8327
Other manufacturing	2,030	5,851	9,535	0.2882	0.4697

* In the absence of available sources for the total working population by sector in 1995, and considering the low growth of the total working population in manufacturing industries between 1993 and 1995, values for 1993 have been used to calculate the wage-earners ratios of the Japanese subsidiaries to total jobs in the sector.

Sources: Toyo Keizai; China Statistical Yearbook; United Nations Industrial Development Organization; International Yearbook of Industrial Statistics

NOTES

[1] Centre d'Economie et de Finances Internationales (Château Lafarge, Route des Milles, 13290. Les Milles) et Université de la Méditerranée. E-mail: teboul@romarin.univ-aix.fr.

2 The Chinese sources used, for foreign investment, are from the *Statistical Yearbook of China*, and indicate the origin of external capital by country, including Hong Kong and Taiwan, by distinguishing loans and direct investments in different types of companies with foreign capital, and also give the distribution by province. Japanese figures on Japanese investment in China, total and by branch, are those provided by the Ministry of Finance.

3 S. Tokunaga, (1992).

4 International Regulation Bank (1992).

5 Note that these are the expected results, not the real results. In reality, Japanese company profits proved to be fairly disappointing but this was not fully comprehended until 1995 and more so in 1996. Taking non-repatriated profits into account, a source of financing investments is justified by the fact that, in contrast to what exists in relations between OECD countries, these investment flows are not accounted for in Japanese FDI to China (or to other non-OECD countries).

6 Jetro (1996); MITI (1996).

7 Vtn-Lao-Khm-Mmr: Vietnam, Laos, Cambodia, Myanmar.

8 This sample appears sufficient to analyze the distribution, but not to evaluate flows in volume. Extrapolated sets of data for spatial distribution of Japanese FDI in China are obtained by approximate means, taking into account the size of the annual sample, by considering that one can distribute the annual total flow to the different regions by presuming that on average, the flow by company was appreciably the same for the different Chinese regions. The use of each company's social capital as a weighting would probably make it possible to render extrapolated sets of data more reliable, but these indicators do not constitute a real guarantee since investments almost systematically associate stock acquisition with loans on the Chinese, Japanese, or third country capital markets; see Jian An-Chen (1992).

9 For 1980, approximately 40% of foreign investments are not attributed by region but by large Chinese corporations or ministries. It essentially concerns the activity of exploration and oil exploitation off-shore which authorizes us to disregard these flows for the analysis of regional distribution.

10 The institutionalization of economic zones enables the equally rapid concentration of capital in a narrow portion of the economic area. Here the Chinese interest joins with foreign investor interest, especially Japanese in the case of the Sino-Japanese industrial park of Dalian (Liaoning). See Toyo Keizai (1995).

REFERENCES

Adams, G.F., "Economic Transition in China: What Makes China Different?" in *From Reform to Growth: China and Other Countries in Transition in Asia and Eastern Europe* (Parts: OECD, 1994).

Banque des Réglements Internationaux, "Evolution récente des paiments et des financements extérieurs de certains pays d'Asie de l'Est", in *Activité Bancaire et Financière Internationale*, BRI, Département Monétaire et Economique, Básle (August 1992).

Chen, J-A., "Japanese Firms with Direct Investments in China and their Local Management", in Tokugaga Shojiro (ed.) *Japan's Foreign Investment and Asian Economic Interdependence* (Tokyo: University of Tokyo Press, 1992) pp. 257–272. *China Statistical Yearbook*, 1985–1995.

Fukusaku, K., Wall, D., and Wu M., *La "Longue Marche" de la Chine vers une économie ouverte* (Paris: OECD, Etudes du Centre de Développement, 1994).

Healey, D., *Les Exportations japonaises de capitaux et le développement de l'Asie* (Paris: OECD, Etudes du Centre de Développement, 1991).

Japan External Trade Organization (Various publications, 1996) Hakusho, Kaigai Chokusestsutoshi (Tokyo, 1996).

Lee, K., "Making another East Asian Success in China", in *From Reform to Growth: China and Other Countries in Transition in Asia and Eastern Europe* (Paris: OECD, 1994).

Lin, C.Z., "The Assessment: Chinese Economic Reform in Retrospect and Prospect", *Oxford Review of Economic Policy*, 4 (1995).

Maruyama, N., *Industrialization and Technology Development in China*, Institute of Developing Economies, Tokyo, Occasional Papers Series, no. 24.

Minami, R., *The Economic Development of China: A Comparison with the Japanese Experience* (Basingstoke: Macmillan, 1994).

MITI (Ministry of International Trade and Industry), Kaigai Jigyo Katsudo Doko Chosa Gaiyo (Tokyo: 1996).

Okurasho (Ministry of Finances of Japan), *Okurasho Kokusaikinyukyoku Nenpo* (Tokyo: 1996).

Naughton, B., "Chinese Institutional Innovation and Privatization from Below", *American Economic Review*, 84 (2) (May 1994).

Rawsky, T.G., "Chinese Industrial Reform: Accomplishments, Prospects, and Implications", *American Economic Review*, 84 (2) (May 1994).

Rawsky, T.G., "Growing Areal Disparities in China: Some Evidence in the Provision", *Oxford Review of Economic Policy*, 4 (1995).

Sano, T. and Tamamura, C. (eds) *International Industrial Linkages and Economic Interdependency in the Asia-Pacific Area (International Input-Output Analysis)*, Institute of Developing Economies Symposium Proceedings, no. 1, Tokyo.

World Bank, *China: Macroeconomic Stability in a Decentralized Economy*, 1995, Washington.

Yamamoto, K. and Igusa, K. (eds) *Industrial Structure and Human Ressource Development in the Asia Pacific Area*, Institute of Developing Economies (March 1995), Tokyo.

Yamazawa, I. (ed.) *New Development of APEC*, Institute of Developing Economies, 1995, Tokyo.

6 Group relationships and business strategy of Japanese trading companies in the Chinese market

Jacques Jaussaud

This chapter focuses on the effects of group relationships on the business strategy of Japan's general trading companies, taking the Chinese market as a case study.

The structure of the multisectoral industrial groupings[1] in Japan (also called *horizontal keiretsu*) is by now well known. They are large industrial groupings whose affiliate companies are present in almost every sector of the Japanese economy. Because of the anti-monopoly law of 1947 prohibiting monopolistic competition, multisectoral industrial groupings in Japan have structured their activities on the basis of cross-shareholding between member firms. Of these groupings, Mitsubishi, Mitsui, and Sumitomo can be considered the direct offspring of the *zaibatsu* following the Second World War, while others, such as Fuyo, Sanwa, or DKB, represent a regrouping around large banks of companies lacking capital for financing rapid growth during the 1960s.

The nine general trading companies in Japan (also known as *sôgô shôsha*) have more or less close relationships with companies within their own groups. However, the nature of these relationships itself is very much open to debate. If one admits that, in general, these relationships were particularly close during Japan's industrialization period until the eve of the Second World War, one can also underline the fact that they have no longer been the same since the country's period of high growth between 1952 and 1973, and particularly during the 1970s and 1980s. These trading companies, generalists in nature, are often regarded as not particularly suited for promoting specialist and sophisticated products that an increasing number of Japanese companies have been able to produce for two or three decades.[2]

Personalized interviews were conducted in Japan during the months of March through June 1995 with executives from both trading companies and other large firms. The executives of the latter category of firms generally explained that *sôgô shôsha* are no longer essential partners, just useful ones in some situations. Executives from the trading companies, on the other hand, insisted on the fact that today the relationships between enterprises belonging to the same group are very seldom of a strategic nature. When they require a particular service which can only be offered by a trading company, industrial companies belonging to the same group as a *sôgô shôsha* often have no hesitation searching outside of its group to find a more competitive company.

Certain available data lead us to believe that this line of discourse is probably biased. Japanese economic presses[3] regularly refer to a large number of investments made by industrial firms in collaboration with the *sôgô shôsha* belonging to their group, even though in some cases these firms are shown to prefer a *sôgô shôsha* outside of their own groups in making such investments. It is also a well-known fact that the Americans are particularly critical of relationships between Japanese industrial groupings, as these have been perceived as constituting "structural obstacles" to opening up the Japanese market to foreign competition since the 1980s. It is thus to be expected that the attitude of the executives interviewed often tended to minimize the alleged importance of such "obstacles".

I aim to explore several research avenues in order to arrive at a more precise definition of the impact of group relationships on the strategy of Japanese trading companies. One such avenue is to study the subsidiaries of Japanese companies created outside Japan and the nature of collaboration these companies have with the *sôgô shôsha*. There exists a great wealth of information in this area.[4] However, the analysis for the present research will be limited to a study of the subsidiaries created in the People's Republic of China (henceforth referred to simply as "China").

The analysis will proceed in the following manner: first, I provide some precision as to why China constitutes an important empirical base for the present research; next, I provide details regarding the research methodology used; and finally, the principal results obtained will be discussed.

CHINA: PRIORITY FOR JAPANESE INVESTMENT IN THE 1990s

Slow growth in Japan and the appreciation of the yen during the first half of the 1990s provoked an explosion of Japanese direct investment in Asia, just as much as production costs increased considerably in Japan during the 1980s.[5] During fiscal 1994 Japanese foreign direct investment (FDI) in the industrial sector in Asia was by far greater than in North America (US$5.18 billion as compared with $4.76 billion according to statistics supplied by the Japanese Ministry of Finance). All sectors considered, it can be said that Japanese investment in Asia during this period was lower compared to investment in North America, but higher compared to that in Europe.

Japanese investment in China exploded during 1992 and 1993. Kawahara (1995) notes, for example, that the Chinese authorities approved 3,400 investment projects from Japan during 1992 (representing a six-fold increase compared to 1991) for the sum of US$3 billion (four times higher compared to the previous year).[6] When one takes into account delays associated with international business, the effective invested sum would be a little less than that which has been indicated above. An amount of $2.56 billion was recorded in 1994, compared with $9.7 billion which represented total Japanese investment in the whole of Asia during that year.[7]

The activities of Japanese enterprises in China can be even better understood by examining the number of subsidiaries created during the 1990s. Table 6.1 provides an overview of this development. It is clear that the average sum invested (for each operation) in China appears to be rather weak compared to those in other countries. However, the total number of investment operations for this country increases rapidly compared to that of the other countries.

Table 6.1 Number of subsidiaries of Japanese firms in selected Asian countries (1991–1994)

South Korea		*China*		*Taiwan*		*Thailand*		*Indonesia*		*India*	
1991	1994	1991	1994	1991	1994	1991	1994	1991	1994	1991	1994
330	390	277	1057	598	789	816	960	333	431	64	71

Source: "Kaigai Shinshutsu Kigyô Sôran", Tôyô Keizai Shimpôsha, 1995

The nine general trading companies were active participants in this development, contributing capital to the creation of a quarter of these subsidiaries in China up until 1994 (24 per cent to be exact, representing 254 subsidiaries out of a total of 1,057).[8] One can understand better the priority given to China by the *sôgô shôsha* by studying Tables 6.2 and 6.3.

Table 6.2 provides an overview of the total number of subsidiaries in 1991 through 1994 by country. Table 6.3 indicates the relative increases, calculated in accordance with the following formula: (number of subsidiaries in 1994 – number of subsidiaries in 1991)/ (number of subsidiaries in 1991 + number of subsidiaries in 1994)/2). Calculation of such an indicator seems to us to be preferable to a simple increase rate which, in the case of China, would reach a much higher value, considering the fact that the total number of subsidiaries created in this country in 1991 was rather small. Our indicator, reduced to some degree by the fact that growth is restored by averages rather than by the value of the variables studied, makes it a lot easier to carry out a comparison of countries. Table 6.3 clearly demonstrates that it is in China that the general trading companies were most active during this period.

The Chinese environment presents a number of difficulties, which induced some Japanese industrial firms to consult the general trading companies for assistance. This relates to issues such as the necessity to negotiate with central and provincial administrative officials, the ever-changing legal system relating to business, uncertainties related to the political objectives in China, and so on. Such issues clearly enhance the position of partners which have already experienced business in the country, and set up relationships with local interests, as have *sôgô shôsha*. In accordance with Williamson's postulation (1985), turning to a general trading company would enable a Japanese firm to reduce transaction costs in this environment.[9] China constitutes an important environment for our investigation for the following reasons: first, it gives us the possibility of assessing if the tendency of Japanese companies to resort to the assistance of *sôgô shôsha* in such a difficult environment is really frequent or not; and second, if and when they do, is it often to a company within their own group or some other alternative?

Table 6.2 The total number of *Sôgô Shôsha* subsidiaries in selected Asian countries (1991–1994)

Number of subsidiaries	South Korea		China		Taiwan		Thailand		Indonesia		India		Western Europe		North America		Total	
	1991	1994	1991	1994	1991	1994	1991	1994	1991	1994	1991	1994	1991	1994	1991	1994	1991	1994
Mitsubishi Corp.	8	6	8	28	9	14	59	64	12	18	3	2	53	66	100	113	379	449
Mitsui & Co.	7	7	12	49	9	13	77	88	27	30	0	0	89	96	160	166	560	698
Sumitomo Corp.	4	7	1	20	5	11	28	39	17	29	3	3	33	41	63	72	260	383
Itochu	9	6	7	52	11	8	30	32	14	21	2	2	51	58	68	79	321	397
Marubeni	6	3	9	30	6	10	28	34	15	23	0	0	56	66	87	89	340	405
Nissho Iwai	5	5	6	24	1	3	15	18	8	12	2	2	25	31	55	57	191	251
Kanematsu	3	1	2	12	1	4	26	8	6	12	1	1	9	11	14	19	94	113
Nichimen	3	2	5	23	1	1	7	7	12	13	3	3	11	12	14	17	97	120
Tomen	4	2	2	7	11	10	20	26	16	21	1	0	26	29	33	48	209	278

Source: "Kaigai Shinshutsu Kigyô Sôran", Tôyô Keizai Shimpôsha, 1995

Table 6.3 Growth indicator by the number of subsidiaries (1991–1994)
Indicator: (number of subsidiaries in 1994 – number of subsidiaries in 1991) / ((Number of subsidiaries in 1991 + number of subsidiaries in 1994)/2).

Number of subsidiaries	South Korea	China	Taiwan	Thailand	Indonesia	India	Western Europe	North America	Total
Mitsubishi Corp.	-0.29	1.11	0.43	0.08	0.40	-0.40	0.22	0.12	0.17
Mitsui & Co.	0.00	1.21	0.36	0.13	0.11	—	0.08	0.04	0.22
Sumitomo Corp.	0.55	1.81	0.75	0.33	0.52	0.00	0.22	0.13	0.38
Itochu	-0.40	1.53	-0.32	0.06	0.40	0.00	0.13	0.15	0.21
Marubeni	-0.67	1.08	0.50	0.19	0.42	0.00	0.16	0.02	0.17
Nissho Iwai	0.00	1.20	1.00	0.18	0.40	0.00	0.21	0.04	0.27
Kanematsu	-1.00	1.43	1.20	-1.06	0.67	0.00	0.20	0.03	0.18
Nichimen	-0.40	1.29	0.00	0.00	0.08	0.00	0.09	0.19	0.21
Tomen	-0.67	1.11	-0.10	0.26	0.27	-2.00	0.11	0.37	0.28

Source: Derived from Table 6.2

METHODOLOGY

Studies of the importance of group relationships in the strategy of *sôgô shôsha* come up against the question of the specificities of Japanese multisectoral industrial groupings. The notion of membership of an enterprise in a multisectoral industrial group is not always clear. And as we explained earlier, the structure of these groups is often made up of minority cross shareholding between companies belonging to the same group, the idea being to protect the interest of each member while shielding it from hostile takeovers (this is particularly the case in the face of increasing liberalization of the Japanese economy following the country's adhesion to the world trading body GATT in 1955, and the OECD in 1964). Companies belonging to the same group can always develop close relationships with one another without this fact being revealed by studying the list of the principal shareholders within the group.

Membership of an enterprise in a multisectoral industrial grouping can be studied based on the following criteria: first, by studying the total percentage capital of the enterprise in question held by the other members of the group; and second, by studying the participation of the enterprise's representatives in the monthly multisectoral group board meetings.[10] Rather than simply examining membership, an alternative approach to the problem would perhaps be to study the intensity of relationships between enterprises belonging to a group.[11] For the purpose of the present chapter, however, the term *membership* will be retained throughout the analysis.

The relations between general trading companies and industrial groupings in Japan are very complex. Mitsubishi Corp., for example, is the trading arm of the Mitsubishi group, and Marubeni that of the Fuyo group. But Tomen, which is the trading company of the Tokai group, is also very close to the Mitsui group. This is explained by the fact that Tomen was created in 1920 as a result of restructuring and re-naming the existing cotton department of Mitsui & Co. Under this arrangement, Tomen became a member of the enlarged executive board of the Mitsui group.[12] Itochu, which used to be close to the Sumitomo group, had to find new partners when Sumitomo Corp. strengthened its position after the Second World War, and became the principal trading company within the DKB group, leaving Kanematsu behind. Nissho Iwai and Nichimen are the two trading companies of the Sanwa group, but Nissho Iwai

Table 6.4 Industrial groupings and *sôgô shôsha*

Industrial groupings	General trading companies
Mitsubishi group	Mitsubishi Corp.
Mitsui group	Mitsui & Co., Tomen
Sumitomo group	Sumitomo Corp.
Sanwa group	Nissho Iwai, Nichimen
Fuyo group	Marubeni
DKB (Dai Ichi Kangyo Bank) group	Itochu, Kanematsu, Nissho Iwai
Tokai group	Tomen

Source: Derived from *Industrial Groupings in Japan*, Dodwell Marketing Consultants (Tokyo: 1992)

participates in the executive board of the DKB group as well. From this discussion, it is clear that the relationships between the general trading companies and the multisectoral industrial groupings are not necessarily exclusive: they are the result of history as well as of strategy. Strong competition can develop between two companies even if they both belong to the same group.

The present chapter aims to test certain hypotheses, developed after an exploratory study made from March to June 1995. The method of data collection comprised personalized interviews with the executives of the respondent organizations. The general hypotheses of the study can be stated as follows:

H1 Japanese companies very often turn to the general trading companies in their efforts towards internationalization.
H2 Group relationships is a determinant factor for the choice of a trading company when the enterprise is a member of a multisectoral industrial group. In other words, if the enterprise requires the assistance of a trading company in its internationalization effort, it would very often choose one belonging to its own group.
H3 Trading companies generally decline developing relationships with partners belonging to competing multisectoral industrial groups.
H4 In the international environment, the *sôgô shôsha* develop relationships with a significant number of Japanese enterprises which are non-members of their own multisectoral groups.
H5 In developing relationships with a Japanese partner who is a not a member of its multisectoral group, a general trading company avoids competing with an enterprise which is a member of its own group.

These general hypotheses will be studied in relation to a particular form of partnership: the creation of subsidiaries in a foreign market. The present investigation will be limited to the Chinese market.

The general hypotheses outlined above will be studied in relation to five new hypotheses, which are the following:

H'1   Japanese companies very often turn to *sôgô shôsha* for assistance in creating subsidiaries in China.

H'2   Relationships determine the choice of a trading company when the enterprise is a member of a multisectoral group. In other words, if it requires the assistance of a trading company in order to create a subsidiary in China, the enterprise very often chooses a trading company belonging to its own group.

H'3   General trading companies avoid creating subsidiaries in China with partners belonging to a competing multisectoral industrial group.

H'4   *Sôgô shôsha* very often create subsidiaries in China in partnership with companies who are non-members of a multisectoral industrial group.

H'5   In creating a subsidiary in China with a Japanese company which is not a member of its multisectoral industrial group, a *sôgô shôsha* avoids competing with an enterprise belonging to its own group.

In order to test the validity of these hypotheses our analyses will be based on a sample of some 1,057 Japanese subsidiaries in China as at the end of 1994. The adopted approach is as follows:

1   Identification of *sôgô shôsha* subsidiaries in China (created in partnership with another Japanese enterprise) using the directory *Kaigai Shinshutsu Kigyô Sôran '95*[13] published by Tôyô Keizai Shimpôsha.

2   Using the directory *Nihon no Kigyô Gruppu*, by the same publisher, we look to which multisectoral industrial group the Japanese partner might belong. Then we compare, where appropriate, this multisectoral industrial group with that of the concerned *sôgô shôsha*.

We are obliged to work with primary sources published in Japanese since the *Kaigai Shinshutsu Kigyô Sôran* directory has not been translated since 1992 (1991 data), yet it is from 1992 that Japanese investment in China begins to intensify. Furthermore, in order to verify the possible membership of an enterprise in a multisectoral industrial group, we cannot limit ourselves to *Industrial Groupings in Japan*,[14] which takes into account of only 1,800 principal enterprises of the groups, whereas the directory *Nihon no Kigyô Gruppu* identifies 15,000.

Looking at hypothesis H'5, we shall require some more sources, as we shall explain in due course.

THE MAIN FINDINGS OF THE STUDY

Regarding H'1, we have already pointed out that the nine *sôgô shôsha* were involved in 24 per cent of the Japanese subsidiaries in China at the end of 1994 – that is to say, in 254 out of the 1,057 identified by the directory *Kaigai Shinshutsu Kigyô Sôran*. Of those 254, 188 have been set up in joint venture with Japanese partners, which is 18.97 per cent of all subsidiaries set up in China by Japanese companies other than the *sôgô shôsha* alone, or in cooperation with non-Japanese partners (Chinese partners, mainly). When they set up subsidiaries in China, in one case out of five (18.97 per cent), Japanese companies other than the *sôgô shôsha* themselves do it in cooperation with one of the *sôgô shôsha*.

Table 6.5 will help us in looking at hypotheses H'2, H'3, and H'4. Regarding H'2, as shown at the bottom of the table, companies have been loyal to the trading company of their own multisectoral industrial grouping, except the Tokai group. Regarding the Sumitomo group, the loyalty rate is only 41.18 per cent; this is a result of the determined strategy of Itochu towards the Sumitomo group companies, as explained above.

Loyalty of *sôgô shôsha* towards their group companies, which refers to H'3, varies widely from one *shôsha* to another. The loyalty rate is high for Mitsubishi Corp. (80 per cent), Mitsui & Co. (60 per cent), and Sumitomo (100 per cent), but is rather weak for the others. It seems that H'3 is relevant for the former *zaibatsu*, but not for multisectoral groups set up around banks, generally regarded as showing less solidarity. This seems to be because of competition between *sôgô shôsha* within some of the multisectoral groups – namely, Itochu, Kanematsu, and Nissho Iwai within the DKB group, and Nissho Iwai and Nichimen within the Sanwa group. Within the DKB group, Itochu is clearly in a strong position compared to the

Table 6.5 Subsidiaries of the *sōgō shōsha* in China, according to the horizontal *keiretsu* of the Japanese partner

	Mitsubishi group	Mitsui group	Sumitomo group	Fuyo group	DKB group	Sanwa group	Tokai group	Sub-total with a partner member of a keiretsu	With a partner not a member of a keiretsu	Without a Japanese partner	Total no. of subsidiaries in China	Loyalty rate of the shōsha to its keiretsu (%)	% with partner not member of a keiretsu	% without a Japanese partner
Mitsubishi Corp.	8	0	0	1	0	1	0	10	10	8	28	80	35.71	28.57
Mitsui & Co.	4	9	0	0	2	0	0	15	22	10	47	60	46.81	21.28
Sumitomo Corp.	0	0	7	0	0	0	0	7	7	6	20	100	35	30
Itochu (*DKB group*)	2	1	5	1	6	1	0	16	30	7	53	37.5	56.6	13.21
Marubeni (*Fuyo group*)	1	0	0	5	1	0	3	10	8	12	30	6.25	26.67	40
Kanematsu (*DKB group*)	0	1	1	0	1	1	0	3	8	1	12	33.33	66.67	8.33
Nissho Iwai (*DKB, Sanwa*)	0	0	4	0	2	4	2	11	11	2	24	45.45	45.83	8.33
Nichimen (*Sanwa group*)	0	2	0	1	1	1	0	5	14	3	22	20	63.64	13.64
Tomen (*Tokai group*)	1	0	0	1	0	0	0	2	5	2	9	0	55.56	22.22
Total per group	16	13	17	8	13	7	5							
Loyalty rate of keiretsu members towards the Shōsha of the keiretsu (%)	50	69.23	41.18	62.5	53.85	57.14	0							

Source: In accordance with the methodology of this chapter

Warning: in two cases, a *sōgō shōsha* has two different partners from two different *keiretsu* for a given subsidiary (Kanematsu and Nissho Iwai); in two cases, a subsidiary in China of a company which is member of a *keiretsu* has two different *shōsha* as partners (Marubeni and Tomen in one case, Nissho Iwai and Nichimen in the other one).

two other *sôgo shôsha* – namely, Kanematsu and Nissho Iwai. Itochu, as indicated several times earlier, has a very clear and determined strategy for China. This has led the two other trading companies to look for partners outside their group in their strategy towards this market. On the other hand, Nissho Iwai and Nichimen compete with each other within the Sanwa group.

Although formulated by executives during the interviews of March–June 1995, this argument does not explain the whole phenomenon. Marubeni, which as a trading company has no competitor within the Fuyo group, has developed business with several Tokai group members, to the detriment of Tomen. This seems to confirm the hypothesis that group relationships do not necessarily limit potential cooperation, both from the point of view of *sôgô shôsha* as well as other types of companies.

In a number of cases, partners of the general trading companies in China are non-multisectoral group members (hypothesis H'4): 35.71 per cent for Mitsubishi Corp., 46.81 per cent for Mitsui & Co., 66.67 per cent for Kanematsu, and so on. Rates are much higher if we calculate them not related to the total number of subsidiaries that *sôgô shôsha* have set up in China, but to the number of subsidiaries that they have set up with Japanese partners. In this approach, the rate is 50 per cent for Mitsubishi Corp., 59.5 per cent for Mitsui & Co., and so on (Table 6.5). Such high rates, however, do not mean that multisectoral group relationships are slack. Such an interpretation would be valid only if cooperation between trading companies and non-group members were more frequent now than it used to be in the 1960s and 1970s; and above all, if such cooperation led to competition with some members of the group of the *sôgo shôsha*. This situation refers to our broader H'5 hypothesis.

We have formulated H'5 as follows: in creating a subsidiary in China with a Japanese company which is not a member of its multisectoral industrial group, a *sôgô shôsha* avoids competing with an enterprise belonging to its own group. In other words, H'5 assumes that there is no *intra-group competition*.

Looking at H'5, we face a methodological problem. What do we mean by *competing*? Does a trading company truly *compete* with a group member if this one has not been willing to set up business in China, leading the *sôgô shôsha* to look for another partner, outside its group? Furthermore, two different companies in the same field of business may not be competitors, when products are different

(different chemicals, for instance) or when positioning differs (Mercedez and Suzuki, for example, in the car industry).

Looking at H'5 requires a precise identification of activities of firms. We have used the CD ROM JADE,[15] edited and distributed by the Bureau Van DIJK (the Netherlands), using Teikoku Data Bank (Tokyo). JADE provides us with accurate financial and non-financial data covering 100,000 Japanese companies. Activities of firms are precisely listed, according to several nomenclatures. We have used the four-digit SIC-US, commonly used in Japan, and which is more precise than the nomenclature provided by Teikoku Data Bank itself.

We have adopted the following approach: for each Japanese partner of a *sôgô shôsha* in a joint venture subsidiary in China, but not member of its multisectoral group, we have:

1 identified using JADE its activities according to the SIC-US codes (one to ten different codes, sometimes more);
2 looked for members of the multisectoral group of the *sôgô shôsha* in the same field of business, using the directory *Industrial Groupings in Japan* (Dodwell Marketing Consultants, *op. cit.*);
3 identified precisely with JADE the activities of such group members (SIC-US);
4 noticed whether there is (or not) coverage between the activities of the partner and those of group members. In case there is no coverage, we consider that there is no intra-group competition.

When there is no coverage between the activity codes, we can say with confidence that there is no competition between the partner and the identified group members in the same field of business. On the other hand, it is much more difficult to reach a decision when there is a coverage, particularly in the case of a partial one. Positioning of products, as underlined above, may be very different. Furthermore, a company may have a minor activity for a given code, when the other registers a great part of its turnover in it. Unfortunately, JADE does not display turnover according to activity codes. Lastly, coverage is often on a code finishing with 9 – a dummy code for activities not already itemized (*3579: office machines, not elsewhere specified*, for instance). Two different companies, listed under such a code, may produce and sell very different products. Such problems lead us to concentrate our attention on the situation of non-competition.

Table 6.6 Subsidiaries of *Sôgô Shôsha* in China, with partners which
are not members of their multisectoral group, and intra-group
competition

Sôgô Shôsha	No. of subsidiaries in joint ventureship with a non-member of the MSG* of the sôgô shôsha	No. of cases in which there is non-competition with a company of the MSG* of the sôgô shôsha	Non-competition situation rate (%)
Mitsubishi Corp.	11	3	27.3
Mitsui & Co.	22	21	95.5
Sumitomo Corp.	0	–	—
Marubeni	9	5	55.6
Itochu	26	21	80.8
Kanematsu	6	2	33.3
Nissho Iwai	17	9	52.9
Nichimen	12	4	33.3
Tomen	6	6	100
Total	109	71	65.1

*MSG: multisectoral group, or horizontal keiretsu.

Source: In accordance with the methodology of the paper

Another limitation to our methodology might be the fact that we
take into account activities of Japanese companies, not those of
their subsidiaries in China. This latter information is, to the best
of our knowledge, neither listed under the SIC-US index code nor
any other used by JADE. This is, however, not a severe limitation
as activities of subsidiaries in China as described in the directory
Kaigai Shinshutsu Kigyô Sôran '95 show that these are almost always the same as those of the mother company in Japan.

Results are shown in Table 6.6. Let us notice first that we have
lost some information between Table 6.5 and Table 6.6. All partners of *sôgô shôsha*, non-members of their multisectoral group, have
not been identified on JADE, because in some cases they do not
appear. In other cases we have number of homonyms (Asahi Kôgyô,
for instance, or Aoki KK, just to mention two cases), and eventually
because in some cases we could not read some seldom used Chinese
characters. As a consequence, Table 6.6 lists 109 subsidiaries which
have been set up by *sôgô shôsha* with partners which are not members
of their group, where Table 6.5 identified 150 such cases.

Out of 109 subsidiaries identified in Table 6.6, 71 are cases in which there is no intra-group competition, that is to say, 65.1 per cent. For the other cases, as explained above, we cannot know: in some cases there is possibly competition, in others not.

It is worth noting that regarding this issue, results vary widely from one *sôgô shôsha* to the next. Non-competition situation rates are high for Mitsui & Co. and Itochu which have many subsidiaries with non group members, and also for Tomen. The rates are low for Kanematsu, Nichimen, and, to a lesser extent, Nissho Iwai. Once again, competition between trading companies within the DKB and the Sanwa groups seems to be the key factor. Kanematsu, under strong competition from Itochu in the DKB group, has to look for partners outside the group in order to develop business in China. Nichimen suffers from a competitive situation once again from Nissho Iwai within the Sanwa group.

From Table 6.6, it is not easy to comment on the case of Mitsubishi Corp. The non-competition rate is very low – 27.3 per cent. We cannot forget the fact that when we look at a particular trading company the number of subsidiaries is very low, which makes interpretation risky. Furthermore, as already stated, only non-competition situations are clear.

We have also divided up Table 6.6 in order to distinguish the cases in which the partner of the *sôgô shôsha* is a member of another multisectoral group from those of which it is not (see Appendix). We then have 37 subsidiaries in the former case and 72 in the latter. The results do not differ significantly in the two cases, but these figures are not easy to compare as the number of subsidiaries for each *sôgô shôsha* is very low – the reason for the two tables in the Appendix.

CONCLUSION

This research throws new light on the question of permanence of group relationships within multisectoral groups in Japan, and more precisely, on the effects of group relationships on the strategies of *sôgô shôsha*. Setting up subsidiaries in China has been taken up in this chapter as a case study.

Group relationships still clearly matter, but we have found significant differences from one *sôgô shôsha* to another. Differences seem to be mainly (but not totally) explained by the nature of competition between trading companies within given groups – the cases of DKB and Sanwa being good examples.

It will be useful to check the consistency of these results by adopting a different approach to the research problem. I have, for instance, adopted in another paper a sector-based approach using the global auto industry as a case.[16] The results appear to confirm this notion widely.

APPENDIX

Table 6.7 Subsidiaries of *sôgô shôsha* in China, with partners which are members of another multisectoral group, and the situation of intra-group competition

Sôgô shôsha	No. of subsidiaries in joint venture with a member of an MSG* other than that of the sôgô shôsha	No. of cases in which there is non-competition with a company of the MSG* of the sôgô shôsha	Non-competition situation rate (%)
Mitsubishi Corp.	2	0	0
Mitsui & Co.	6	6	100
Sumitomo Corp.	0	–	—
Marubeni	5	2	40
Itochu	10	6	60
Kanematsu	2	0	0
Nissho Iwai	7	4	57
Nichimen	4	1	25
Tomen	1	1	100
Total	37	20	54

* MSG: multisectoral group, or horizontal keiretsu.

Source: In accordance with the methodology of the chapter

Table 6.8 Subsidiaries of *sôgô shôsha* in China, with partners which are not members of any multisectoral group, and intra-group competition

Sôgô shôsha	No. of subsidiaries in joint venture with a company not a member of any MSG*	No. of cases in which there is non-competition with a company of the MSG* of the Shôsha	Non-competition situation rate (%)
Mitsubishi Corp.	9	3	33.3
Mitsui & Co.	16	15	93.7
Sumitomo Corp.	0	–	–
Marubeni	4	3	75
Itochu	16	15	93.8
Kanematsu	4	2	50
Nissho Iwai	10	5	50
Nichimen	8	3	37.5
Tomen	5	5	100
Total	72	51	70.8

* MSG: multisectoral group, or horizontal keiretsu.

Source: In accordance with the methodology of the chapter

NOTES

[1] Catherine Figuirères, "Les Groupes multisectoriels: un atout maître", *Revue Française de Gestion*, 91 (November–December 1992).
[2] See, for example, D. Haber, *Les Sogo Shosha* (Paris: Economica, 1993) pp. 192ff.
[3] See *Nihon Keizai Shimbun*, and particularly the English edition, *Nikkei Weekly*.
[4] See, for example, the directories of enterprises edited by Tôyô Keizai Shimpôsha, mentioned elsewhere in this chapter.
[5] J. Jaussaud, "L'Economie du Japon et des NPI d'Asie", *Grand Larousse Annuel*, 1993.
[6] T. Kawahara, "Booming Investment in China", *Japan Economic Almanac*, Nihon Keizai Shinbunsha, 1995.
[7] M. Ishizawa, "Overseas Investment", *Japan Economic Almanac*, Nihon Keizai Shinbunsha, 1996.
[8] "Kaigai Shinshutsu Kigyô Sôran", Tôyô Keizai Shimpôsha, 1995.
[9] See Williamson, *The Economic Institutions of Capitalism* (New York: Free Press, 1985.)
[10] *Industrial Groupings in Japan* (Dodwell Marketing Consultants, Tokyo, 1992) p. 36.
[11] H. Haakansson, (ed.) *International Marketing and Purchasing of Industrial Goods: A European Perspective* (John Wiley, 1992).

12 The Mitsui group has two executive boards: a limited board with 26 members, and an enlarged board with 74 members. See *Industrial Groupings in Japan*, Dodwell, *ibid.*

13 *Kaigai Shinshutsu Kigyô Sôran*, 1995, Toyo Keizai Shimpôsha, *op. cit.*

14 Periodically published by Dodwell Marketing Consultants, Tokyo. Last edition 1996/1997.

15 JADE (CD ROM), *Japan Accounts and Data on Enterprises*, Bureau Van DIJK, 1997.

16 Jacques Jaussaud, "Sociétés de Commerce et groupes multisectoriels: des relations complexes – le cas de l'automobile", in *Japon Pluriel*, Actes du Second Colloque de la SFEJ Editions Philippe Picquier, 1998.

REFERENCES

Dodwell Marketing Consultants, *Industrial Groupings in Japan* (Tokyo: 1992) p. 36.

Figuière, Catherine, "Les Groupes multisectoriels: un atout maître", *Revue Française de Gestion*, 91 (Nov.–Dec. 1992).

Gerlach, M., *Alliance Capitalism, the Social Organization of Japanese Business* (Berkeley: University of California Press, 1992).

Haakansson, H. (ed.) *International Marketing and Purchasing of Industrial Goods: A European perspective* (John Wiley, 1992).

Haber, D., *Les Sôgô Shôsha*, Economica, 1993.

Ishizawa, M., "Overseas Investment", *Japan Economic Almanac*, Nihon Keizai Shinbunsha, 1996.

Jade (CD ROM), *Japan Accounts and Data on Enterprises*, Bureau Van DIJK, 1997.

Jaussaud, J. "L'Economie du Japon et des NPI d'Asie", *Grand Larousse Annuel*, 1993.

Jaussaud, J. (1998), "Sociétés de Commerce et groupes multisectoriels: des relations complexes – le cas de l'automobile", in *Japon Pluriel*, Actes du Second Colloque de la SFEJ, Editions Philippe Picquier.

Kawahara, T., "Booming Investment in China", *Japan Economic Almanac*, Nihon Keizai Shinbunsha, 1995.

Tôyô Keizai Shimpôsha, *Kaigai Shinshutsu Kigyô Sôran, 1995* (Tokyo, 1995).

Tôyô Keizai Shimpôsha, *Nihon no Kigyô Gruppu, 1995* (Tokyo, 1995).

Williamson, O.E., *The Economic Institutions of Capitalism* (New York: Free Press, 1985).

7 Industrial distribution channels in the People's Republic of China market

Sam Dzever[1] and Wang Zhengyi[2]

This chapter examines the changes that have recently been introduced in the distribution channels for industrial products in the People's Republic of China (PRC), and assesses their overall impact on organizational buyer–seller relationships in this environment. Data for the study were collected during the months of May through July 1996. The sample comprises 72 organizations (local and joint-venture distributors/wholesalers) drawn from the Tianjin and Beijing areas, the sources of which were the following directories: *Zhong Guo Zhi Ming Qi Ye Lu* (A Shortlist of Companies in China), and *Tianjin Zhi Ming Qi Ye Lu* (A Shortlist of Companies in Tianjin). Industrial products handled by these distributors included the following: machines, materials, capital equipment, office equipment, parts, and hand/power tools. The study addressed itself to the following specific issues: the nature and degree of competition between private distributors and state-owned purchasing agencies, the extent to which private distributors have equal access to foreign exchange relative to the state-owned purchasing agencies, the extent to which industrial distribution channels can now be said to be shorter and more efficiently run as compared to the situation before the reforms, import licences, the degree of freedom foreign suppliers have in choosing distributors, and the degree of government control over the running of the channels. Analysis of this nature is important and has significant implications for industrial marketing strategy in this environment.

BACKGROUND

Lambin (1993) maintains that an adequate understanding of the distribution system in any given market constitutes an important factor in properly understanding how it works, the reason for this being that in most markets, the physical and psychological distance between producers and consumers is often so great that the use of intermediaries (distributors and other facilitating agencies) becomes an essential element in the efficient matching of the supply and demand segments in the market place. These intermediaries are required because manufacturers are unable (or unwilling) to assume by themselves, at a reasonable cost, all the tasks and activities implied by a competitive exchange process. The author then goes on to suggest that distribution may be described as:

> organized structures performing the tasks necessary to facilitate exchange transaction. Their role in a market economy is to bridge the gap between manufacturers and end-users by making goods available where they are needed and under the appropriate terms of trade. The functions of distribution channels is to create time, space, and state utilities which constitute the added value of distribution.

A description of the functions of distribution such as this assumes, of course, a competitive market environment. And as the PRC moves from a completely planned economic system to a market-driven one, the role of distribution will no doubt assume an added importance.

Significant changes have occurred in the PRC distribution system following economic reforms first introduced in the late 1970s. These changes are in relation to both consumer and industrial products and have important implications for marketing strategy in this environment. This chapter aims to make a contribution towards a better understanding of this problem with regard to the industrial market.

AN OVERVIEW OF THE MAJOR REFORMS IN THE PRC'S ECONOMY SINCE THE LATE 1970s

The PRC economy has seen major restructuring since the late 1970s, the aim of which has been to steer it towards market mechanism. Among the most important of these measures have been the opening up to the outside world and the encouragement of foreign investment. Special Economic Zones (five in all) have been created especially for foreign investment. To these are to be added 16 "open coastal cities" stretching from Dalian in the north to Beihai in the south. The objective of the government in these policy initiatives was to put into place favourable investment climate in order to attract foreign capital through direct investment as well as joint-venture enterprises with local firms.

Coupled with these developments has been the gradual easing up of trade restrictions in several sectors of the economy, thus making them more receptive to foreign investment. And with the creation of these favourable conditions, three "upsurges" are said to have occurred in the PRC economy since the early 1980s. The first was in 1984, followed by a second in 1988, and a third in 1993. A PRC government publication (1993) notes that under this arrangement, some 83,000 joint-venture projects were approved in 1993 worth US$111.43 million. And, according to Warner (1994), up to 100,000 joint-venture projects were approved by the government from 1991 through 1993.

The PRC government is seeking to modernize a number of state-owned enterprises in its current Five-Year Development Plan. The modernization of these industries will lead to an increase in demand for various types of industrial products, a significant number of which can only be obtained from foreign sources.

Along with these macroeconomic developments have been significant changes in the distribution system since the early 1980s. As noted earlier, this chapter is concerned specifically with analysis of the industrial distribution channels. Before turning to this question, however, it would be useful first to provide an overview of the major changes that have occurred in the wider distribution system since this period. This overview will then become the basis for discussing the more specific issues to be addressed in relation to the objective of the chapter.

THE STRUCTURE OF THE DISTRIBUTION SYSTEM IN THE PRC MARKET

The structure of the distribution system in China following the founding of the People's Republic was a direct reflection of the planned system that prevailed in the other sectors of the economy. Kwan *et al.* (1994) note that following the founding of the People's Republic, measures were immediately taken by the authorities "to abolish the practice of individual commerce in China. Private wholesalers were largely replaced by either state or collectively-owned wholesale agencies". And with the transformation of private retailers to state cooperatives, the state was able to attain hegemony over production and distribution of various commodities in the economy.

This monopolization led to a host of problems, the most important of which was the fact that in the absence of any form of market forces, consumer demand could only be estimated and companies (which were, of course, all state-run) were instructed to produce in accordance with that estimate. And as the state did not always have access to the most up-to-date information upon which it could base its estimates, it became clear that "the composition, quality and specification of commodities" did not reflect correctly the nature of demand. As a result, "apart from the high costs incurred . . . the long channels of distribution [created] time lag between supply and demand. Consequently, goods produced were not marketable and consumers were deprived of desired products" (Kwan *et al.*, 1994).

The government considered at this stage that the principal function of distribution was primarily in relation to supplying basic commodities (mostly foodstuffs) to consumers. Under these conditions, distribution was organized as a three-tier structure with the Ministry of Commerce at the helm. The Ministry of Commerce was the state organ charged with the overall responsibility of supervising the distribution of all commodities in the economy. Directly under this ministry were the various state-owned distributors. The three-tier structure was made up of the following levels:

- first-level purchasing and supply organizations (located in the cities of Tianjin, Shanghai, and Guangzhou);
- second-level purchasing and supply organizations (located in the provincial areas); and
- third-level wholesalers (located in smaller cities and counties).

Under this system, the first-level purchasing and supply organizations bought goods from within the country and from overseas supply sources which it further distributed down the system to the second-level purchasing and supply organizations. The latter, in turn, forwarded the goods to the third-level wholesalers who further distributed them to the various retail outlets located throughout the country, and finally to the end-users. In the rural areas, these outlets were organized primarily as cooperatives. Kwan *et al.* (1994)

further observe that "the retailers were only allowed to buy from the wholesalers within the dictated region" and that "supplies from elsewhere were brought in only as a last resort".

This procedure was used in relation to both consumer and industrial products. For the latter category, however, it was often the case that the end-user having recognized the need for a particular product (either new or replacement) would place a purchase order directly with the appropriate wholesaler (that is, the wholesaler with whom it had its normal business relations). The wholesaler would then forward the order to the appropriate first-level purchasing and supply organization who then would draw up a shortlist of possible supply sources, select a supplier, and purchase the needed item. Once acquired, the product was then forwarded (through the appropriate channels as described above) to the end-user. It must be added, however, that orders of this nature were rare and often the preserve of a selected group of end-users who operated in "key industries". Other types of organizational users had to conform with the types of sourcing arrangement which by now were firmly established in the consumer distribution system – estimate demand and then produce or purchase the needed product in order to meet that demand. But, as earlier noted, there was a severe lack of reliable information relating to just what sorts of products were needed, by which enterprises, and at what times. The result was that often demand could not be met, and in the worst cases, companies ended up with products they did not need.

It became clear that the system needed, as a matter of urgency, some major reforms. Macroeconomic reforms first introduced by the government during the latter part of the 1970s then became the basis for restructuring the entire distribution system.

Three major changes have since occurred in the system. These are:

1 the decentralization of the three-tier authority;
2 significant reforms in the retailing outlets; and
3 the elimination of the fixed price system.

Let us take a brief look at each of these changes.

The decentralization of the three-tier structure constitutes one of the most important policy reforms in this sector. The Ministry of Commerce no longer has exclusive control of the system. Under the new arrangement, both state purchasing agencies and private firms are allowed to engage in distribution activity. This suggests that channels are now relatively shorter, more direct, and possibly better managed. Under the old system, the Ministry of Foreign Trade appointed a purchasing agency and assigned to it the responsibility of sourcing products internationally on behalf of the end-users. Following these reforms, however, the initiative to purchase a product comes directly from the end-user which appoints a purchasing organization to negotiate with the suppliers on its behalf. Various intermediaries still exist in the market place, but on the whole their role now appears to be primarily restricted to the more commercial aspects of the decision process (price negotiations, contract arrangement, agreement regarding delivery schedules, and so on). Responsibility for the more technical aspects of the decision process are generally assumed by the end-users themselves. Indeed, it is often the case that it is the end-user who draws up a shortlist of suppliers and then submits this to the purchasing agency with the instruction that it negotiate the best possible price. From these changes it would appear that foreign suppliers now have better access to the end-users compared to the previous situation.

Important changes have also occurred in the retail outlets during the last few years. It has been observed that under the new system a significant number of the small-scale state-owned companies are being restructured into private or collective ownerships. These enterprises are now relatively freer to choose their own supply sources, in addition to being allowed to introduce a new system of staff compensation based on real contribution to the organization.

The abolition of the fixed price system means that government retail stores now have relative freedom to choose their own supply sources. This is an important development which has significant implications for foreign suppliers in this market as it opens up new possibilities of establishing direct buyer–seller relationships of a long-term nature.

The PRC government has given particular attention to various infrastructural projects in its current Five-Year Development Plan. This entails significant increases in demand for various types of industrial products, a large number of which can only be obtained from foreign sources. The Ministry of Foreign Trade has been assigned responsibility for purchasing various products with respect to all major infrastructure projects.

We can summarize the most important changes that have occurred in the distribution system for industrial products in this market since the early 1980s in the following manner:

- Private wholesalers and retailers are allowed to engage in the distribution of various industrial products in the market place.
- There appears to be some degree of competition between private distributors and government-owned distributing agencies in international sourcing of new or replacement products.
- Private distributors now appear to have better access to foreign exchange due to the easing up of government restrictions.
- There appears to be some flexibility on the part of the authorities in evaluating import licence applications from private distributors.
- Channels appear to be shorter, direct, and possibly more efficiently managed.
- The government appears to have lessened its control over the running of the channels, making it easier for foreign suppliers to establish direct relationships with the end-users.

These issues constitute the subject matter of the present study and we shall return to a more detailed appraisal of them following a brief review of the literature.

THE INDUSTRIAL MARKET IN THE PRC: A REVIEW OF THE LITERATURE

A cursory study of the available literature suggests that there is a serious lack of empirical studies related to the distribution system in the PRC market. This applies equally to both the industrial and consumer markets. And as the PRC's economy becomes more open to international competition, this issue will no doubt become an urgent one for research, since foreign marketers need to have up-to-date information regarding channels in order to enable them design appropriate competitive strategies in this environment.

Among the more recent empirical works analyzing different aspects of the PRC's industrial market are: Kaynak and Kucukemiroglu (1992); Kwan *et al.* (1994); Walter and Mingxia (1995); Chang and Ding (1995); Yadong Luo (1995); Davies *et al.* (1995); Mummalaneni *et al.* (1996); and Dzever (1997).

METHODOLOGY

As mentioned in the introduction, the present study was conducted using distributors in the Beijing and Tianjin areas. The sources of the data were drawn from the following directories: *Guo Zhi Ming Qi Ye Lu* (A Shortlist of Companies in China), and *Tianjin Zhi Ming Qi Ye Lu* (A Shortlist of Companies in Tianjin), both published by the government of the PRC in 1996. The distributors contacted included both state-owned purchasing agencies and private wholesale/retail organizations. A structured mail questionnaire in English was translated into Chinese and mailed to a shortlist of respondent organizations (in all, 150) selected at random from these directories. The questionnaire was not pretested on a smaller sample before the full-scale survey. The criterion for selecting respondents was that they had, during the last few years, been involved in the distribution of an industrial product purchased from a foreign supply source. The questionnaire was generally addressed to the person indicated in the directory as the "contact" person. In a few cases, however, it was necessary to place a call to the organization to explain the nature of the research and request the name of the person to whom the questionnaire could be addressed. And as one of the researchers lived and worked in the Tianjin area, finding out who the appropriate "contact person" was in the respondent organization was a relatively straightforward task.

The questionnaire was divided into two sections. The first section dealt with personal and organizational characteristics of the respondents. The personal characteristics related to issues such as age, sex, education, and the nature of function the respondent had in the organization. In order to guide respondents, the following functions were suggested: "manager", "buyer", "other". In the case of "other", respondents were asked to specify.

Organizational characteristics related primarily to issues such as whether they were state-owned or private distributors, joint-venture enterprises, or "other". (In the case of the latter, respondents were again asked to specify.)

The last part of this section of the questionnaire dealt specifically with issues related to the types of industrial products imported. To guide respondents, the following categories were suggested in the questionnaire: machines, capital equipment, office equipment, raw/processed materials, parts, hand/power tools, "other" (in which case respondents were asked to specify). These products were selected on the basis of the fact that they related mostly to infrastructural projects, in addition to the fact that they were most often mentioned in the directories. Furthermore, and as has already been mentioned, the PRC government has accorded infrastructure projects its highest priority in the current Five-Year Development Plan. The development of these projects would no doubt require significant imports of various types of industrial products. As a result, it can be expected that the government would be more flexible to the possibility of purchasing from various foreign sources.

The second section of the questionnaire contained eight specific statements, and respondents were asked to indicate their preferences on a five-point Likert scale in the following manner:

1 = Strongly disagree
2 = Disagree
3 = Neither agree nor disagree
4 = Agree
5 = Strongly agree

Usable responses were received from 72 firms, representing 48 per cent of the sample. (Some questionnaires were discarded on the basis of insufficient information, or respondents declined to provide answers to key sections of the questionnaire as a means of maintaining client confidentiality, or had not engaged in the distribution of industrial products for a sufficient duration of time in order to hold a "realistic" opinion, and so on). The respondents displayed the following personal and organizational characteristics:

Sex	Frequency	Percentage
Male	54	72
Female	18	25
Age	Youngest	Oldest
	22	54

The majority of the respondents were aged between their mid-30s and mid-40s.

Function in the organization:

Manager	Buyer	Other
45	26	1

Organizational characteristics:

Private importers/wholesalers	State-run importers/wholesalers	Other
16	55	1

The types of products handled by the respondents generally included those specified in the questionnaire. A significant number of them imported several categories of the products, while others concentrated primarily on one particular category.

The eight specific statements on which respondents were asked to indicate their preferences were the following (these roughly corresponded to the issues which had been the subject of much debate since the reform of the sector):

1 The reform of the distribution system in the PRC market has made it possible for private distributors to import industrial products without first seeking the approval of the authorities.
2 Following the reform, there appears to be more open competition between private distributors and government-owned importing agencies in international sourcing of industrial products.
3 Following the reform, it appears that private importers have less difficulty in obtaining foreign exchange approval from the authorities.
4 In assessing applications for foreign exchange, the authorities do not give preference to government-owned importing agencies but, rather, consider all applications on their own merits.
5 Because of the reform, distribution channels are now better managed, making it easier for products to reach end-users quickly.
6 Because of the priority given to the indicated products in its current Five-Year Development Plan, the government appears to be more accommodating in evaluating import licence applications from private distributors.
7 As a result of this reform, industrial distribution channels are no longer strongly controlled by the government, and foreign suppliers can now freely choose distributors in the market place and be confident that their products will be handled expertly whether these are private or government-owned organizations.
8 Following the reform, channels now appear to be shorter and more efficiently run compared to the previous situation.

For data analysis purposes these variables can be restated in the following manner:

1 = Import
2 = Competition
3 = Forex
4 = Authorities
5 = Channels
6 = Priority
7 = Confident
8 = Efficient

RESULTS

The statistical tool used to analyze the data is SPSS. We first calculate the means of the respondents' preferences relative to each of the indicated variables; thereafter a correlation analysis is performed on the data. The results of these analyses are presented below.

Table 7.1 provides an overview of respondents' preferences relative to each of the eight variables. As can be observed, the variable with the highest mean score is "efficient". This indicates a relatively high level of agreement to the statement that, following the reform, channels are now shorter and more efficiently run compared to the previous situation.

The next variable is "confident", which has a mean score of 3.84 and a standard deviation of 0.85. The result indicates a high level

Table 7.1 Mean scores and standard deviation of respondents' preferences

Variable	Mean	Std. Dev.
Efficient	3.92	0.88
Confident	3.84	0.85
Channels	3.75	0.98
Competition	3.50	0.95
Authorities	3.39	1.08
Priority	3.39	1.15
Forex	3.25	1.12
Import	2.71	1.07

of agreement among respondents to the statement that as a result of the reform, channels are no longer strongly controlled by the government and that foreign suppliers can now freely choose their own distributors (whether state-owned or private), and be confident that their products will be handled expertly. This finding is significant because under the three-tier system it was often the case that neither the importing firm nor the foreign supplier had a choice in the matter. Business relations were largely "dictated" by the authorities – the Ministry of Foreign Trade, the Planning Commission, and the State Council (the latter in cases of large infrastructural projects). In a politically determined structure of this nature, neither the end-user nor the supplier had direct relationships. The Planning Commission simply drew up a shortlist of suppliers (very often these were from the countries with whom the government wanted to develop political relations), appointed the appropriate importing agency, and instructed it to purchase the required product on behalf of the end-user.

Our findings suggest, however, that following the reforms there appears to be greater freedom for both end-users and suppliers to establish direct business relationships in the market place.

Next is the "channels" variable, which recorded a mean score of 3.75 and a standard deviation of 0.98. The variable indicates the responses of the importers/distributors to the statement that because of the reforms channels are now better managed, making it easier for products to reach the end-users quickly.

Following immediately after this variable is "competition", with a mean score of 3.50 and a standard deviation of 0.95. The result indicates that respondents agreed (to some extent) with the statement that there is now freer competition between private distributors and government-owned purchasing agencies in international sourcing of industrial products. In theory, this means, for example, that if a state-owned enterprise has a need for an industrial product and wishes to utilize the services of an intermediary to help it source internationally for the product, it will choose the intermediary which has the highest competitive advantage (that is, an intermediary which can find a supplier with lower prices, better services, better possibilities of establishing close buyer–seller relationships of a long-term nature, and so on) rather than based on whether it is a state-owned or private distributor.

The variables "authorities" and "priority" recorded precisely the same mean score (3.39) and standard deviation of 1.08 and 1.15

respectively. The variables indicate respondents' preferences to the statements that (1) in assessing foreign exchange applications, the authorities do not make a distinction between state-owned and private distributors, but simply consider all application on their own merits; (2) because of the priority given to industrial products in the current Five-Year Development Plan, the government appears to be more flexible in evaluating import licence applications from private distributors.

It is very clear from the findings of these two variables that the restructuring of the distribution system has not brought about significant changes in the way the authorities assess either applications for foreign exchange or import licences made by private distributors. It appears that these distributors still have significant difficulties in getting their foreign exchange applications approved by the authorities. Furthermore, the government still appears to be reluctant to approve applications for import licences from private distributors.

The findings suggesting that the authorities still clearly distinguish between private distributors and government-owned organizations in assessing applications for foreign exchange is confirmed by the findings related to the "forex" variable. Here respondents were asked to indicate their preferences to the statement that, following the reform, it appears that private importers have less difficulty in obtaining foreign exchange approval from the authorities. This variable recorded a mean score of 3.25 and a standard deviation of 1.12, coming almost at the bottom of the list.

The variable which occupies the bottom position, however, is "import", which has a mean score of 2.71 and a standard deviation of 1.07. The variable indicates respondents' preferences on the statement that the reform of the distribution system has made it possible for private distributors to import various kinds of industrial products without first seeking the approval of the authorities. These findings indicate once again that, despite the reform, there is yet to emerge a significant improvement in the position of the government when it comes to its assessment of private distributors in this market. This, in turn, suggests that despite the reform a situation of free competition is yet to emerge in the distribution channels for industrial products in the PRC market. These findings are reinforced by the results of the correlation coefficient of the variables shown in Table 7.2.

The table shows correlation coefficient of the variables with a

Table 7.2 Correlation coefficients for variables 1–8

	Authorities	Channels	Compete	Confident	Efficient	Forex	Import	Priority
Authorities	1,0000 (71) P = ,	,0310 (71) P = ,797	,3035 (71) P = ,010	,2124 (70) P = ,078	,0192 (71) P =,874	,2192 (71) P = ,066	,2454 (71) P = ,039	,3456 (70) P = ,003
Channels	,0310 (71) P = ,797	1,0000 (72) P = ,	,2569 (72) P = ,029	-,1295 (70) P = ,285	,2704 (72) P = ,022	-,0894 (72) P = ,455	,0448 (72) P = ,709	-,0291 (71) P = ,810
Competition	,3035 (71) P = ,010	,2569 (72) P = ,029	1,0000 (72) P = ,	,2978 (70) P = ,012	,2181 (72) P = ,066	,4757 (72) P = ,000	,1737 (72) P = ,144	,0884 (71) P = ,464
Confident	,2124 (70) P = ,078	-,1295 (70) P = ,285	,2978 (70) P = ,012	1,0000 (70) P = ,	,0693 (70) P = ,568	,2957 (70) P = ,013	,1371 (70) P = ,258	,3144 (69) P = ,009
Efficient	,0192 (71) P = ,874	,2704 (72) P = ,022	,2181 (72) P = ,066	,0693 (70) P = ,568	1,0000 (72) P = ,	,2767 (72) P = ,019	,2127 (72) P = ,073	,2781 (71) P = ,019
Forex	,2192 (71) P = ,066	-,0894 (72) P = ,455	,4757 (72) P = ,066	,2957 (70) P = ,013	,2767 (72) P = ,019	1,0000 (72) P = ,	,4026 (72) P = ,000	,4815 (71) P = ,000
Import	,2454 (71) P = ,039	,0448 (72) P = ,709	,1737 (72) P = ,144	,1371 (70) P = ,258	,2127 (72) P = ,073	,4026 (72) P = ,000	1,0000 (72) P = ,	,2917 (71) P = ,014
Priority	,3456 (70) P = ,003	-,0291 (71) P = ,810	,0884 (71) P = ,464	,3144 (69) P = ,009	,2781 (71) P = ,019	,4815 (71) P = ,000	,2917 (71) P = ,014	1,0000 (71) P = ,

Notes: (Coefficient / (Cases) / 2-tailed significance).
, designates that a coefficient cannot be computed.

two-tailed significance observed at the level of less than 0.05. The table indicates that there exist strong linear relationships between the following variables: priority/forex, priority/authority, import/forex, forex/competition, and confident/priority.

DISCUSSION

This study has demonstrated that significant changes have occurred in the industrial distribution channels in the PRC market following economic reforms since the early 1980s. These changes relate specifically to issues such as relative freedom on the part of importers to establish direct relationships with foreign suppliers. Government agencies (such as the State Planning Commission, the Ministry of Foreign Trade, and the State Council) now have minimal intervention in the development of industrial buyer–seller relationships in the market place. On the other hand, it appears that the reforms have yet to take effect as far as the position of private distributors is concerned. These distributors still have problems obtaining government approval for import licences, foreign exchange, and so on. These obstacles still exist, and it is open to discussion as to what extent one could say that there is free competition between government-owned purchasing agencies and private distributors in this market. As far as the efficient management of the channels are concerned, the study has found this to be the case. This has been brought about primarily as a result of these reforms, which have also contributed significantly to the shortening of the channels, making them more accessible to foreign suppliers.

IMPLICATIONS

These findings have important implications for industrial marketing strategy in this environment. In designing competitive strategies, foreign marketers of industrial products have to keep in mind that it is now possible to have direct access to the prospective end-users in the market place. And in evaluating strategic partners, it is important to choose one which has ready access to foreign exchange, and one which has a considerable number of business relationships within the channels. These matters are important for successful industrial marketing strategy in this environment.

LIMITATIONS

The study does not constitute a sufficient basis for generalizing on the implications for industrial marketing strategy in the wider PRC market since it was limited to a specific geographical area. In order for the findings to have much wider implications, we need a larger sample preferably drawn from several geographical areas in the country. Despite these limitations, it is our hope that the study has made a modest contribution toward a better understanding of the PRC distribution system and its impact on industrial marketing strategy in this environment.

NOTES

[1] The Norwegian School of Management, Oslo, Norway, and IAE Poitiers, France.
[2] Nankai University, Tianjin, People's Republic of China.

REFERENCES

Chang, K. and Ding, C.G. "The Influence of Culture on Industrial Buying Selection Criteria in Taiwan and Mainland China", *Industrial Marketing Management*, 24 (1995).

Davies, H. *et al.* "The Benefits of 'Guanzi': The Value of Relationships in Developing the Chinese Market", *Industrial Marketing Management*, 24 (1995).

Deng, S. and Wortzel, L.H. "Import Purchase Behaviour: Guidelines for Asian exporters", *Journal of Business Research*, 32 (1995).

Dzever, S. "Industrial Procurement Practices of Taiwanese Firms in the Chinese Market", in S. Dzever and J. Jaussaud (eds) *Perspectives on Economic Integration and Business Strategy in the Asia Pacific Region* (Basingstoke: Macmillan, 1997).

Kaynak, E. and Kucukemiroglu, O. "Sourcing of Industrial Products: Regiocentric Orientation of Chinese Organizational Buyers", *European Journal of Marketing*, 26 (1992).

Kwan, P. *et al.* "Distribution of Consumer Products in China", Paper presented at the conference "The Future of China", INSEAD (Fontainbleau, France: 1994).

Lambin, J.J. *Strategic Marketing: A European Perspective* (London: McGraw-Hill, 1993).

Mummalaneni, V. *et al.* "Chinese Purchasing Managers' Preferences and Trade-offs in Supplier Selection and Evaluation", *Industrial Marketing Management*, 25 (1996).

New Star Publishing, *China's State-owned Enterprises Enter Market* (Beijing, 1993).

Walter, P.G.P. and Mingxia, Zhu "International Marketing in Chinese Enterprises: Some Evidence from the PRC", *Management International Review*, 35 (1995).

Warner, M. "Economic Reform, Industrial Relations and Human Resources Management in the People's Republic of China in the Early 1990s", Paper presented at the conference "The Future of China", INSEAD (Fontainebleau, France: 1994).

Yadong, L. "Business Strategy, Market Structure, and Performance of International Joint Ventures: The Case of Joint Ventures in China", *Management International Review*, 35 (1995).

8 China's emerging markets
Investment strategies of Taiwan's companies
Robert Taylor

THE SETTING

The strategies of Taiwan's companies investing in China are necessarily conditioned by the political and regulatory environments prevailing both on the Chinese mainland and in the Republic of China (ROC).

While military action in the Taiwan Straits prior to and during the island's presidential elections in March 1996 appears to have adversely affected trade and investment between the two countries in the short term, as indicated by recent statistics, economic cooperation would seem set to expand in the long run, if ongoing trends in the 1990s are taken into account. During the months from January to August 1996 Taiwan–mainland trade totalled US$14.02 billion, a 0.66 per cent increase over the same period in 1995. Taiwan's investment in the mainland also increased in value over the same period.

THE POLITICAL AND REGULATORY ENVIRONMENT IN CHINA

Since the initiation of the open door policy in 1978 the Chinese government has sought to encourage foreign investment through various financial incentives, and Taiwan's companies have to date invested mainly, though not exclusively, in Fujian and Guangdong, the provinces immediately opposite the Taiwan Straits, where there are strong linguistic and cultural affinities with the people of the island. The full advantages of investment have, however, not always been realized, due to poor physical infrastructure and an inadequate legal framework, factors at least partially reflected in the geographical and industrial sector concentration of foreign capital input. While the Chinese authorities have continually sought to remedy such deficiencies, regulations issued in 1995 represent a significant new departure by reordering industrial priorities.

Ever sensitive to any perception of economic exploitation by foreign powers, the Chinese leaders have now issued regulations which go further than previous controls in classifying foreign direct investment. There are four categories – recommended, authorized, restricted, or prohibited. Recommended sectors, for example, include energy and transportation systems, projects using advanced technology, export-orientated production, agricultural development, and programmes to open up the resources of China's mid-western hinterland. Nevertheless, foreign investment in previously controlled tertiary sectors like air cargo and shipping is now being permitted. In summary, these priorities reflect the determination of the Chinese authorities to correct the structural imbalances of foreign investment which they see as biased sectorally towards labour-intensive industries and real-estate development, and regionally towards China's coastal areas.

In addition to the promulgation of such measures designed to attract foreign investment in sectors crucial to China's economic development, the central government is also taking steps to improve the macroeconomic controls necessary in a market economy and ensure that laws are consistently applied nationally and locally, the latter being an issue of particular concern to foreign investors. An area of relevance, for instance, is efficient tax collection. Simultaneously, however, the authorities are reassessing concessions to foreigners in order to ensure that benefits they enjoy in China do not confer unfair advantages in competition with domestic Chinese enterprises.[1]

The above legislation applies with equal force to all overseas investors but, seen in tandem with other developments, such priorities could be regarded as potentially advantageous to Taiwan's companies. It is noteworthy that a number of Chinese officially inspired sources, one of which is referred to later in this chapter, discusses at length Taiwan's economic model, suggesting how the changing product life-cycles and new high-tech commodities characteristic of the island's current stage of development fit China's industrial priorities.

Moreover, while political uncertainty remains as a result of China's military belligerency in the Taiwan Straits in early 1996, the leadership in Beijing has been refashioning institutional mechanisms for the intensification of economic cooperation with the island. In the absence of diplomatic relations, given that both leaderships claim to be a government of China, Beijing's unofficial body, the Economic and Trade Coordination Committee for the Two Sides of the Straits, has been accorded enhanced responsibilities to expand the introduction of capital from Taiwan and bring about further political contacts in the interests of reunification on Communist terms. This institution is now taking over some of the functions of the political body, the Association for Relations across the Taiwan Straits. Thus economic lines of communication are to be extended through strengthening contacts between industrialists and intellectuals on Taiwan and their counterparts on the mainland through information exchange and professional training.[2]

Nevertheless, political considerations pervade all aspects of cross-Straits economic relations. Despite incentives given, for instance, by local governments, to investors from the island, the Law for Protecting Investments by Taiwan Compatriots, as its name suggests, is designed to treat such industrialists and entrepreneurs as special domestic investors.[3] In fact, whatever mutual benefit may spring from such capital input, China's policy has a hidden agenda. There is little doubt that the Chinese leaders have used promises of further trade and investment as incentive for political consensus, especially from Taiwan's leaders. A Taiwan source claimed access to a Chinese Communist Party (CCP) internal document which allegedly asserted that the mainland's trade with Taiwan was designed to force the island's investors to pressure their government towards acceptance of unification on Communist terms, by which the island's leaders would eschew any claim to be the government of the whole of China.[4] At the same time the Chinese leaders in Beijing are adamant that Taiwan's government reject completely any popular call for the island's political independence.

THE POLITICAL AND REGULATORY ENVIRONMENT IN TAIWAN

While Taiwan's investment in and trade with the Chinese mainland has been increasing rapidly in the 1990s, it has been, in official parlance, indirect and channelled through Hong Kong, and the island's government has shown itself ambivalent towards the further development of economic relations. The leaders of the Republic of China on Taiwan share with their mainland counterparts the one China concept but interpret it differently; the Beijing view equates that one China with the People's Republic, while in Taipei both sides are considered equivalent parts of a single China.[5] In economic terms the two entities are complementary: Taiwan has the spirit of entrepreneurship, technology, and capital; China, cheap labour, natural resources, and, potentially, a huge domestic market. In the minds of the island's leaders there are two anxieties: the first is that Taiwan's industry will be "hollowed out"; and the second refers to excessive dependence on China. That such investment could put Taiwan at a disadvantage in any future political negotiations has induced caution and conservatism among the island's elite.[6] Thus, in the words of Taiwan's President, Lee Teng-hui, there is to be no political surrender, and closer economic relations are to further mutual interests, establish bilateral trust, and thereby gradually attain the goal of peaceful reunification, but on Taiwan's not Communist terms.

The creation in the early 1990s of two institutions to oversee economic relations, the Mainland Affairs Council of the Executive Yuan, Taiwan's Cabinet, and the Straits Exchange Foundation, itself attests to such ambivalence. The Council is in charge of coordinating and implementing policy; the Foundation is an administrative body, facilitating private cross-Straits scientific and cultural exchanges, processing travel documentation, and acting as an arbitrator in trade disputes. The purpose of both bodies is to promote commerce.

The leaders of the ROC on Taiwan have three main motives in promoting economic relations with the mainland. The first, in terms of treatment here, securing a role for the island in growing regional economic integration, is inextricably linked to the other two, rectifying trade imbalances and facilitating economic restructuring. The Asian Development Bank, for example, has recently noted that economic links between Asian countries are intensifying, and there is increasing dependence on trade with the sub-region formed by Taiwan, Hong Kong, and China. In addition, a report by the American consultancy firm, McKinsey, commissioned by the ROC government, has stated that Taiwan is well placed to play a key role in such integration in a number of spheres: manufacturing, financial services, telecommunications, and transportation. The island is a candidate for such a role, given its key advantages. As its economy is restructured, Taiwan will be well equipped to attract high-tech manufacturing as well as create research and development centres for value-added products, because of its highly educated and disciplined labour force. Growing discretionary income will ensure an attractive, even if limited, domestic market. An already vigorous stock market offers potential for the establishment of a regional financial centre in Taiwan. Geographical location offers an ideal focus for telecommunications and media. Finally, Taiwan has the capacity to become a transportation and distribution centre for sea cargo and an airline hub for both passengers and freight. In any bid to become a regional transportation, communications, and services hub, however, Taiwan could face fierce competitors, like Hong Kong and Singapore, which are as yet superior in legal infrastructure, administrative efficiency, and research and development. Moreover, there remains a major barrier to a role for the island as a regional hub; there are no direct transportation links with China, and Hong Kong controls a large proportion of transhipments, handling container cargo very efficiently.[7] The colony's status in this respect, will, of course, change with its retrocession to China in 1997.

The role envisaged by Taiwan's government has been outlined in the Asia-Pacific Regional Operations Centre Plan, a comprehensive project proposed by the ROC Cabinet in January 1995 to optimize the island's economic prospects. Under the plan, the island would become a specialized regional centre for manufacturing, sea and air transportation, financial services, telecommunications, and regional enterprise. As a first step towards the realization of that plan, the Taiwan authorities have unofficially been sounding out the Chinese government which has reportedly expressed interest in cooperating in a scheme to turn Taiwan's ports into what the ROC leaders call offshore transhipment centres, the first to be designated being the southern city of Kaohsiung. Significantly, the term "offshore" is used to signify that the transhipped cargo will not pass through ROC customs, so that the operations cannot be construed as direct shipping between Taiwan and the mainland, which the island's government still prohibits. The establishment of such offshore transhipment centres is an integral part of the ROC government's plan to turn the island into a sea transportation hub, and would allow foreign and flags of convenience vessels to ship cargo between Taiwan and the mainland, as long as the cargo originated from or is destined for a third party. In addition, Economics Ministry officials have been quoted as saying that if the

transhipment centre plan is successful, legislation may be introduced to designate certain areas as special offshore zones in which
direct exchanges of manpower and products between Taiwan and
the mainland may be undertaken. Such proposals may be seen as
tentative moves towards future direct transportation with the mainland, trade with which is becoming even more crucial for Taiwan's
economic health.[8]

Taiwan's trading relations naturally reflect its stage of economic
development. In recent decades the government has pursued an
export orientation, and to remain competitive on world markets,
the island's manufacturing has moved from labour-intensive textile
industries to more value-added sectors. Japanese investment has
played a key role in this transition, and Taiwan's export products
remain heavily dependent on technology and components from Japan.
But in general the products have been sold not to Japan but to
Western nations, and consequently Taiwan's foreign trade deficit
with that country has been growing. As sectors like electronics will
continue to rely on high quality and competitively priced Japanese
inputs and while Japan's markets remain notoriously difficult to
penetrate, there seems little hope of immediately reducing Taiwan's
adverse trade balance. One solution is to target further the Chinese
market; already Taiwan's investment there is fuelling exports of
capital goods to the mainland.

Thus Taiwan's deficit with Japan must be seen in the context of
the island's world trade. In the 1980s, for instance, Taiwan's trade
deficit with Japan was offset by the trade surplus with the United
States. As the trade deficit with Japan increased, the surplus with
the United States also went up. But since 1987, while Taiwan's
deficit with Japan has continued to climb, the surplus with the United
States has in general been declining. Palliatives, however, have been
growing direct trade with Hong Kong and indirect trade with China
via the British colony. Statistics indicate these trends. In 1995 Taiwan
suffered a US$14.68 billion trade deficit with Japan, according to
Japanese customs statistics cited in a report by the island's Board
of Foreign Trade. In addition, Taiwan's trade surplus with the
United States dropped by 10.4 per cent over the previous year to
US$5.64 billion in 1995. Imports were rising faster than exports. In
contrast, Taiwan–mainland trade, conducted mostly through Hong
Kong, totalled US$20.99 billion in 1995, with the island exporting
US$17.8 billion worth of goods, while importing US$3.1 billion worth
of mainland products. As a result, Taiwan enjoyed a trade surplus

of US$14.7 billion, an increase of 14.8 per cent over 1994. In summary, mainland trade has offset Taiwan's deficit with Japan and moreover contributes to a world surplus for the island. In 1994 Taiwan's trade with China accounted for 9.2 per cent of the island's world trade.[9] In addition, during the first eight months of 1966 the mainland remained the largest source of Taiwan's global trade surplus.

While calling for diversification and cautioning against excessive reliance on the mainland market, government officials have been intensifying dialogue with China's Ministry of Foreign Trade. Surpluses have been fuelled by Taiwan's ventures in China which are importing from the island industrial raw materials, man-made fibre and yarn, machinery, electronics, and electrical appliances for their mainland operations. Surpluses, however, may prove a mixed blessing. The Chinese are exercised by trade imbalances and in February 1996 Wu Yi, the Trade Minister, announced a policy of gradually curbing the deficit with Taiwan. But while this will temporarily cut Taiwan's surplus, as mainland exports increase, the Minister simultaneously promised to improve the mainland's investment climate. In response, Taiwan's Economics Ministry has stated its intention of approving the entry of further categories of imports from China, in addition to the 2,901 materials and product sectors already authorized. Moreover, exports of machinery to the mainland may be reduced following the imposition of higher import duties by the Chinese government. Finally, exports from ventures in China with Taiwan investment may in time further reduce the island's surpluses.[10]

Against this background it is possible to discuss moves towards a Taiwan–mainland industrial division of labour which bodes well for two-way trade and investment. As will be shown in a later section, the sectoral pattern of Taiwan's capital input in China is evolving accordingly and will thus be to some extent at least influenced by the ROC government's external economic strategy. In turn, Taiwan's current official economic policy towards the mainland is only partly in response to the business lobby, as the government must also take into account wider political implications. Business and government no longer speak with one voice. Thus, while not wishing to stem the mainland investment tide, the government has emphasized diversification of national partners and drafted a plan to promote economic cooperation with South-east Asian countries, the so-called Southern strategy. But the complementarities and synergies with China cannot be denied. In early 1994, on the trade front, the government announced new market opening measures. Whereas previously importation of mainland goods had required an import licence issued by the National Trade Bureau, reforms were now being instituted and would pass through three stages, involving a visa system, then a scheme to list negative factors, and, finally, free trade. The transition would take two years. Meanwhile, in September 1995, the ROC government announced measures to allow the indirect importation of an additional 1,432 industrial items from China, even though many agricultural products and some chemicals remained restricted, given the need to protect local producers.[11] In conclusion, although giving the mainland's commodities a more open market will reduce the trade surplus with China, Taiwan's companies will be able to obtain cheaper raw materials and semi-finished products, which could improve the international competitiveness of the island's own exports.

Similarly, in spite of the ROC government's ambivalence, there is growing acknowledgement of the advantages of investment in China. As Taiwan's economy is restructured, a division of labour is emerging. China has a large land area, cheap labour, even if with relatively low productivity, and a government policy encouraging investment. Taiwan, in contrast, has limited space and manpower, and there are calls for stricter anti-pollution legislation. The island is moving away from labour-intensive industries, and as its mainland investment increases, more of its semi-finished products can be produced in China, with resulting cost benefits. Accordingly, the ROC government has latterly been increasing the number of sectors where capital input is permitted. By the end of 1994, for example, Taiwan's companies were allowed to invest in over 4,000 industrial items, over 160 agricultural products, and 14 service industries on the mainland. Most of the approved investment categories included items that were in over-supply in Taiwan. Thus allowing production in China would not threaten to "hollow out" Taiwan's industrial base. The mainland, however, presented a potential threat in some sectors like petrochemicals, textiles, and pharmaceuticals, and if such industries increased their Chinese investments, it could have a negative impact on Taiwan's economy. To meet this threat, one official source has suggested that the government actively pursue a division of labour policy by which Taiwan's companies, especially in high-tech and capital-intensive sectors, upgrade local industry while they apply to invest on the mainland. Local industries would thereby retain their interests in Taiwan and simultaneously benefit from China's low labour costs, thus enhancing their international competitiveness. Reflecting moves towards a division of labour, the government has recently been augmenting the number of categories in which entrepreneurs may undertake investment in China. Such categories fall mainly within the textile, machinery, construction materials, and consumer electronics sectors.[12] The scope, then, for investment by Taiwan's companies on the mainland has been extended, with parameters set by ROC government policy.

The relationship between government and business in Taiwan, in the context of foreign direct investment, is evolving according to the pace of economic change on both the island and the mainland. In Taiwan the state has played a key role in major economic enterprise. Thus, not surprisingly, political considerations have often helped determine the direction of overseas investment flow. Large companies, in close connection with government, have been more cautious, and with greater choice, by virtue of reputation, in selecting an investment location, have tended to follow official dictates, but smaller firms have often proved more entrepreneurial when perceiving profitable opportunities. This is why, until recently, Taiwan's investors on the mainland have been small and medium-sized enterprises, with an average capital input of about US$1 million.[13] Increasingly, companies in all categories have their own strategic agenda, capitalizing on the economic restructuring process in Taiwan itself in addition to the opportunities perceived in the context of China's current stage of development. Taiwan's companies started investing seriously in China in the late 1980s, motivated by rising factor input costs, particularly labour, at home. In order to remain competitive on international markets, they had to move into more capital- and skill-intensive manufacturing sectors and services, while transferring labour-intensive operations offshore. Significantly, in this context, manufacturing represented 39.7 per cent of Taiwan's gross domestic product in 1986 but by 1992 this figure had fallen to 32.9 per cent, and the period also saw the concomitant rise of the service sector. Exports, often labour-intensive products, played a key role in Taiwan's economic take-off, and there are signs that the Chinese Communists are adopting a similar strategy, moving into manufacturing sectors recently vacated by newly developed countries like Taiwan. In fact, writers in Chinese official journals have alluded to the opportunities presented by investment in China, given Taiwan's current stage of development. China's advantage is low labour costs, although it is freely admitted that its quality is inferior, a factor that can threaten productivity. Moreover, unlike Taiwan, which has a highly educated population suited to high-tech service industries, China has a variety of educational levels which can accommodate the needs of labour-intensive ventures and capital-intensive investment. In addition, China suffers from a surplus of rural migrants to the cities, displaced by a rationalizing agriculture, which can only be absorbed by secondary and tertiary industries.[14]

THE STRATEGIES OF TAIWAN'S COMPANIES IN CHINA AND THEIR IMPLICATIONS

Investment by Taiwan's companies in China will now be broadly assessed according to the criteria of raw material and component sourcing, technology transfer, and profitability. According to an ongoing study by Taiwan's Chung-Hua Institute for Economic Research, these three factors are all determined by the short-term orientation of most investing companies. The report concluded that, as of early 1994, Taiwan's companies tender on short-term projects in China, mostly in labour-intensive processing industries. This was because Taiwan's ventures were on average able to reap a profit in just 1.17 years, faster than their foreign counterparts, equivalent figures for Singaporean companies being 1.31 years, Japanese firms 1.33 years, Hong Kong and Macao firms 1.35 years, and US enterprises 1.51 years. Significantly, however, only 6.3 per cent of the profits Taiwan's companies make in China are channelled back to the island. This short-term mentality manifests itself in various ways. Taiwan firms prefer to rent factories, while other foreign investors tend to use the production facilities of their mainland partners or acquire land to build their own plants. In addition, production is often characterized by classic assembly operations, components, and raw materials being sourced from Taiwan. Thus the products, whether plastics, food, or electronics, are already close to the maturity stage when factory production begins in China. For new products research and development is conducted in Taiwan, after which the goods are finished on factory assembly lines in China, where the manufacturers can reduce costs by using cheap labour and taking advantages of anti-pollution laws much less rigorous than those in Taiwan.

Findings suggest that as much as 60 per cent of the Taiwan-funded factories on the mainland acquire their production technology from parent firms on the island. Only 30 per cent utilize the technology of joint-venture partners. In contrast, the report claimed that 40 per cent of the relevant Hong Kong, American, and Japanese firms obtained technology from their home base. Such sourcing methods on the part of Taiwan's companies aid short-term profitability but may be already proving a double-edged sword; heavy reliance on technology from Taiwan may eventually slow flexible response to market change and expose products to disadvantage in competition. Similarly, only 45 per cent of Taiwan's companies obtain finance from mainland banks and only 9 per cent tap into the monetary resources of mainland partners. Once again the short-term view is evident, but obtaining funds from Chinese banks may well increase as the mainland's financial institutions are reformed and long-term company strategy is formulated by Taiwan's firms in China. Furthermore, the island's companies are yet to integrate themselves fully into the Chinese market. According to the institute's report, only 35 per cent of the products manufactured in China by firms from Taiwan are sold on the mainland market, and of the remaining 65 per cent, 12 per cent are sent to Taiwan, 14 per cent to the United States, and 13.2 per cent to Hong Kong. Europe and Japan each account for 7 per cent. Undoubtedly, "short-termism" is a factor in not targeting fully China's domestic market, but also to be taken into account are low profit margins on mainland sales, local currency depreciation, difficulties in ensuring payment from customers, and an antiquated distribution system only just being reformed. But export-orientated industries can easily make money only as long as the vagaries of international markets allow.[15]

In fact, a number of Taiwan's companies are now taking the long-term strategic view that China is potentially one of the largest markets in the world, and these are notable exceptions to the features outlined in the report cited above, and changes in investment orientation have been gathering momentum in the last two years. Attracted by the huge Chinese market, Taiwan's industrialists and entrepreneurs are coming to the conclusion, like Japanese strategists, that success in China is only possible in the long term. In the consumer goods context such commitment is already being aided by Chinese concessions to foreign participation in the distribution sector. A case in point is Taiwan's Vigor International Incorporated which, operating via Hong Kong, entered the mainland market after having obtained a licence from Disney Enterprises to use their trademark in manufacturing and selling products in China. Under the trademark Vigor has designed and produced such products as children's clothes, shoes, and toys, and sold them through more than 100 stores in China, including 36 direct sales stores and 80 franchise stores. Further retail outlets are planned. The company's president attributes Vigor's success in retailing to medium-range pricing and long-term market research.[16]

Investors in Taiwan's computer industry also target the Chinese domestic market but are additionally examples of capital-intensive and skill-intensive operations. In 1992 investment by Taiwan's companies in that industry was growing more rapidly in China than in the ROC. Moreover, whereas earlier such investors had preferred ASEAN countries like Malaysia and Thailand, in 1993 and 1994 Taiwan's information electronics industry was beginning to shift its focus to China. A long-term commitment is suggested by the fact that more and more stages of the production process are being moved to the mainland. Furthermore, computer component suppliers have been following their customers and this will ultimately benefit China's own development. In addition, not only have power supply devices, monitors, and mainframes gradually become production staples but a computer software industry is now being developed on the mainland by Taiwan's information industry, using factory-type quantity production methods. In fact, information electronics is one area of potential synergy. China's scientists can launch artificial satellites but are unfamiliar with large-scale microcomputer production and sales. China's Minister of Electronics Industry has acknowledged that Taiwan's computer technology is a model for emulation. Even if in the long run China will move out of such a pursuer mode, in the immediate term cooperation with Taiwan is crucial for the future development of China's electronics industry.

In turn, relocation on the mainland has undoubted benefits for Taiwan's computer companies, the ability to employ highly qualified manpower and target huge markets in China as well the United States and Japan, to which such products are being increasingly exported, being but two, as stated by the leaders of major companies like Acer, based in Beijing. There are, however, risks. The production technology provided by Taiwan's firms is transforming the mainland's information electronics industries, and quite soon the former's differential advantage may be lost. The danger is that China will become a competitor. As yet the mainland cannot compete with Taiwan in high-quality electronics products as a whole but its industry is progressing rapidly. Thus, if at least some stages of the manufacturing process are not retained in Taiwan, there could be long-term adverse effects on the latter's economy. Finally, as Taiwan's manufacturing in China moves beyond assembly towards knowledge-based operations, not only will low-skill employment be further reduced in Taiwan but even software specialists will be trained on the mainland. When that stage is reached, local staff will be competent to direct Taiwan's plants in China and managers from the ROC may be replaced. This could have serious implications for Taiwan as high-tech industries become the backbone of its economy.[17] The key to Taiwan's economic survival lies in maintaining a lead in capital- and skill-intensive sectors like information technology, and, as discussed, there are already signs that the island's investors are addressing these issues strategically.

INVESTMENT TRENDS

It is now possible to summarize the above trends in the mainland investment of Taiwan's companies under a number of headings and to suggest future directions. The criteria are: geographical location, industrial sector, and capitalization. Taiwan since the late 1980s has been one of China's major capital suppliers, and in early 1996 an ROC government source estimated that investment exceeded US$20 billion, including capital from over 25,000 companies, although the caveat must be entered that government-approved projects account for only a third of the estimate. According to current estimates, Taiwan, with investment exceeded only by Hong Kong and the United States, may in fact be China's largest investor, since much of the British colony's capital input derives from companies in the ROC.[18] Certainly, China is now the main destination for Taiwan's foreign investment, which now represents about 10 per cent of the total invested on the mainland, placing the ROC within the top three investors.[19]

To date, Taiwan's investment has been heavily concentrated regionally, with 60 per cent accounted for by the southern provinces of Fujian and Guangdong. Fujian is a natural partner; its labour surplus contrasts with Taiwan's shortage, many of the island's investments being, up until recently, labour intensive. Enterprises from Taiwan in a number of sectors, including shoemaking and textiles, have transferred production to Fujian, and latterly so have electronics and other high-tech industries. In an echo of earlier stages of Taiwan's own development programme, the island's Hsinchu Hi-Tech Park has signed contracts with Xiamen Torch High Tech Park to set up a joint operation. In addition, Taiwan's companies have invested more than US$1 billion in Fujian's agriculture, representing 60 per cent of the province's total foreign funds in that sector. Economic cooperation is being intensified, and the province now provides more than 60 per cent of essential goods for daily consumption in Jinmen (Quemoy) and the Matsu Islands, near the mainland but controlled by Taiwan.[20] Another major investment site is the province of Jiangsu, where 20 of the leading 100 enterprises in Taiwan have invested. Here again the trend is towards technology and capital-intensive enterprises. Importantly, in accordance with Chinese government priorities, energy, transportation, and infrastructural sectors have begun to attract more and more of the island's investment in Jiangsu, as elsewhere. Referring to investment in the province, a mainland source reported that by the end of June 1995 the Jiangsu provincial government had approved the establishment of 5,622 enterprises, founded by Taiwan's companies, capitalized in total at US$7 billion.[21]

Taiwan's investors have also been targeting other provinces and cities on the coast. Since 1992, however, there has been a trend towards greater dispersion of Taiwan's investment, and a Chinese source indicated in 1995 that the island's investors have been involved, albeit minimally, in remote provinces like Xinjiang, Gansu, and Yunnan, even though entrepreneurs are naturally cautious about pouring funds into inland areas, where infrastructural development remains rudimentary. This trend may be set to continue, given the Chinese government's policy of encouraging investment in the hinterland rather than the south-eastern coast in order to ameliorate regional inequalities of wealth.[22]

A trend towards greater geographical dispersion is accompanied by a change in the industrial and sectoral focus of Taiwan's companies. China's current developmental priorities are less favourable to foreign investment in labour-intensive manufacturing, and Taiwan's investors in that sector are facing increased competition from other foreign investors as well as lower profit margins due to new tax legislation, credit tightening, and tougher labour laws. Moreover, wage costs are rising in labour-intensive manufacturing. Thus Taiwan's mainland manufacturers are increasingly focusing on China's capital-intensive heavy industries and technology-intensive electrical and machinery sectors. Taiwan's enterprise thus seek to gain competitive edge through upgrading technological capability in capital-intensive sectors and improving quality in consumer goods manufacturing.[23] There has also been a discernible move from short-term profit-making to a long-term investment planning orientation. These trends were reflected in new investments by Taiwan's companies in China during 1995. The Republic of China Investment Commission noted that electronics and information products, Taiwan's most competitive manufactures globally, had replaced labour-intensive goods and foodstuffs as the island's companies' largest new investments on the mainland during the first ten months of 1995. For example, during that period the Commission approved mainland investment applications worth US$861 million by electronics and information products manufacturers. The next largest investments were in food products, valued at US$648 million and aimed at exploiting the potentially vast mainland market. The third investment group included rubber and plastic products, capital input for which reached US$275 million.[24]

High-tech investment and further targeting of China's domestic market indicate a longer-term orientation among Taiwan's companies, and this is perhaps nowhere better illustrated than in commitment to China's developmental priorities like agriculture and infrastructure, where there is already involvement by governments on both sides of the Straits. Agricultural cooperation and exchanges have been taking place for seven years, in spite of periodic deterioration of cross-Straits relations, especially in early 1996. Under semi-official auspices Taiwan's companies have launched more than 2,000 investment projects in the mainland's agricultural sector. In 1996 relevant government bodies on the mainland are taking further steps to promote such cooperation. There are to be more tecnological exchanges, and selective production cooperation projects will be initiated in provinces as far apart as Fujian, Anhui, Sichuan, and Liaoning.[25] Furthermore, one of Taiwan's companies is active in the creation of infrastructure on the mainland. The Everyman Group, one of the world's leading marine shippers, has received ROC government approval to construct a container depot in Shanghai, and the feasibility of similar projects for the Chinese cities of Tianjin and Qingdao is under consideration by the group. The development of such facilities, when seen in conjunction with the proposed construction of offshore transhipment centres in Taiwan itself, may be regarded as a prelude to the eventual establishment of direct transportation links.[26]

Additionally, the authorities on the two sides of the Straits have agreed to cooperate in resource exploitation – witness the agreement to explore for oil in an area between south Taiwan and the Guangdong coast.

Geographical dispersion and the establishment of capital- and skill-intensive enterprises both demand improvements in China's infrastructure. Participation in these sectors by Taiwan's companies will necessitate higher capital outlays, usually beyond the reach of individual companies. In fact, since 1994 a number of Taiwan's industrial concerns have been considering cooperation with Japanese and US interests.[27] Already the scale of Taiwan's investment in the mainland is increasing. Hitherto, until the mid-1990s, the average value of such projects was about US$1 billion, much lower than equivalent investments by ROC companies in South-east Asia. Recent applications approved by the ROC's Economic Ministry's Investment Commission include investments in a tyre factory, a video cassette recorder venture, and a food processing plant, all exceeding US$5 million in value.[28]

The strategic focus of Taiwan's companies has shifted from short-term profit to the long-term targeting of China's domestic market.

SUMMARY AND CONCLUSIONS

This chapter has examined the investment strategies of Taiwan's companies targeting China's emerging domestic markets. It was shown that these are to some extent still constrained by the lack of diplomatic relations between the two Chinese governments. Such strategies must also take account of the political and regulatory environments in Taiwan and China. Since the two economies may be seen to a great extent as complementary, the respective governments have devised institutional mechanisms whereby investment by Taiwan's companies may be facilitated. Investment, however, is still officially indirect and undertaken via Hong Kong.

The concessions offered by the Chinese to other foreign investors apply equally to Taiwan's manufacturers. Taiwan's companies have technology and capital, China, abundant labour. The island's entrepreneurs also have the advantage of linguistic and cultural affinity, attributes not possessed by other foreign investors. Largely on the basis of labour-intensive manufacturing, the island has become one of the top investors on the mainland.

It was demonstrated, however, that mainland investment presents both political and economic challenges for Taiwan, and it is here that the island's government and its industrialists remain in potential conflict. There is the anxiety among government officials that close economic integration will lead to political unification on Communist terms. In addition, Taiwan's industries may be hollowed out as its technological expertise and employment are transferred to the mainland. This becomes potentially more likely as Taiwan's investors move from labour-intensive to capital- and skill-intensive sectors.

Taiwan's investors are also adjusting their investments in accordance with China's developmental priorities, including high-tech industrial and infrastructural sectors. A new tax regime and employment laws in China are factors in high wage costs, especially in labour-intensive sectors. While until recently Taiwan's investment had been mainly concentrated in textile and electronics assembly plants in the southern provinces of Fujian and Guangdong and focused on producing largely for export markets, the island's companies are now moving into high-tech value-added sectors, goods being aimed at China's vast potential market. This change in industrial or sectoral focus and growing interest in China's infrastructure have led to a greater geographical dispersion of Taiwan's capital. There is also higher capital input in individual ventures. A new long-term perspective on the part of Taiwan's investors may also presage future economic cooperation under the auspices of the two governments. Such an optimistic scenario, however, presupposes that, on the passing of Deng Xiaoping, there is neither a protracted succession struggle nor a military confrontation severe enough to reverse or curtail the economic open door policy pursued by China's leaders since 1978.

NOTES

[1] Industrial priorities and macroeconomic controls are discussed in Kato Kozi, "Implications of China's Evolving Industrial Policy for Foreign Investment", JETRO *China Newsletter*, 1995, no. 119, p. 1, and JETRO China-Northeast Asia Team, "Investment Roundup", *ibid.*, 1996, no. 120, p. 204.

[2] Details concerning the Economic and Trade Coordination Committee are given in a report in a Taiwanese newspaper, *Lien Ho Pao*, and reproduced in *Summary of World Broadcasts*, 13 February 1996.

[3] For the law relating to Taiwan's investors, see Deborah Shen, "Peking's Investment Law Vague", *Free China Journal*, 18 March 1994.

[4] The internal CCP source is discussed in *Joint Publications Research Service*, 10 March 1994.

[5] Christie Su, "As Tensions Ease, Taipei focuses on Cross-Straits Ties", *Free China Journal*, 26 April 1996.

[6] See, for example, the discussion in G.L. Clark and W.B. Kim (eds) *Asian NIEs and the Global Economy* (Baltimore: The Johns Hopkins University Press, 1995) p. 259.

[7] I have examined issues concerning Taiwan's role in Asian regional integration at some length in my book *Greater China and Japan* (London: Routledge, 1996).

[8] A number of sources have analyzed the Asia-Pacific Regional Operations Centre Plan. See, for example, Susan Yu, "Peking Buoys ROC Shipping Project", *Free China Journal*, 6 October 1995; and Christie Su, "ROC Calls for the Mainland to Cooperate over Shipping", *ibid.*, 15 December 1995.

[9] Deborah Shen, "Deficits with Japan, Korea Grow", *Free Chinese Journal*, 9 February 1996; figures for trade with the United States appear in Deborah Shen, "Record Year for Foreign Trade; Surplus Back on a Growth Track", *ibid.*, 12 January 1996; two-way trade across the Taiwan Straits is reported in a Central News Agency, Taipei, source, "Taiwan to Cut Trade Surplus with China by Increasing Imports", as carried in *Summary of World Broadcasts*, 5 February 1996. For trade with China as a percentage of Taiwan's world total, see "Taiwanese Officials Urge Exporters to Reduce Dependency on Chinese Market", a report from the Central News Agency, Taipei, 25 September 1995, as carried by *Summary of World Broadcasts*, 27 September 1995.

[10] Recent Taiwan – mainland trade negotiations are examined by Deborah Shen, "Military Exercises by Mainland Put a Damper on Trade Activities", *Free China Journal*, 9 February 1996. For the imposition of import duties by the Chinese, see "Trade with Taiwan Continues to Increase", from a Central News Agency, Taipei, source, as reproduced in *Summary of World Broadcasts*, 12 July 1995.

[11] Assessment of current ROC government policy appears in "Cross Strait Trade Policies Analyzed", *Chin Pao* (The Mirror), a Hong Kong journal, no. 2, 5 February 1994, pp. 80–81, carried by *Joint Publications Research Service*, 6 April 1994. The importation of more categories of mainland goods is discussed in "More Restrictions on Chinese Imports Dropped", Central News Agency, Taipei, as reported in *Summary of World Broadcasts*, 27 September 1995.

[12] The twin themes of economic restructuring and division of labour are pursued by Kelly Her, "Biggest Taiwan Project in Mainland Gets Go Ahead", *The Free China Journal*, 11 November 1994.

[13] G.L. Clark and W.B. Kim (eds) *Asian NIEs and the Global Economy* (Baltimore: The Johns Hopkins University Press, 1995) p. 261.

[14] *Ibid.* See also Shen Yi, "The Upgrading of Taiwan's Production and the Mainland's Economic Development", *Guomin Jingji Guanli Yu Jihua* (Management and Planning of the National Economy), 1995, no. 9, pp. 178–184. Similar themes are also pursued by Satoshi Imai, "Comparison of Western, Overseas Chinese and Japanese Ventures", *China Newsletter*, no. 119, (1995) p. 15.

[15] Allen Pun, "Study Looks at Mainland Projects", *Free China Journal*, 4 March 1994.

[16] Deborah Shen, "Chinese Economies Tend towards Mutual Reliance", *Free China Journal*, 7 January 1995.

[17] Investment by Taiwan's computer companies on the mainland is discussed in "New Triangular Relationship: Deterioration of Taiwan Firms' Two Sides of the Strait Advantange", *Tien-Hsia* (Commonwealth), December 1993, no. 12, pp. 21–31, as reproduced in *Joint Publications Research Service*, 10 March 1994. I have examined the possible adverse consequences for Taiwan's economy arising from computer manufacturing investment on the mainland in my book *Greater China and Japan* (London: Routledge, 1996).

[18] For total investment, see Kelly Her, "More Businessmen from Mainland to Visit", *Free China Journal*, 26 April 1996; references to government-approved investment appear in a report from Taiwan's News Agency CNA, "Plans for Further Deregulation of Controls on Investment in China", as reproduced in *Summary of World Broadcasts*, 10 February 1996. Taiwan-derived Hong Kong investment is mentioned in Deborah Shen's article "Chinese Economies Tend towards Mutual Reliance", *Free China Journal*, 7 January 1995.

[19] R. Garnaut, E. Grilli, and J. Riedel (eds) *Sustaining Export Oriented Development* (Cambridge: Cambridge University Press, 1995) p. 263. Taiwan's stake is given by Satoshi Imai, "Comparison of Western, Overseas Chinese and Japanese Ventures", *China Newsletter*, no. 119 (1995) p. 15.

[20] For the concentration of Taiwan's investment in Fujian and Guangdong provinces, see *China Newsletter*, no. 119 (1995) p. 24; the scope of Taiwan's companies' investment in Fuijan appears in a report from the Xinhua News Agency in Beijing, "Fujian and Taiwan Intensify Economic and Trade Co-operation", as reproduced in *Summary of World Broadcasts*, 6 September 1995.

[21] "Taiwan Businessmen Invest Heavily in Jiangsu Province", *Xinhua News Agency*, as reported in *Summary of World Broadcasts*, 30 August 1995. Statistics concerning enterprises appear in "Taiwan Invests over Seven Billion Dollars in Jiangsu", *Xinhua News Agency*, as reproduced in *Summary of World Broadcasts*, 27 September 1995.

[22] For details of nationwide investment by Taiwan's companies, see Shen Yi, "The Upgrading of Taiwan's Production and the Mainland's Economic Development", *Guomin Jingji Guanli Yu Jihua* (Management and Planning of the National Economy), no. 9, (1995) pp. 178–184.

[23] These issues are analyzed in Kelly Her, "Taiwan – Mainland Trade Flourishes", *Free China Journal*, 7 July 1995.

[24] Deborah Shen, "Record Trade with Mainland in 1995", *Free China Journal*, 6 January 1996.

25 "China – Taiwan Co-operation in Agriculture Reviewed by Chinese Agency", a Xinhua News Agency report, as carried in *Summary of World Broadcasts*, 20 January 1996.

26 See Kelly Her, "Shanghai Cargo Depot Approved", *Free China Journal*, 26 August 1994.

27 The Chinese mainland perspective concerning such emphases appears in a survey of Taiwan's potential role in China's development published in *Gongye Jingji* (Industrial Economics), no. 11, (1995) pp. 136–137.

28 The US$5 million figure is given by G.L. Clark and W.B. Kim (eds) *Asian NIEs and the Global Economy* (Baltimore: The Johns Hopkins University Press, 1995) p. 261. Statistics for recent diverse investments by Taiwan's companies appear in Kelly Her, "Shanghai Cargo Depot Approved", *Free China Journal*, 26 August 1994.

Part III

Country-based Analysis – India

9 India

Fifty years after independence

Aline van Beveren

On the eve of India's fiftieth Independence anniversary, a statement by its first Prime Minister, Pandit Nehru, is still up-to-date:

A long time ago we made a trust with destiny and now the time has come when we shall redeem our pledge. At the stroke of the midnight hour, when the world sleeps, India will awake to life and freedom. A moment comes but rarely in history when we shall step out from the old to the new, when an age ends and when the soul of a nation long suppressed finds utterance.

India has always aroused strong reactions (positive and negative) and conflicting feelings. The country has often appeared as a place of contrast, rather difficult to understand. It is a country as large as a continent, where religions, languages, and customs so different from one another coexist. What can one say about the geography and cultural diversity of a country which recognizes 15 official tongues? So many differences exist in India, all of which contribute to the "value" and identity of the country.

To most Westerners India is almost like a dream. Starting with the writers and novelists of the eighteenth and twentieth centuries, who hasn't fought with Captain Corcoran, who hasn't admired the courage of the Maharani of Jhansi or the adventures of heroes along the spice route, or those who took part in the lives of the Moguol emperors or Maharajas, like Benoît de Boigne with the Scindia family in Gwalior?

Contracts found in India's geography and various cultures are also present in its economy, as are extremes and paradoxes. India has a world-wide task force that is well known for its dynamism and exceptional education (the country's engineers, for example, are ranked among the best in the world). But it is also a country with almost 40 per cent of the world's poorest population.

Following its independence, and under the leadership of Prime Minister Jawaharlal Nehru, India developed a socialist economy and a will for autonomy which culminated in the conclusion of the non-alignment movement in 1955. Two main tendencies were important in the development of the new economy: on the one hand, the Five Year Plan emphasized the development of agriculture and heavy industries; on the other, it encouraged a mixed system of both private and public sector enterprises. Major private groups linked to families such as the Tatas and the Birlas were established during the British Raj in the nineteenth century and grew in a protected environment following the country's independence. This typical approach to development has often been referred to as "self-reliance" but is largely regarded as outdated nowadays. At the time, however, foreign participations in Indian firms were limited to 40 per cent of the total capital, and procedure for obtaining approval from the authorities were long and difficult (Foreign Exchange Regulation Act, 1973). In order to protect its economy, India opted for a limitation on imports through quotas and custom duties.

On the heels of these measures came the nationalization of the major commercial banks in 1969 by Prime Minister Indira Gandhi. The immediate consequence was the development of a public banking system orientated towards borrowings and preferential interest rates for "priority" sectors such as agriculture.

Despite a relatively controlled economy, India remains a democracy. It is a state where rules and regulations have particular significance. This is especially the case with regard to business, where the rules are mainly derived from British common law. This means that a contract is a contract and that rules and procedures allow people to settle business in a stable framework.

Today India is once again on the world stage thanks to the reforms process and the globalization of its economy. When P.V. Narasimha Rao took over power in June 1991, he wasn't very much welcomed in India and abroad. Many commentators predicted that he would not stay in power for long as the Prime Minister, and to some he was only a puppet to be manipulated by the Congress party. His election was largely due to the assassination of Rajiv Gandhi on 21 May 1991. Against all odds Narasimha Rao remained in power as the Prime Minister until May 1996, when he lost the general election. However, he started the reform process in all sectors of the economy – an "irreversible movement", as stated by the Prime Minister during his visit to Paris in June 1995. The movement has been continued by the new government even after the cabinet reshuffle of April 1997.

Today India represents one-fifth of the world's population, and is ranked tenth in terms of global economic power. To many French investors, India is still marked by regulations, a complex bureaucratic system, and high custom duties and interest rates. A number of litigations against French businesses in this environment have tended to reinforce this viewpoint as well as to poison Indo-French business relationships.

The country is not an easy scene for any foreign investor. An Indian businessman (Jagdish Parekh) once observed that "The Indian economy is like a coconut – it is hard on the outside, but once broken one can enjoy the taste of sweet liquor". It is a flavoured fruit for one who has patience. But if there are still difficulties one needs to be reminded of the progress made in the reform process. This relates to both the economy and the daily lives of the people. A brief comparison of the situation today as against 15 years ago would show just how important the liberalization process is.

Fifteen years ago passenger cars made in India were called "Ambassador" or "Premier Padmini" (both models were from the 1950s) and were primarily the preserve of the upper classes; the middle classes vehicles were the scooter or the bus. Today India is driving the Maruti, and an increasing number of foreign auto-makers are setting up joint-venture enterprises with local firms. Notable examples include: Mercedes Benz with Telco; Peugeot with Premier Automobile Ltd (to manufacture the Peugeot 309); Ford with Mahindra and Mahindra; and Fiat with Premier Automobile Ltd.

In the 1980s, the drinks most consumed by the youths of India were called "Campa Cola" and "Thumbs Up". Today Pepsi-Cola and Coca-Cola have invaded the Indian market through marked advertising campaigns. And American television series are becoming more commonplace on Indian television.

Today in India the typewriter has largely been replaced by personal computers and the Internet. My purpose here is not to analyze these changes as a way of progress for India or, for that matter, to identify a lack of identity and the Americanization of the country. Nevertheless India, this giant with agile feet, is changing and moving forward fast – the implications of which include changes in mentality as well as increased inequality among the populace.

Reforms are under way on the economic side as well. Since 1991, the government has undertaken significant structural reforms in many sectors of the economy. These reforms are a follow-up (but on a much larger scale) to the work started in the 1980s by Prime Ministers Indira and Rajiv Gandhi, the aim of which was to give the country a new dynamism and move it rapidly towards a new era – the twenty-first century. The 1991 movement is taking on a new dimension: it is irreversible and is moving the country rapidly towards a market economy after 40 years of a planned economic system. The new policy will provide India with a strong basis for industrial growth and economic independence. It has also given the country the opportunity to emerge as one of the world's most dynamic economies.

Despite many clichés and a particular development path, India can no longer be considered a socialist economy but rather a mixed one, where both private and public sectors have an important role to play in the development of the economy. Today India isn't "cancelling" its past, but, rather, it is adopting new conditions and measures in order to meet international norms and requirements.

India is a member of the World Trade Organization (WTO) and is ready to enter the twenty-first century with a new economic agenda. The changes brought about as a result of the 1991 restructuring are considerable: majority stakes in Indian companies for foreign investors, the possibility of creating 100 per cent owned subsidiaries, abolition of the licence system, the setting up of a VAT system (MODVAT), incentives regarding private investment, deregulation of the interest rates system, development of free trade zones (Export Oriented Units, Export Processing Zones), new opportunities for the middle classes, and so on.

Most sectors of the economy have been liberalized since 1991. An ambitious programme of privatizations is under way which will allow a reduction of the budget deficit with cuts in public spending. The financial sector is also facing a complete restructuring, with deregulation of interest rates, adoption of international ratios such as the Cooke ratio, possibilities for private sector investments, increases in the local establishment of foreign financial institutions, and the possibility for these to invest in the Indian capital market.

In addition to the above, many sectors which were formerly reserved for public enterprises have now been opened to private investment. These include the agro and food-processing industry, as well as infrastructure sectors considered a priority for the government. There are also a number of facilities which have been earmarked especially for those who wish to invest in the priority sectors. Of these should be mentioned software and computer-related activities which have benefited from special regulation regarding the free trade zones. "Software technology parks" are being actively encouraged by the government as a way of promoting rapid development of the software industry in the country. Benefits to be gained under this regulation include low customs duties for equipment imports and various tax concessions. Export Processing Zones have also been created as a way of regrouping the increasing number of export-orientated companies. These benefit from special tax concessions, import facilities, and the ability to export 25 per cent of their total output under the Domestic Tariff Agreement (DTA) regulation.

Regarding foreign investment, a number of measures have been taken by the government. These include: significant reductions in custom duties, facilities to set up wholly-owned subsidiaries or joint-venture enterprises with local firms, and easy access to the administration concerned with investment approval and registration. Foreign direct investment in priority sectors enjoys in most cases automatic approval from both the Reserve Bank of India and the Indian Central Bank for stakes up to 51 per cent of the capital (since February 1997). Automatic approval can be given for up to 74 per cent of the capital of the newly created company.

As indicated earlier, this procedure relates solely to the priority sectors. For sectors other than these, requests for authorization must submitted to the Foreign Investment Promotion Board (now directly under the Minister of Industry) for approval. It concerns projects with an amount lower than INR6 billion. When it is higher, authorization must be granted by the Cabinet Committee on Foreign Investments. These approvals are given within a few weeks of application, and investors can ask for more than 51 per cent or 74 per cent of the total capital (and in exceptional cases up to 100 per cent of the capital).

The system of taxation has also undergone some structural changes. This relates in particular to the adoption of a modified system of Value Added Tax (MODVAT). The government's plan is to introduce a full VAT system soon.

On the monetary side, the Indian rupee is convertible on current account and on capital account only for foreign investors. The current budget (1997–98) allows for full convertibility of the rupee on capital account.

A quick study of the pattern of consumption for consumer goods would show that the Indian market is a large one. There has been a marked decrease in expenditure on food items and an increase for those which belong to other fields such as health and consumer goods. About 70 per cent of the population still lives in rural areas. This does not preclude their access to various consumer goods nor to television advertisements (either through the national networks or special mobile video equipment).

The Indian middle class is estimated to consist of about 250 million people, among which about 90 million are said to have incomes equal to the average household in Europe. Even if India likes foreign consumer goods, especially American ones, there are some specificities with regard to this environment which are worth noting. For example, with regard to the agro and food-processing industry, one must always take into account the number of vegetarians in the country, and the fact that air conditioning is a must in all cars, the caste system, religions, among other factors. These are all elements which call for an adaptation of the products to local traditions and customs. McDonalds, for example, has changed its well-known "Big Mac" to "Veg Burger" and "Maharaja Mac", replacing beef with mutton. To all these modifications should be added the already mentioned restructuring in sectors such as banking, infrastructure, agriculture, food processing, and so on. Let us take a close look at some of these sectors.

THE BANKING SYSTEM

The banking system is one of the wheels of India's economic development and of its international integration. The banking system is directly under the control of the Reserve Bank of India and the Indian Central Bank, the latter with its capital in Bombay. The Central Bank has a crucial role in India's banking and monetary system, as it is often involved in the nation's monetary and financial policy.

The banking system in this country is divided into two main categories; namely, commercial banks and financial institutions, each of which has its own diversity. The commercial banks are made up of nationalized banks as well as private banks, following the liberalization of foreign banks in the country. The first such bank to be established was the Hong Kong & New Zealand Grindlays Bank.

Financial institutions comprise primarily development banks, insurance companies (still closed to foreign investment), and other private financial establishments located in the different states. The insurance sector is very much in the news today as the Finance Minister Chidambaram wishes to liberalize and open it up to foreign participation. But some political parties (such as the Communist party of India) are very much against this idea, despite pressure from world bodies (such as the World Bank, the International Monetary Fund), foreign investors, and even some foreign governments.

The nationalizations of 1969 have had direct consequences on the banking sector – a sector largely dominated by the central government. Following this process the activities of banks in the country have very much been modified. For example, there has been the development of the so-called "social banking" system: that is, an increasing role for the banks in rural and social development programmes (such as special loans at low interest rates for agriculture often made without expectation of profit). Banks are thus largely considered as units aimed at providing subsidies to all the underdeveloped sectors of the economy. They have to give a fixed percentage of their loans to priority sectors, and they have to encourage the development of their networks all over the country even in small, non-profitable areas. The fact that banks have to lend to some sectors at preferential rates and have to open non-profitable branches has had a negative effect on profitability and the quality of services they offer. Above all, some loan programmes launched on a large scale by the central government have jeopardized the financial stability of the banks. From 1969, private banks had a minor role in the economy until the reform process started in 1991. They are now trying to improve their role in the economy.

The most dynamic of this sector, however, are the foreign banks, which have 140 branches in almost all of the major cities in the country. Despite the limited number of branches and several obstacles, foreign banks have rapidly increased their activities and the variety of services and products they offer. Their growth rates and profitability far exceed those of Indian banks. The government has announced its decision to allow the expansion of foreign banks, especially in facilitating the opening up of new branches.

The second category of financial institutions concerns development banks, whose aim is to cater for long- and medium-term needs of the country. They are being encouraged by the government to set up joint-venture arrangements with foreign companies.

The Indian banking system has undergone some major changes in the last few years, in particular with the launching of new products and services and the determination to follow the example of international banks.The development of this sector has been facilitated on the one hand by the reform policy, and on the other, by changes in consumer attitudes towards banks in general. Recent increases in the middle classes have led to the introduction of new products such as credit cards in order to meed the needs of new clients. Regarding companies' needs and markets, Indian banks have recently come under strong competition from foreign banks established in the country, have had to improve the quality of services they offer, and enlarge the range of products and services offered (for example, portfolio management, factoring, and so on). With these changes, it is clear that the banking system in India is on the way towards full modernization and diversification.

The Narasimham Committee Report – named after the former Governor of the Reserve Bank of India (RBI) – has put forward a number of proposals aimed at further restructuring and developing the Indian banking system. Among the most important of these are the following:

- A reduction of the Statutory Liquidity Ratio (SLR) and Cash Reserve Ratio (CRR) – instruments of control over the financial reserves of the banks. These measures have already been implemented.
- A new policy which makes establishment of branch offices of foreign banks in India easier.
- A reappraisal of the structure of Indian banks. The committee has proposed three or four major banks which could become international-sized banks (the State Bank of India (SBI) which is among these has already established a branch office in Paris); eight to ten national banks in charge of universal banking activities in the country; and local banks with activities targeted at the rural areas.
- The two-heads control system over banks from the RBI and from the banking division of the Ministry of Finance should be cancelled and put into the hands of a single body.
- Banks and financial institutions should adopt a solubility ratio, in particular the Cooke ratio.
- Transparency regarding bank accounts.

- Abolition of the branch licensing policy concerning the setting up of new agencies.
- Progressive deregulation of interest rates.
- A reduction in the number of loans given to the priority sectors.
- Obligatory computerization of the banking system – an environment which is becoming more and more competitive.

All these points have today been achieved or partially achieved; others are on the way.

The liberalization of this sector, which is too heavily controlled and administered, is deemed appropriate for the reforms process launched throughout the economy.

The liberalization of the economy would not have been possible without the reform of the banking sector. A rapid movement in the deregulation and liberalization process would have been negative. The financial scam of 1992 and its consequences over the financial stability of number of banks are a witness to this movement and its problems.

INFRASTRUCTURE

The infrastructural sector is a crucial one for India's development. The size of the country in itself makes this sector an important one and a priority for the government.

Transportation

Despite one of the biggest railway system in the world, few lines in the Indian railway system are today electrified, and most of them date to the British Raj. The immediate negative consequences of this are frequent delays, in addition to the fact that many towns are today without railway stations. For companies this situation can have catastrophic effects, as each firm has to take into account both its suppliers and raw materials resources, as well as the final consumer location, not all of which are always located in the same area. Companies have therefore to be careful about delays in transportation, in addition to being obliged to invest heavily in stocks in order to offset possible problems in transportation arrangements. All of these problems are costly and often place a significant constraint on the finances of the organizations.

The situation with the road system is no better. Indian roads are not adapted to the evolution of the country's market for automobiles. There has been a 25 per cent increase in the number of automobiles on Indian roads in the last year, yet there are only a few miles of highways in the country, most of which are centred around the major cities. The system of road construction has not been modernized in years and the government is now in the process of opening up this sector as well to foreign investment.

Air transport has seen some restructuring since 1992 with the liberalization of the air traffic system. Private airlines have grown up, but still foreign airlines are not allowed to participate in this development. And those that have tried (such as the German carrier Lufthansa) have decided to terminate all forms of collaboration with local carriers. The air crash at Delhi airport in November 1996 underlines the urgent need for modernization in this sector.

Telecommunications

Important restructuring is also needed in this sector. It is a priority area for the government, and foreign investment is allowed up to 100 per cent of the total capital.

The density of telephone lines in India is one of the lowest in the world – 0.8 lines per inhabitant as against the world average of 10 lines per inhabitant. It is not uncommon to wait for months, even years, before getting a phone connected in India. Even after obtaining a phone line there are no guarantees that one would succeed in placing a phone call, as line failures are frequent. With the network in such a bad condition, it is not surprising that cellular phones are becoming increasingly popular.

The priority given to this sector has provided new opportunities for foreign firms, and France is well placed to participate in this development particularly in the telecommunications sector. France Telecom was one of the few foreign companies granted a concession in 1994 to operate a cellular phone network in eight cities in the country. In addition, Dassault Automatisme et Télécommunications received authorization during the same year to install a public network (the so-called "bipbop" network) in the cities of Bombay and Delhi. To these is to be added Alcatel, which has had a long presence in this environment and has already completed several projects in collaboration with its joint-venture enterprise Alcatel-Modi.

AGRICULTURE

Another priority sector is agriculture and the agro food-processing industry. Agriculture has an important role in the Indian economy, contributing a little over 30 per cent of the gross domestic product (GDP). Nearly 70 per cent of India's working population are employed in this sector. After Independence, one of the Nehru is major objectives was that India should attain self-sufficiency in agriculture. It is clear that this objective has now been achieved. This said, it must be added, however, that despite the "Green Revolution" launched in the 1960s, India is still largely dependent on climatic conditions (especially the monsoon season) for its agricultural output. And significant inequalities still exist between states as far as mechanization in this sector and technological development are concerned. Punjab, for example, is a prosperous agricultural state benefiting from the Green Revolution and its ability to utilize its river network positively for irrigation purposes. The same cannot be said of Bihar, for example, which still uses traditional methods in its agricultural sector.

India is one of the leading producers of tea, sugar, fruits, and vegetables on a global basis (the last two product having a tremendous need for foreign investment). The sector ranked second and third respectively for rice and cereals production. Technology and transportation problems still represent major challenges in India's agricultural sector. Export percentages are low, as a significant part of the output is intended for local consumption. The government is currently encouraging local consumption of products which were traditionally meant for export, the most notable example being tea. Coffee, on the other hand, is produced primarily for export. Some states have built up their image on production and distribution of one product – jute, in the case of West Bengal, for example.

The various sectors described above are only a few examples of India's path to development and of the opportunities these provide for foreign investment.

CONCLUSION

The general elections of May 1996 were once again a clear witness to India's democratic system. The BJP coalition government with Mr Vajpayee as the Prime Minister did not put an end to the reform process. It is clear that should the contrary become the case this will no doubt jeopardize the country's effort to modernize its economy and make it more attractive to foreign investment. It will most likely also make it difficult for India to receive favourable attention from international lending organizations.

India is an emerging economic power, and no company interested in the Asia-Pacific region can afford to ignore this increasingly important market. It is a country of contrasts where centuries-old traditions thrive side by side with modern technology. Two worlds are said to exist in India today. The first is the India of 200,000 villages – that is, Mahatma Gandhi's India, India's soul with its traditions, the heart of India's cultures and religions. And the second is India of the metropolises (Bombay, Delhi, and so on) – a modern India, looking towards the twenty-first century. India is a mosaic of cultures, all of which contribute to building its identity. Its age and its experience have given the country a knowledge and a holiness which could inspire us all. The French novelist Michel Tournier once observed that "India is the foreign country *par excellence*"; it is a difficult country with a multicultural society.

Western stereotypes about India are often caused by lack of information. To invest here it is important to know the country. Economics and business are often linked with the cultural side of life in this environment. Culture has significant influence in the Indian economy – a point not to be ignored by foreign investors when considering this market.

10 Liberalization policy and change of government in India

Pascale Boureille

With a population of almost a billion inhabitants, the Indian market is a considerable one. Even though a large part of the population still lives below the poverty level, because of the development in the productive structures a middle class has emerged that today represents, according to estimates, between 100 to 300 million persons. In many sectors of the economy, supply still lags behind demand.

Up until the 1980s/1990s this important market was very difficult to access as trade and foreign investment were highly regulated. During the 1980s, and particularly during the first half of the 1990s, political liberalization,[1] even if it did not replace the strong administrative system, introduced some fundamental changes, and provided foreign firms with new opportunities for export and investment. All sectors of the economy were affected by the reforms.

It is at the business policy level that the first reform was introduced, and this was well before 1991. The policy was particularly favourable to exporters of production equipment as well as high-technology products, which were either not found in the country or were of relatively higher priced by international standards. Imports of these products and technology were subject to very stringent controls in order to ensure that "non-essential" products which could easily be manufactured locally were not being imported. As a result of these measures, exporters can be said to have indirectly supported production costs which were much higher than those of their foreign competitors for manufactured products.[2] It was thus as a way of supporting the export sector that the liberalization measures were introduced, in the beginning very selectively (from 1960 to 1970), and later in a more comprehensive manner in the 1980s. From 1991, and as a measure of reintroducing competition which was inhibited by protection, that the liberalization policy was

165

enlarged. It became possible to import foreign manufactured parts even if a substitute could be found locally: the principle of local "non-availability" which constituted the basis of India's commercial policy since Independence was thus gradually replaced. Only imports of consumer products are still subject to this regulation. But in this sector, as in the other sectors of the economy, foreign investment and transfer of technology are facilitated when they do not involve financial participation as they are quasi-automatically approved.

Until the beginning of the 1990s, India's industrial policy rested on three principal regulations: the Industries Development and Regulation Act (IDRA, 1951); the Monopolies and Restrictive Trade Practices Act (MRTP, 1969); and the Foreign Exchange Regulation Act (FERA, 1973). The first required preliminary authorization for the creation of all enterprises. It reserved all infrastructure projects as well as basic industries in the hands of the public sector. Existing private enterprises were not replaced; however, they were not allowed to expand their production capacities. Other sectors, such as textile and craft industries, were reserved for small and medium-sized enterprises. The second limited the expansion of production capacity for private enterprises. It provided for state control of the structure of the clothing industry as well as avoiding the development of monopolies. As the third regulation limited participation of foreign companies to 40 per cent of the paid-up capital[3] in Indian firms, it ensured that national sovereignty was preserved.

This system of regulation (which was regarded as an impediment to productivity gains and competitiveness of Indian firms, growth in general,[4] and without necessarily bringing an end to the creation of monopolies[5]) was progressively abolished from 1991.

Today industrial permits are required for 15 products, representing only 15 per cent of the value added for the manufacturing sector. These comprise mainly products of a strategic nature, dangerous chemicals, and products which are considered to be non-essential.[6] The MRTP regulation no longer exists; this makes company mergers easier.

As a result of an amendment introduced in the FERA regulation, foreign investors can now retain the majority of the capital in an enterprise situated in Indian national territory (an authorization is required if the majority shareholding is more than 51 per cent of the paid-up capital). Only the defence, atomic energy, carbon, petroleum, transportation, and minerals industries are still reserved for the public sector. In other infrastructural sectors, such as electrical energy, roads, ports and airports, and telecommunications, private investment (including foreign investment) is actively encouraged. The participation of private investment (both foreign and local) can be up to 49 per cent in the telecommunications sector, 50 per cent in the mining sector (with automatic authorization granted), 100 per cent in the electrical energy (under conditions for preliminary authorization). The manufacture of clothes is no longer exclusively reserved for small and medium-sized enterprises. Large enterprises which export up to 75 per cent of their total production output can now also participate in this sector.

Regarding the financial sector, until 1991 the banks were essentially part of the public sector (90 per cent of the deposits, and all active banks).[7] They were subjected to very stringent regulations. It was the state which fixed interest rate levels. Cash Reserve Ratio (CRR – that is, the level of reserves that commercial banks were required to deposit with the Central Bank) were relatively high, almost at the same level as the Statutory Liquidity Ratio (SLR – namely, part of deposits which were compulsorily required for the purchase of public titles). It was on the other hand necessary to devote part of the credit to "priority" sectors. Also, in 1991, 63.5 per cent of the supplementary deposits was put on reserve, and 40 per cent of the available resources for credit was devoted to the "priority" sectors.

Between 1991 and 1996 CRR and SLR increased respectively from 15 to 14 per cent and 38.5 to 25 per cent. CRR was replaced within the non-residents' deposits.[8] Since 1994, the banks have been free to determine interest rates for loans exceeding 200,000 rupees. Rates for loans under this sum are between 12 and 13.5 per cent. The government has also allowed the creation of private banks. Nine such banks have been created since 1994.

At the capital market level, a new control authority was created in February 1992 – the Securities and Exchange Board of India (SEBI), which has been charged with the responsibility for further reform in the sector. In the future all enterprises created under SEBI (whether of Indian or foreign origin) will have free access to the Indian capital market. They will also be able to fix title prices freely. Indian enterprises are, on the other hand, authorized to issue their titles in the international market.

Finally, measures have also been taken at the fiscal policy level; namely, in favour of foreign investment (tax deductions, exemption from taxes on export revenue, temporary tax exemptions on all revenues in certain sectors of the economy, and so on). But certain reforms also concern local producers, as the system of indirect taxes which existed until then was not favourable to local enterprises due to its complexity, and, above all, the level of taxes imposed on intermediary products.[9]

Even if numerous uncertainties still exist (such as political evolution, infrastructural development, and growth), and bureaucratic rigidities persist, all of which have the tendency to discourage potential foreign investors, these reforms together favour the development of trade and investment. Commercial liberalization and the privatization process offer new opportunities, while the reforms of the financial and banking sectors facilitate the necessary conditions for financing trade and investment, to which are to added the fiscal advantages outlined earlier. Import and investment levels have witnessed significant growth since 1991 (see the section below). However, while the Indian market is a little easier to access as a result of the modification of the competitive rules, the reforms have also introduced new constraints. The fiscal reforms which aimed to reduce production costs for national enterprises fall under this category, and the same applies to the reforms in the financial sector which will make access to local financing of enterprises easier (see the section beginning on page 000 below).

THE RESPONSE OF FOREIGN INVESTMENT

The opening up of the economy from 1992 has been met with a favourable response from the business community. There has been a significant increase in imports and foreign direct investment (FDI).

Imports

After a net decline (in 1991/92) in both dollar value and volume of net purchases abroad (due to temporary restrictions imposed in order to address the balance-of-payment crises), thanks to the strengthening of the liberalization process and growth in the economy,[10] there was a return to growth in imports, as can be seen in Figure 10.1.

The United States remained the principal supplier (approximately 10 per cent of all imports), followed by Germany (7.6 per cent),

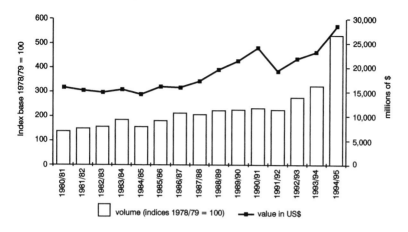

Source: *Economic Survey 1995/96*

Figure 10.1 Developments in the volume of imports (value in US$)

and Japan (7 per cent). With a total of 2 per cent of imports, France occupied ninth position, representing a decline relative to 1991. Of these suppliers, it should be noted the role of the petroleum-exporting nations (together they had 20 per cent of all imports), and particularly Kuwait, whose total import share increased from less than 1 per cent to more than 5 per cent between 1991 and 1995.[11]

It should be noted that petroleum still represents almost a quarter of the total import value, even though it has declined relative to the situation in 1990s (30 per cent). Despite the lifting of quantitative restrictions and reduction of import tariffs, the share of intermediary products, apart from petroleum, has been relatively stable since 1991 (almost 24 per cent, with a peak of 26.8 per cent in 1993/94). This increase in imports was particularly beneficial to agricultural products (from 2 to 5 per cent of total imports from 1991 to 1995) and capital goods (from 21.8 to 26.5 per cent).[12]

Foreign direct investment

A marked increase in transfer of technology was recorded during the same period, a large part of which was realized by way of FDI (as shown in Figure 10.2).

Since 1991, there has been a significant increase in the total amount

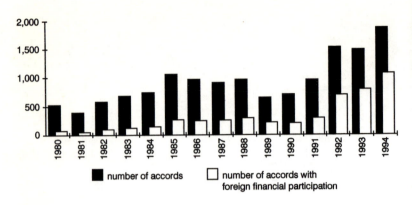

Figure 10.2 Number of collaborations approved by the government, 1980–1994

Sources: EPW Research Foundation (1995); *Economic and Political Weekly*, XXX (50) (16 December) p. 3190; Department of Scientific and Industrial Research, *Handbook of Foreign Collaboration Approved during 1981–1989*, Government of India, New Delhi, p. xxxi

of FDI in India. During 1995, this amount stood at US$1.3 billion, compared to $150 million at the beginning of the decade. (It is important to note, however, that this increase is still below the amount fixed in relation to the government's overall objective.)

The geographical origins of FDI have remained unchanged. The United States remains the major net investor (with a share of between 30 and 40 per cent of the total FDI approved by the government), followed by Japan (5–15 per cent), the United Kingdom (5–15 per cent), Germany (approximately 7 per cent), Italy (5 per cent), and Switzerland (5 per cent), to mention only the principal investors.

This transformation is different, however, as far as sectoral orientation of the investment is concerned, primarily as a result of the opening up of certain sectors of the economy to private capital (both local and foreign). The influence of FDI in the privatization process in particularly significant in sectors such as electrical energy and refining. The total number of FDIs approved by the government between 1991 and 1995 were the most numerous in these sectors (10.2 per cent for electrical energy, and 10.9 per cent for refining), followed by the agricultural sector (13.3 per cent), and metallurgical industry (12.2 per cent).

Table 10.1 Sectoral distribution of collaboration agreements approved by the government between 1991 and 1995 (percentages)

Metallurgical industry	12.20
Electrical energy	10.20
Refining	10.90
Electrical equipment	7.00
Telecommunications	6.60
Automobile	2.00
Other transportation	3.30
Non-electrical machines	4.40
Chemical industry	9.50
Agric & food industry	13.30
Construction materials	2.70
Financial services	7.90
Tourism	5.20
Others	4.80
Total	100

Source: Compiled from EPW Research Foundation (1995); *Economic and Political Weekly*, XXX (36) (9 September 1995), p. 2227, fig. 2

Almost a quarter of the total FDI were in the agriculture and food, automobile, and electrical equipment industries. These industries also represent the sectors with the highest consumption demands in India.

The telecommunications sector, which has recently been opened to FDI, has tremendous potential. At the beginning of 1995, 6.6 per cent of the total FDI approved had been in this sector; at the end of that year, however, this share had increased to 30 per cent.[13]

But if the opening up of the Indian economy has facilitated access to the market, it has also brought about new rules of competition for foreign companies in this environment.

LIBERALIZATION AND CONDITIONS FOR COMPETITION

If the reform recently introduced is, above all, to re-establish internal and external equilibrium in the economy, it has also ameliorated the competitiveness of national enterprises in this market. The conditions for competition have therefore been directly modified.

The expansion of the range of products which can be imported have opened up new possibilities for foreign companies (especially with respect to production and equipment products), but at the same time it has created new opportunities for local manufactures and competitive conditions for local firms. Reduction of import tariffs and indirect taxes have tended to improve the competitive prices of Indian products. In facilitating the expansion of production capacities and thus the realization of economies of scale, the suppression of the MRTP regulation will be dealt with in the same fashion. In order to open up the economy further, competitive conditions have been modified as seen by the increasing number of foreign producers being attracted to the Indian market either as exporters or investors.

Independently, elements affecting the physical supply capacity of Indian firms or their competitive prices, the country's long-term import motives (and particularly in relation to equipment), should be diminished by reforms in the financial sector, and in particular, the banks.

Financial constraints constitute one of the principal motivating reasons for the import of equipment even if these can be found locally. One of the cases that have been extensively discussed is that which relates to central electrical equipment. The state enterprise Bharat Heavy Electrical Limited (BHEL), whose products are well known to be comparable and sometimes superior to its foreign counterparts, is a good example.[14] In making new equipment purchases the State Electricity Boards[15] often turn to foreign companies rather than BHEL.

The reason for this apparently unjustified choice (particularly from the point of view of the public sector) is due to the inability of the State Electricity Board (often operating at a deficit),[16] but also the unwillingness of the banks, to finance these investments. In the case of the State Electricity Board, there exists at this level a legal constraint as they are not allowed to borrow directly from the commercial banks. It can be imagined that a modification of the regulation will ameliorate this problem. But what preoccupies the government most is how to lessen inflationary tensions, or a restricted monetary policy which limits investment opportunities. The capacity for local financing is also limited by the level of available local resources.

Within this framework, when the State Electricity Boards is under constraint (as are all the other enterprises whose investment needs are always large), it turns to other sources of financing. Local suppliers of equipment, in this case BHEL, are generally not in the position to be granted credit. The State Electricity Board could turn to the central government for its financing by way of budget deficit. But inflationary constraints and concern on the part of the government (concern which existed well before 1991) limit this avenue for credit.[17] What remains is the possibility of external means of financing, but this often involves the import of equipment even if this could be produced locally. It is thus the case that when credit is obtained through bilateral cooperation it often obliges India to purchase the needed equipment from the donor country. It is also the case when credit is provided by the supplier. Only credit obtained from the World Bank allows BHEL to enter markets, thus allowing the company to compete internationally and locally.[18]

Foreign companies have gained additional competitive advantage through this bias, in addition to that which they already have in the areas of cost, quality, image, brand, performance, and so on. But with the reform in the banking sector (especially as it relates to a reduction in the rate of obligatory reserves) and the liberalization of the capital market, combined with the privatization process of the public sector, new opportunities for financing ought to be possible for Indian investors. The need to import foreign equipment in order to obtain credit will be reduced, and foreign suppliers will, by the same token, lose much of the competitive advantage they have hitherto enjoyed relative to their local counterparts. It is too early to measure the impact of the reform in the financial sector on the competitiveness of foreign firms relative to their local counterparts, but for those who are concerned with this issue, this development in the banking policy is certain to generate some interest. Other reforms and their impact on the competitive conditions, and strategy towards the Indian market, ought also to be affected by the new political reality.

THE NEW POLITICAL REALITY AND ITS IMPLICATIONS

The Congress Party of India, which has been in power almost without interruption since Independence (both at the central and state levels), showed some serious weaknesses during the regional elections of 1995, until its defeat in the general elections of 1996. The advancement of the Bharatiya Janata party (BJP) and the arrival in power of the centre-left coalition are also bound to modify the conditions for accessing the Indian market.

The advancement of the Bharatiya Janata party (BJP)

The weakness of the Congress party which became evident at the beginning of 1995 was evidence of a bitter dispute within the party, created largely as a result of the policy of Prime Minister Narashima. Other than the laxity related to intercommunity tensions and emerging corruption, the dissidents particularly opposed the politics of liberalization (starting at the beginning of 1991), which contributed to aggravation of the problem of social inequality which they felt should have, on the contrary, been reduced. These dissensions, combined with the concern of a large part of the population regarding the ability of the reforms to ameliorate the situation, were well received by the opposition.

The Congress party lost the states of Karanataka, Andhra Pradesh, Maharashtra, Gujarat, and Bihar during the regional legislative elections of 1995. This setback was to the benefit of the Hindu nationalist parties. In Bombay, for example (the capital of Maharashtra, the most industrialized state in India) it was the fascist party Shiv Sena which succeeded – a party close to BJP and well-known for its hostility to foreign investment.

All these developments have not helped the politics of liberalization in terms of foreign investment, and the government of Maharashtra awaits to have a controlling advantage. Soon after its arrival to power it annulled (in order to renegotiate) the accord signed between Maharashtra State Electricity and the American firm Enron for the construction of an electricity generating plant at Dabhol, the largest foreign investment project ever authorized in India (US$2.5 billion for a generating capacity of 2025 megawatts) and for which work had already began.

To be addressed were the following issues:

- the prohibitive cost of the project, given that profit-rate level effectively guaranteed was higher than that which Enron has demanded (34 per cent as against 30 per cent, before taxes, which in itself was much higher than that which the firm could obtain in the United States);
- very high price levels of energy sold to Maharashtra State Electricity Board which has responsibility for electricity distribution in the state;
- the fact that the price was determined in US dollars introduced exchange-rate risks;

- and the fact that because gas was imported, this created very high currency costs.

This affair has rekindled hostile arguments against multinationals. The advantage of returning to local enterprises rather than foreign ones, from the point of view of balance of payments, has been well documented in the Indian economic literature.[19] According to Morris (1996), if the contract for the construction of the Dabhol electrical plant had been granted to an Indian firm, in this case BHEL, rather than Enron, the import content of the project would have been 20 per cent instead of 80 per cent.

Despite the uncertainty surrounding the capacity of Indian firms to fulfil their commitment, the Enron affair has in the meantime not halted a marked increase in foreign investment, which has doubled since 1995. Even though the liberalization process has rekindled the debate between partisans and opponents of FDI, the affair has tended to strengthen the position of the latter as it has brought together a large part of the leftist parties which constitute the new coalition power at the central government level. This makes negotiations with Indian partners very difficult.

Change of majority at the central government level

Even though he multiplied his efforts such as accelerating measures to reduce poverty, the Prime Minister Narashima Rao and his government, which remained in power for a few months before the general elections of 1996, were never convincing. The Congress party never managed to regain the confidence of the people and it obtained only 139 of the 534 seats in Parliament. The BJP, on the other hand, was able to confirm its rapid advancement, obtaining a large part of the seats in Parliament (not sufficient, however, to form a new majority). In the end a centre-left coalition (the United Front) was formed, with the support of the Congress party, and H.D. Deva Gowda became its head.

The new Prime Minister has already assured investors that he will continue the liberalization process already started. He has, however, also indicated that the new coalition which he represents was brought to power under a much more restrictive programme. In connection with the Enron affair, the left-wing parties demanded that all projects which were under way should be re-examined and submitted to the same scrutiny as Enron if the terms of the agreement were very unfavourable to national interests. It has particularly denounced the Torrent project in Gujarat, but the BJP which is the ruling party in this state does not wish to grant this request.[20]

The leftist coalition also promised to control foreign investment better, hoping to put a stop to import of products which are considered non-essential (in terms of satisfying the general demand of the population).[21] However, as we have shown, if the increasing part of foreign investment is orientated towards primary industries and infrastructure sectors, consumer product sectors (both durable and non-durable) are also very much coveted. If a very selective policy is put into place this will mean not only that renegotiation of contracts will be difficult (as the negotiating power of Indians will be reinforced), but also that certain sectors will be closed.

The measures already taken by the new Finance Minister, P. Chidambaram, seem to point rather towards a strengthening of the liberalization process, including the consumer sector. But a good number of the parties upon which the new parliamentary majority rests still remain hostile to this policy. However, the climate is less uncertain at this level.

CONCLUSION

As can be witnessed by the increase in imports and particularly the unprecedented foreign investment, the widening of the liberalization process which was put into place in 1991 has made the Indian market very attractive. Combined with the increase and diversification of demand, the opening up (both external and internal) of the market has brought about new opportunities for foreigners, whether suppliers of products and technology or investors.

But it has also brought about new constraints. Not only has it increased the number of foreign actors in the market place and limited progressively certain of the advantages enjoyed by Indian producers (difficult and costly access to foreign products, high taxes on intermediary products, high interest rates, and so on), but also it ought, on the other hand, to favour a reduction of import motives, particularly with respect to equipment.

As promised during the election campaign, the new Prime Minister since June 1996 has put into place a very selective policy with respect to the opening up of the economy. One can envisage that investment will become much more difficult in the consumer sector, to the advantage of infrastructure. But if the uncertainty at this level is generalized, and following on the precedence created by the Enron affair, investors will expect their Indian clients to provide guarantees not to close during contract negotiation.

NOTES

[1] The purpose of this chapter is neither to discuss the fundamentals of the policy of liberalization nor its logic, but rather its consequences for foreign businesses in the country. It is important to underline, however, that even if its roots go back to the 1980s, the programme of structural adjustments which were put into effect from 1991 was brought about by the balance-of-payment problems as well as the conditions set down by the International Monetary Fund.

[2] This is part of the problem of anti-export bias which has been analyzed particularly by scholars such as Singh (1964), Bhagwati and Desai (1970), Bhagwati and Srinivasan (1975).

[3] There is a dispensation for enterprises that export 100% of their production (for which foreign participation can be up to 100%) and for certain priority sectors.

[4] For more details on this point, one can refer to the work of the following authors: Ahluwalia (1985, 1991), Bhagwati (1993), Bhawati and Srinivasan (1993).

[5] Mani (1992).

[6] Carbon and lignite, petroleum products, alcohol, sugar, oils and animal fats, tobacco, asbestos products, wood decorative products, certain leather, paper, defence electronic equipment, industrial explosives, pharmaceutical products, electronic recreational products.

[7] CFCE (1995) p. 62.

[8] *Economic Survey 1995/96*, p. 48.

[9] Report of the Chelliah Committee (1993).

[10] A return to growth driven by increase in imports of production equipment.

[11] *Economic Survey 1995/96*, p. 48.

[12] *Economic Survey 1993/94* and *1995/96*.

[13] *The Nikkei Weekly*, 18 March 1996.

[14] See Chandra (1994), Morris (1996).

[15] The State Electricity Boards are dependent on the state governments rather than the central government. They have in most cases a monopoly of electricity generation in the states to which they belong.

[16] See Parikh (1995) p. 2545.

[17] Morris (1996) has observed that this concern for inflation is unfounded considering the reduction of this bottleneck which allows the increase of electricity production and the continued generation of revenue which, in turn, allows it to be self-financing.

¹⁸ Morris (1996).
¹⁹ Concerning the Enron affair, see the critical analyses of Gosh, Sen, and Chandrasekhar (1995), and Morris (1996).
²⁰ Purkayastha (1995).
²¹ This idea can also be found in the BJP programme. However, contrary to the policy of the leftist parties, it is favourable to deepening the internal liberalization process in order to benefit private initiative.

REFERENCES

Ahluwallia, I.J. (1985), *Industrial Growth in India: Stagnation since the Mid-Sixties*. Oxford University Press, Delhi.

Ahluwallia, I.J. (1991), *Productivity and Growth in Indian Manufacturing*, Oxford University Press, Delhi.

Bhagwati, J.N. (1993), *India in Transition. Freeing the Economy*, Clarendon Press, Oxford.

Bhagwati, J.N. and Desai, P. (1970), *India Planning for Industrialization, Industrialization and Trade Policies since 1951*, Oxford University Press, London.

Bhagwati, J.N. and Srinivasan, T.N. (1975), *Foreign Trade Regimes and Economic Development: Anatomy and Consequences of Exchange*, A Special Conference Series on Foreign Trade Regimes and Economic Development, Vol. I, National Bureau of Economic Research, New York.

Bhagwati, J.N. and Srinivasan, T.N. (1993), *Economic Reform in India*, Ministry Of Finance, Government of India, July, in Kapila, U. (1994), *Recent Development in Indian Economy. The Ongoing Economic Reform*, Academic Foundation, Delhi.

Boureille, P. (1994), *Relations entre importations et développement: le cas de l'Inde*, Thèse de Doctorat, Université Pierre Mendés France, Grenoble II.

CFCFE (1995), *Inde*, Les éditions du CFCE, Paris.

Chandra, N.K. (1986), "Modernisation for Export-Oriented Growth A Critique of Recent Indian Policy", *Economic and Political Weekly*, XXI, 29, July 19, pp. 1272–1273.

Chandra, N.K. (1994), "Capital Development and crisis of the Indian Economy", document miméographié.

Chaudhuri, S. (1995), "Government and Transnationals. New Economic Policies since 1991", *Economic and Political Weekly*, XXX, 18–19, May 6–13, pp. 999–1011.

Chelliah Committee (1993), *Tax Reform Committee. Final Report 1 & 2*, Ministry of Finance, Government of China, New-Delhi, January.

Economic Survey 1994–95, Ministry of Finance, Government of India, New-Delhi.

Ghosh, J., Sen, A., Chandhasekhar, C.P. (1995), "Life after Enron", *Economic and Political Weekly*, XXX, 33, August 19, pp. 2038–2041.

Mani, S. (1992), New Industrial Policy, Barriers to Entry, Foreign Investment and Privatisation, *Economic and Political Weekly*, XXVII, 35, August 29, pp. M.86–M.94.

The Nikkei Weekly, March 18, 1996.

Morris, S. (1996), "Political Economy of Electrical Power in India", *Economic and Political Weekly*, XXX, 20, May 18, pp. 1201–1210 and 21, May 25, pp. 1274–1283.

Ministry of Commerce (1994), *Export and Import Policy: 1 April 1992–31 March 1997*, Government of India, March.

Nayyar, D. (1993), "Economic Reforms in India: A Critical Assessment", International Labour Organisation and Asian Regional Team for Employment Promotion, New-Delhi document miméographié.

New Industrial Policy Statement, Government of India, New-Delhi, July 24, 1991.

Reserve Bank of India, *Report on Currency and Finance*, Bombay various issues.

Parikh, K.S. (1995), "Enron Episode: Lessons for Power Policy", *Economic and Politial Weekly*, XXX, 41–42, October 14–21, pp. 2543–2546.

Planning Commission, *Eight Five Year Plan*, Government of India, New-Delhi.

Purkayastha, P. (1995), "Enron: The Drama Continues", *Economic and Political Weekly*, XXX, 31 and 32, August 19, pp. 2042–2044.

Reserve Bank of India, *Report on Currency and Finance*, Bombay various issues.

Sen, S. and Das, R.U. (1992), "Import Liberalisation as a Tool of Economic Policy in India since mid-eighties", *Economic and Political Weekly*, 27, 12, March 2, pp. 585–595.

Singh, M. (1964), *India's Export Trends and the Prospects for Self-Sustained growth*, Clarendon Press, Oxford.

11 Biotechnology and the Indian pharmaceutical industry
Integration and impact

Shyama V. Ramani[1] and
M.S. Venkataramani[2]

ABSTRACT

Against the background of important changes under way in the pharmaceutical industries of advanced countries brought about, in part, by advances in biotechnology, this chapter seeks to examine how well-prepared the Indian pharmaceutical industry is to integrate biotechnology techniques to create new drugs. Tracing the evolution of the industry, the chapter proposes a classification of firms according to their technology strategies, revealing the risk-averse attitude of Indian firms. Then it illustrates that while key steps taken by the government of India to promote biotechnology research in public institutes and university departments are laudable, failure on the part of the government to forge effective networks between industry and research institutions for the commercialization of research is a major weakness. Thus integration of biotechnology remains mainly at the level of distribution of imported diagnostic kits and therapeutics with little impact on the industrial structure of the Indian pharmaceutical sector.

INTRODUCTION

Modern biotechnology refers to a set of techniques such as genetic engineering, cell and tissue cultures, protein synthesis, and enzymology that involve manipulation of the genetic patrimony of an organism. They have emerged from recent developments (since

181

1975) in the biological sciences such as biochemistry, biophysics, molecular biology, microbiology, cellular biology, and genetics. The use of biotechnology has had three types of impact on the pharmaceutical industry. It has led to integration of biotechnology techniques in the production process, creation of new products, and a revolution in the nature of the search process for the creation of new chemical entities.[3] At least ten of the new products constitute radical innovations with a market value of more than US$100 million.[4] All of the top ten biotechnology drugs have been developed by small American companies created by scientists, but often commercialized by an established multinational pharmaceutical firm.

India's pharmaceutical industry is the twelfth largest in the world today and the market accounts for US$2.5 billion.[5] It registered an average annual growth rate of 15 per cent over 1990–1995.[6] The actual value of the industry's production should be deemed even higher when viewed in the context of the regulation on drug prices that keeps prices artificially low in India.[7] Among the developing countries, India is one of the few that can boast of internationally renowned scientists and research institutes, but there is a nagging anxiety that if India lags behind in the creation of technological competence in such a key area as biotechnology, the economic and social upliftment of its people would slow down and a sort of neocolonial dependency on advanced countries might result, with its attendant negative economic and political implications.

Thus the issue of the Indian pharmaceutical industry's prospects in the ongoing "technological race" is beginning to stimulate serious discussion in the government, research, and business communities. What is the present state of the Indian pharmaceutical industry, and how prepared is it to meet the challenging task of integrating biotechnology for new product innovation and commercialization? What are the different technology strategies pursued by Indian firms to achieve this objective, and what is their impact? What is the role and impact of the Indian government? What is the impact of the multinationals in the Indian market? These are the questions we attempt to answer in this chapter. Evidently, firms do not evolve in a vacuum; they are shaped by their strategic interaction with other agents in the market such as their competitors, their suppliers, their consumers, researchers from public institutes, and the government. In this context, the chapter is organized as follows. The first section takes a very brief look at the integration of biotechnology in the pharmaceutical sectors of Europe and America and the evolution of the Indian pharmaceutical sector between 1948 and 1988. Then the second section delineates the role of the Indian government and the public research laboratories. This is followed in the third section by an examination of the structure of the pharmaceutical market, and the technology strategy of Indian firms. Finally, conclusions are summarized in the last section.

In this chapter, the term "Indian pharmaceutical company" refers only to firms whose ownership and control rests with Indian nationals. Companies in which control rests in the hands of foreign nationals of multinational corporations (MNCs) are excluded from purview. There are 12 MNCs among the top 50 pharmaceutical companies in India in terms of sales and only seven of them find a place among the top 20.[8] No MNC figures in the top ten in respect of net profits, with the long-established British major, Glaxo, occupying only the eleventh place. MNCs have been excluded from the present study because they have been content, till the present, merely to market drugs developed in their home bases, and have made no attempts to develop R&D meaningfully in India.

Integration and impact of biotechnology: the international context

The first companies to base themselves entirely on modern biotechnology techniques were American start-ups in the pharmaceutical sector, such as Genentech (created in 1976), Genex (created in 1977), and Biogen (created in 1978), formed by scientists who were aware of the potential economic profit that could issue from investment in their fields and who were able to attract financial support from equally imaginative venture capitalists.[9] Such new biotechnology firms (NBFs) pursued an aggressive knowledge-deepening technology, improving their knowledge base in their chosen scientific field and patenting their discoveries.

As it was realized that dramatic scientific "breakthroughs" might be few and quick returns were unlikely, the needed level of support from venture capitalists was not forthcoming for the NBFs. They had to turn to major corporations, who in turn were awakening to the importance of acquiring and deepening competence in biotechnology. Thus in the late 1980s strategic alliances began to be formed between the American NBFs and the large MNCs (both American and European), with the large firms financing the research of the NBFs, in return for some kind of production and marketing rights. Such cooperation was necessary because, while the early NBFs possessed the scientific competence, they had neither the capital nor the complementary competencies to conduct clinical trials, undertake the prolonged processes of getting regulatory approval, up-scale the manufacturing, create the market, and actually market the product. The large diversified firms were willing to pick up the bill for the R&D expenditure because it represented a means for them to implement "scope economies" in basic biotechnology R&D. By financing R&D projects with what represented to them small or moderate sums of money, rather than buying out NBFs or incurring in-house investment costs, the large firms could investigate the potential of NBF projects without committing themselves too deeply and expensively to any particular technology and thereby avoiding the negative effects of a "technological lock-in".

With the learning that occurred in pursuing such aggressive technology strategies, the picture changed again by the early 1990s. Some of the highly successful NBFs vertically integrated into manufacturing and a few became fully integrated firms, marketing their own product. A number of NBFs whose work was deemed promising were acquired by the large diversified firms. Large firms established strong in-house research competence in their areas of interest and began to match the expenditure of the NBFs. Thus by integrating research and production activities the large firms concerned could avoid a competitive externality whereby their collaborators gained tacit knowledge of the production process. Similarly, by integrating into production the NBFs could also avoid exposing themselves to opportunistic behaviour of and a dependency relationship with their collaborators. Furthermore, vertical integration enabled both kinds of firms to reduce the transaction costs of outsourcing, develop the business competence necessary to evaluate the allocation of resources within the firm to the different types of technologies, and maximize the profit from commercialization of innovations.[10]

The integration of biotechnology among the other latecomer countries of the developed world were characterized by a variety of evolutionary patterns. In Britain, biotechnology was spearheaded by the academics; in Germany, the large firms played an active role; in Japan, it was the government; in France, it was the government in tandem with the academics and industrialists, and so on.[11] While the United States is still clearly in the lead in the integration of biotechnology in the pharmaceutical industry, in terms of scientific publications, firms in the biotechnology sectors, people employed in the biotechnology sectors, firms involved in the creation of radical innovations and so forth other countries of Europe and Japan are making determined efforts to close this gap.[12] On March 1994 the European Commission published a communication "On the Outlines of an Industrial Policy for the Pharmaceutical Industry", which is a reflection of a growing feeling that steps should be taken to promote in Europe a "research-friendly environment that rewards innovation".[13] In Japan vigorous efforts are under way to improve industrial competence in pharmaceuticals and conduct R&D in biotechnology. The leading Japanese companies, Takeda, Fujisawa, and Yamanuchi, are reported to be developing important new drugs and formulating plans to enhance significantly their global marketing potential.[14] These technological developments have made it clear that the "future competitiveness" of the top companies in the international market will be determined, in a large part, by their capacity to create and commercialize innovations.

Thus in the developed countries the integration of biotechnology in the pharmaceutical sector has been achieved through in-house R&D and market transactions, as well as strategic alliances, with the nature and degree of government intervention varying between the different countries. New firms whose R&D or manufacturing process is based entirely on biotechnology have been created. Large firms have commercialized innovations through in-house research efforts, strategic alliances, mergers, and acquisitions and outright purchase of technology.

Such integration has had four types of impact on the final market. First, it has resulted in both incremental and radical product and process innovations. The product innovations fall into three categories – diagnostics, therapeutics, and gene therapy, in increasing order of technological sophistication. Diagnostic kits are products that interact with a certain body fluid (blood, urine, and so on) to reveal the existence of a particular medical condition. Therapeutics are basically medicines, and in this case, medicines that have been produced using some biotechnology techniques. Gene therapy refers to products (and processes) that modify the genetic patrimony of certain cells of the human body to produce a desired effect. Diagnostic kits have been developed for the major diseases, but because of their limited market size, they have not made such an impact on the pharmaceutical sector as the therapeutics. Gene therapy is currently more in the realm of research rather than commercial application.

Second, it has resulted in change in the nature of the search process for the creation of new chemical entities. For instance, traditional extensive processes of screening and selection for the creation of chemical entities have been replaced by "rational drug design", whereby drugs are created through the study of chemical and biological forms at the molecular level .

Third, as was mentioned before, new firms entirely based on biotechnology have been created. This has increased not only market competition but also the industrial competence of the country concerned.

Finally, integration of biotechnology has given rise to a new organizational form for the commercialization of innovations; namely, that of strategic alliances between firms of different competencies and between firms and public laboratories. While strategic alliances have long been prevalent at the manufacturing and marketing stages, it is for the first time that such levels of cooperation are being observed at the R&D level. However, it is not yet clear as to what extent or time this organizational form will be persistent in the biotechnology sectors.

Evolution of the Indian pharmaceutical industry, 1945–1995

When India attained its independence in 1947 it had a pharmaceutical industry of only very modest size with a market of about $28.5 million.[15] There were several Indian-owned companies in the field but their operations were on a much smaller scale than those of foreign companies. The production of pharmaceuticals involves two phases: the manufacture of basic ingredients that are called "bulk drugs" and their subsequent "formulation" for the final use by consumers in the form of tablets, capsules, syrups, injectibles, drops, and sprays. No Indian company was a major factor in either field at the time of Independence and there was heavy dependence on imported foreign drugs which were marketed either by MNCs already established in India or by local agents of other MNCs that did not have a local presence. In order to reduce the dependence on imports and on Western MNCs, at least for vitally needed antibiotics, the government of India undertook large investments to establish public sector enterprises.[16] The most important among these were Hindustan Antibiotics Limited (HAL) and Indian Drugs and

Table 11.1 Market share of drug sales of the 30 leading companies in India, 1976[19]

Rank	Name of company	Market share (%)
1	Sarabhai	7.1
2	Glaxo (UK)	6.2
3	Pfizer (US)	5.9
4	Allembic	4.2
5	Hoechst (Germany)	3.6
6	Lederle (US)	2.5
7	Parke-Davis (US)	2.3
7	Abbot (US)	2.3
7	Ciba-Geigy (Swiss)	2.3
8	Sandoz (Swiss)	2.2
9	Burroughs-Wellcome (UK)	2.1
10	Boots (UK)	2.0
10	Suhrid	2.0
11	Unichem	1.9
11	E. Merck (US)	1.9
11	John Wyeth (US)	1.9
11	M&B (US)	1.9
12	SKF (US)	1.6
12	German Remedies	1.6
12	MSD	1.6
12	Warner Hindustan	1.6
12	Roche (Swiss)	1.6
12	Bey's	1.6
13	East India	1.5
14	TCF	1.4
14	IDPL	1.4
15	Himdays	1.3
15	Raptakos	1.3
16	Ranbaxy	1.2
17	Boehringer-Knoll	1.1

Pharmaceuticals Limited (IDPL). The move was useful and timely but it was not a comprehensive response to the country's healthcare needs. The Indian pharmaceutical market continued to be dominated by MNCs for nearly 30 years even after the country attained independence (see Table 11.1).

As late as 1976, among the top 20 firms which held 57.19 per cent of the pharmaceutical market, there were only four Indian firms. The foreign multinationals formulated their drugs in India, importing the bulk drugs from their home countries. It was their contention that the locally available bulk drugs were not of the desired quality. This led to drug prices that were regarded as too high by the consumers as well as by the government. In response the government introduced price control for a long list of "notified" drugs that were deemed essential. The control regime was continually opposed by both MNCs and the fledgling Indian companies. They argued that high import duties were largely responsible for pushing up prices and that price controls discouraged the flow of investment into the industry by depressing the earnings of companies.

Desirous of developing the indigenous pharmaceutical industry at a much faster pace, the Indian government enacted the Indian Patents Law in 1972. It was a landmark development and the course adopted was no different from what a far more advanced country like Japan had put in place to promote its own pharmaceutical industry.[17] The Act ensured patent protection only to production processes and not to the products themselves. Thus Indian firms were legally free to make products developed by foreign corporations as long as they involved a different manufacturing process. The Indian move, as in that of Japan, was clearly to encourage local companies to cater to the domestic market more effectively and profitably, and eventually to export their products to developing and Communist-bloc countries which did not recognize the product patents of Western countries.

Initially the multinationals did not see the new Patent Act as a threat to their market position, as they assumed that it would be beyond the technological competence of the Indian pharmaceutical companies to do "reverse engineering" and formulate products equivalent to those of the MNCs.[18] The MNCs had underestimated the capability of Indian technologists and the entrepreneurial skills of Indian businessmen, and overestimated the appeal of their brand names, for the price-conscious consumer. The consumer was quite willing to go for a lower-priced Indian product with its own brand name made by a local company. Within a few years Indian companies began increasing their market share dramatically. The long-established firm Glaxo, which had occupied the top position all along, was displaced in 1995 by the fast-growing Indian company Ranbaxy. Other MNCs also found themselves pushed lower in rankings among the top pharmaceutical firms in the country, as shown in Table 11.2 below. In 1995 the top 20 firms by market share, included 13 Indian firms and held 33 per cent of the market. The country was almost totally self-sufficient in formulations and 80 per cent self-sufficient in bulk drugs.[20]

Table 11.2 Market share of drug sales of the 20 leading companies in India, 1995[21]

Rank	Name of company	Market share
1	Ranbaxy	7.0
2	Glaxo India	4.4
3	Lupin	3.0
4	Cipla	2.7
5	Hoechst India	2.6
6	Dabur	2.4
7	Pfeizer	1.9
7	SOL Pharma	1.9
7	Ambalal Sarabhai	1.9
8	Torrent	1.8
8	Dr Reddys	1.8
8	Allembic	1.8
9	Knoll	1.7
9	HAL	n.a.
10	Kopran	1.6
10	Ipca	1.6
10	SmithKline-Beecham	1.6
10	Burroughs-Wellcome	1.6
10	Cadila	n.a.
11	Parke-Davis	1.3

India woke up to the potential of biotechnology around the same time as most countries of Western Europe. The initial move came from the government with the creation of the National Biotechnology Board (NBTB) in 1982 at the instigation of certain influential members of the academic and industrial communities. The industry was slower to react. As late as 1991, in the Department of Scientific and Industrial research's *Compendium of 100 Major In-House Research Centres*, only one company – namely, the pharmaceutical company Wockhardt LTD – mentioned biotechnology as an area of research interest. The criterion for inclusion in the compendium was R&D expenditure of $28,000 and above.

According to the *Research Profile of Biotechnology Activities in India 1993*, published by the DBT, there were only 47 companies active in biotechnology, 10 per cent of which were equipment suppliers. The latest *Directory of Biotechnology Industries and Institutions in India 1994–1995*, published by the Biotech Consortium India Ltd, indicates that there are 97 production units and 45 equipment suppliers. Despite the claim of the DBT in the foreword of its directory that the profiles "includes capital employed, turnover, import/export, manpower employed" and so on, the information given is incomplete and on several points non-existent. Information is given only on 69 of the production units, while little more than names and addresses are given for the rest. BCIL does not state what criteria it adopted to decide that a company is qualified to be included in its listing; the impression lingers that any company that sought to be included was included.[22] The *Biotech Industry Guide* released by the DBT speaks (without giving addresses or details) of 459 units active in the biotechnology sectors.

While our inquiry on the issue is still under way, we have identified 102 firms as being involved to a greater or less degree, in biotechnology, of which 43 are pharmaceutical firms, whose size and resources display considerable variance. Several of the pharmaceutical companies are also seen to have diversified into other fields like agriculture, agribusiness, chemical and environmental sectors, and even into areas of commerce totally unrelated to healthcare like power and real estate.

STRATEGY OF THE INDIAN GOVERNMENT

The strategy of the Indian government can be grouped into three stages: realization stage, building scientific competence, and reaching out to the private sector.

Stage 1: In India the push to develop the biotechnology sectors came from reputed scientists who had been brought into the administration. In 1982 Dr S. Varadarajan, then secretary of the Department of Science and Technology headed the National Biotechnology Board (NBTB). Its objectives were (1) to identify priority areas in biotechnology, (2) to identify infrastructural needs, and (3) to implement a coordinated programme to realize certain national objectives. To this end, a number of pilot programmes were proposed in the sixth (1981–1985) and seventh (1986–1990) Five Year Plans.[23] However, during its four years of existence from 1982–1986, the NBTB seems to have achieved only objectives (1) and (2). The pharmaceutical industry did not figure high in the thinking of the board, and the non-association of any competent scientist or industrialist from the pharmaceutical sector in its deliberations had its own consequences.

Stage 2: In 1986, the NBTB was replaced by a separate government department called the Department of Biotechnology (DBT). It functioned under the aegis of the Ministry of Science and Technology. The main reason for this evolution seems to have been the realization that biotechnology is a generic technology whose progress requires the development of a variety of competencies in a variety of scientific disciplines. In order to achieve this coordinated development, an agency working in tandem with the Ministry of Science and Technology was deemed necessary. It set out to implement the objectives of the earlier body, such as development of competence in genetic engineering, control or eradication of major communicable diseases through creation of vaccines, increase in food production (especially milk), attainment of self-sufficiency in edible oils, and creation of scientific competence in techniques that were not capital intensive. The establishment of the DBT served as a signal that the government considered biotechnology to be a priority area for development. It was welcomed by academics and national laboratories as well as industrialists.

The first target was to create a core of researchers competent in biotechnology. Grants were given to the network of research institutions and university departments to undertake biotechnology-related projects. Grants were also provided to selected teaching and research institutes partially supported by the government, such as the Indian Institute of Sciences, Indian Institutes of Technology, All India Institute of Medical Sciences, National Chemical Laboratory, Tata Institute of Energy Research, Tata Institute of Fundamental Research, and so on. The DBT also participated in the creation of new institutions such as the National Institute of Immunology, the Centre for Cellular and Molecular Biology, National Facility for Animal Tissue and Cell Culture, and the International Centre for Genetic Engineering (in collaboration with UNIDO). No grants were, however, available from the DBT for the modest R&D establishments that were being set up by some pharmaceutical majors.

Stage 3: Finding that the response of the industrial establishments was quite modest and driven by its own rhetoric on the market economy, the government of India promoted a public company known as the Biotech Consortium India Ltd (BCIL) in December 1990. It was set up jointly by the DBT, government-sponsored financial institutions like the Industrial Development Bank of India, the Industrial Credit and Investment Corporation of India and "about 30 industries, mainly in the private sector". BCIL was to "foster and promote a close and productive linkage between industry and

R&D institutions (including universities) to convert the concepts and ideas in the field of biotechnology into products to enable them to reach the market". It would assist "financially or otherwise the innovation, ... "development" ... and commercialization of biotechnology". In a similar fashion it would assist in the setting up of research facilities or projects in the biotechnology field and "sell the know-how generated ... on certain conditions". It was to fulfil the same functions as the venture-capital companies in the US; that is, promote the creation of firms by not only providing venture capital but also the complementary competencies required by scientists to set up firms. While BCIL has had some success in promoting awareness about global developments in biotechnology relating to industry, it has yet to receive from Indian pharmaceutical companies the attention that had been hoped for.

Impact of government strategy on the integration of biotechnology in the pharmaceutical sector

From the above analysis we are led to conclude that, while the Indian government has played a decisive role in the creation of "awareness" of the potential of biotechnology and the development of scientific competence, it has had a very limited direct impact on the integration of biotechnology in Indian industry or the creation of industrial competence at large. Between 1988 and 1993, the DBT approved 295 projects and committed funds worth $11.5 million for research, of which four technologies have been transferred to the private sector. Infrastructural investment was undertaken to develop a critical mass of manpower with scientific competence and the final product markets were controlled to benefit the consumers, but there remained an enormous lacuna in the effort required to transform scientific competence into technological competence. There were no well-thought-out, practical goals set nor were plans made for the effective utilization of competent manpower to reach such goals. Prioritization, selection of the most important areas, concentration of resources and personnel, and accountability for fulfilment of tasks remained inadequately tackled. While this indispensable intermediate exercise to transform scientific competence into technological competence was largely skipped, the government concerned itself with the final product markets and fiscal measures such as price control and distribution to "benefit the common people".[24]

Table 11.3 Patents obtained by public research institutions

Type of institution	Patents in 1980–85	Patents in 1985–90	Patents applied for or obtained in 1990–95
CSIR	0	9	1
ICAR	0	0	2
ICMR	0	0	0
Universities	0	0	0
Autonomous institutions	0	12 all by NII	1
Industrial labs	0	0	1

University–firm linkages remained very poor. No reform of the public sector research establishment was undertaken. The government-run research labs had a poor record of commercialization of innovations, as shown in Table 11.3. Furthermore, the table shows that most of the technology transfers from public laboratories to the private sector have been due to the institute NII (the National Institute of Immunology), which was created during the 1980s to build competence in biotechnology. In order to stimulate public research–firm linkages, from recent times, all public labs have to earn one-third of their projected budget through contracts with industry. Though the elite institutes of research have been moderately successful in generating funds through links with the industry, this has not been realized for many of the public laboratories. An examination of the biotechnology directory issued by the DBT also reveals that most of the laboratories are working on a variety of topics and problems, which in itself indicates that there is no strategy of development of a particular core competence by each institute.

The government did not recognize any responsibility to promote collaboration between the public sector laboratories and the private sector firms, unlike in advanced countries. Neither did it involve the industrial community in the making of strategy for biotechnology. In its role as the promoter of "socially relevant" research and production, the government neglected to involve industrialists from the public and private sectors in the formulation and implementation of its strategy.

Finally, the thrust of government strategy was on agriculture rather than healthcare, because of the former's intrinsic importance to the economy and the existence of a good record of indigenous research accomplishment. The meagre research output of pharmaceutical enterprises and the minor role of pharmaceuticals-related research in the large government-supported research establishment had their inevitable impact on the resources made available to the pharmaceutical industry. There was also none from the industry itself to make the point that a determined effort should be made for developing new drugs through biotechnological techniques, even for the major diseases afflicting the people of the Third World.

TECHNOLOGY STRATEGY OF INDIAN FIRMS

The term "technology strategy" can have various definitions.[25] We refer to technology strategy as the organization of a firm's research and product portfolios in order to achieve a particular set of objectives. In terms of formulation of technology strategy, the Indian firms did not inherit any tradition of creation of incremental or radical innovations through public or private research. Commercialization of research through creation of innovations was virtually an alien concept to the top bureaucrats, public researchers, and firms. Captains of industry, with very few exceptions, regarded themselves as "practical" men and were far more interested in surefire ways of making quick profits than in committing funds for R&D where returns were distant and quite uncertain. Industrialists had little contact with researchers in public institutes and university departments, whom they regarded as denizens of ivory towers engaged in work of no immediate relevance for industry. Since the Indian government had presided over what was in many respects a "command economy", as distinct from a market economy, the industrialists were deeply involved with getting permits, licences, and quotas, and clamouring for fiscal and customs duty concessions for themselves.

That was the state of affairs that has begun to change only in the last few years. The transition towards a market economy began by the renewal and reduction of many controls and regulations, and the ardent solicitation of foreign investments. This in turn led the Indian firms in the pharmaceutical industry to formulate strategies to take advantage of the growth of the domestic market, to seek export markets, to meet competition from existing Indian firms and new entrants, as well as from MNCs, and to prepare themselves for the implications of a change in the patent law under which the industry had been able to make rapid progress. Thus, while the pharmaceutical giants of Europe and the USA examined the possibilities of integrating biotechnology in the context of their established research centres and their tradition of investing in R&D to try to create technological innovations in the medium run, Indian firms started from the position of using R&D as a means to promote their competitiveness in the very short run. R&D that Indian companies were willing to undertake was aimed at technology absorption, improvement of processes in imported technology, and import substitution through reverse engineering of items not covered by patent under Indian law and of those whose patents had expired.

In what follows we identify six different types of technology strategies of Indian firms in the pharmaceutical sector. Each is illustrated by one or more actual cases, the information on which was obtained through some direct interviews with industrialists and government officials, annual reports, government surveys, business and trade journals, and secondary data. The strategies are not to be regarded as mutually exclusive, since many Indian companies pursue more than one of the strategies.

Technological competence without significant process innovation or new product development

There are three types of firms that engage in little or no R&D while being technologically adequate for their overall objectives (by "little investment" we refer to less than 1 per cent of turnover invested in R&D): (1) small-scale units; (2) mid-size firms which concentrate on their production and market strategy; and (3) mid-size firms which produce or market the patented products of Western pharmaceuticals. As an optimistic estimate, except for about 100 firms, the rest of the pharmaceutical industry falls into this category.

Small-scale sector

The firms in the small-scale sector have neither the resources nor the interest to invest in R&D. They survive because of the reservation of certain drugs for the small-scale sector and their lower cost of production owing to lower overheads and wages paid. These small units then sell their product to the medium-size and large firms. As intermediate sellers they have no incentive to invest in R&D and their survival strategy consists of maintaining their present buyers and seeking additional ones.

Focus on production and marketing

Many of the medium-sized companies which have substantially larger resources than those in the small-scale sector stick to a strategy aimed at maintaining and increasing market share through expanding capacity for their profitable products, improving production efficiency, cutting down costs, and improving their marketing practices. Even many of the medium-sized companies maintain their market share because of their cost-efficient production and enhance their market positions through their production and marketing strategy rather than through investments in R&D. For instance, IPCA laboratories is among the top 20 firms in India in terms of market share while spending about 0.5 per cent of its turnover on R&D. Its core competence lies in the production of anti-malarial drugs, in which it controls 42 per cent of the market share. Its substantial growth and market share are explained by the growth of its export and its backward integration from formulation to bulk drugs.

Strategic R&D and manufacturing alliances with foreign firms

The chairman of the large and fast-growing Piramal group, Ajay Piramal, frankly acknowledges[26] that margins in the pharmaceutical industry do not warrant commitment of his company's resources to R&D. For him a much more profitable course for growth and prosperity is to continue to make its range of bulk drugs and to seek alliances with suitable foreign partners in order to get access to their patented products for marketing in India.

Usually, an Indian company's criterion for entering into an international strategic alliance is access to the foreign company's patented drugs to be produced and marketed in India under its name, or access to the commercial network of the foreign company to export the Indian product abroad. On the other hand, in order to attract foreign companies as an outsourcing base, the Indian unit has to signal its quality through gaining regulatory approval from a foreign country, usually a US FDA approval. It can also offer the use of an extensive sales network to market the foreign product or a jointly created product. For instance, Piralmal acquired Roche products and is marketing drugs patented by Roche while negotiating a possible alliance with Bristol, Myers & Squibb.

Entry into biotechnology through strategic alliances

There are also dedicated biotechnology firms which have been created with foreign collaboration. For instance, the company Transgene Vaccine is developing a hepatitis B vaccine in India with imported technology from the German company Braun Biotech. Another DBF, Reproductive Biotechnologies Pvt, is developing a contraceptive vaccine in collaboration with an American company Zonagen, using the latter's patented technology.[27] There are many who have diversified into biotechnology through selling a foreign product. Both public sector (such as IDPLs) and private sector companies (Astro Drug, Lupin, Dr Reddy's labs) are marketing diagnostic kits made abroad.

Technological competence with process innovation but not new product development

These refer to a set of middle sized companies whose competitive advantage lie in their ability to do "reverse-engineering" or bring down costs through process development. The companies make their profit through independent production of an already discovered drug. In the bulk drug market, prices of certain commodities systematically fall following "sprints" in the technological race. For instance, a competent Indian bulk drug manufacturer may discover how to make an already discovered Western drug. By bringing the price down and being the first to sell on the market, the innovating firm rakes in a winner's margin. This puts into motion an intense race among other technologically competent firms, and the prices fall further as more and more bulk drug manufacturers copy the process. The companies which manage to innovate in the second or third rounds obtain lower margins. Thus speed of introduction of a "me too" version is crucial to a firm's success. Companies in this category evolve their strategy taking this phenomenon into account.

Several top-ranking Indian pharmaceutical firms owe their success to effective implementation of such a strategy. Cipla, holding the fourth largest market share in the Indian market, produces, among other drugs, "Vincristine", an anti-cancer drug.[28] India used to export dried leaves of *Vinca rosea*, and out of them Eli Lilly used to make Vincristine in capsule form, sold in India for $2.28 each. Cipla improved and scaled up this known process to make tablets costing less than a dollar and also exported the drug to some foreign countries.

Another example of a company that has successfully developed its own processes to produce drugs patented in the West is SOL Pharmaceuticals. It claims to have research staff working around the clock. It was the first in India to take up commercial production of some of the new molecules like Astemizole and Fluconazole. SOL also copied some new molecules like Lomefloxacin, Lansoprazole, and Amlodipine, reducing their prices by half.[29]

A firm that has been attracting praise for its enterprise and dynamism is Dr Reddy's Laboratories. It developed new process for certain drugs that were initially discovered and sold by foreign multinationals, forcing them to lower their prices as it developed cheaper substitutes. Among the successful products are Quinolone, an antibacterial drug, Ciprofloxacin, an antityphoid drug, Enam, a blood-pressure-lowering drug, and Omex, an anti-ulcer drug.

These firms have not shown a willingness at this stage to integrate biotechnology in their R&D efforts. The most technologically competent firms among them take note of the fact that an intense technological race is ahead of them to replicate about 40 Western drugs with a present market value of more than $15 billion that are going off patents in the next five years.[30] They are gearing themselves for the race by strengthening their R&D centres, expanding their production capacities, and formulating marketing strategies.

These firms have not diversified into biotechnology thus far because their core competence is in organic and synthetic chemistry and not molecular biology. They perceive the costs of diversifying and developing core competence in biotechnology to be rather high. Thus their short-term strategy is to tap the tremendous market potential of replicating the already discovered drugs based on chemical technology, that will go off patents.[31] They may consider integrating biotechnology once the opportunities for making quick and high profit from processing already known drugs are exhausted.

Technological competence with process innovation and new product development

Among the top 50 pharmaceutical firms there are a few which have committed resources to maintain forward-looking R&D centres staffed by persons with the technological competence to engage in efforts to create innovations. The choice for creating product innovations comprises four possibilities: (1) creating the least sophisticated product innovations in biotechnology, namely, diagnostics; (2) creating new chemical entities to compete at the international level; (3) investing in the creation of products for the Third World, that the Western pharmaceutical companies are not strategically interested in, such as therapeutics for tuberculosis, malaria, filariasis, leprosy, snakebites, and so on; and (4) diversifying into biotechnology through a sector with quick returns such as plant or tissue culture.

Creating diagnostic kits

Diagnostics are the easiest types of biotechnology product innovations to commercialize in the pharmaceutical sector, because they are subject to much less stringent regulatory rules, owing to the fact that they only involve tests with body fluids and are not imbibed by humans. The size of the market for diagnostics is smaller than for therapeutics, but their cost of production is also lower and they require substantially less time for commercialization. Moreover, the major thrust of the DBT programme in healthcare also is research in immunodiagnostics, which has resulted in the creation of diagnostic kits by a number of public laboratories. These were then transferred to private sector companies, making this sector distinct for its successful record of transfer of technology from public laboratories to private firms.

Table 11.4 Transfer of technology from public laboratories to Indian firms

Laboratory	Product developed by laboratory	Firm to which it is transferred
NII	Diagnostic kit for liver abscess	Cadilla
NII	Diagnostic kit for blood grouping	Cadilla
NII	Leprosy immunomodulator	Cadilla
MGIIMS	Diagnostic kit for filariassia	Cadilla
NII	Diagnostic kit for hepatitis B	Lupin s
NII	Diagnostic kit for typhoid fever	Lupin
Rajasthan Univ.	Novel peptide from bitter gourd	Lupin
NII	Diagnostic kit for pregnancy detection	Ranbaxy (marketed)
NII	Animal birth control injection	Kapi
CDRI	Diagnostic kit for Leishmanissla	Span diagnostics
CDRI	Phenyl acetyl carbinol from benzaldehyde	Altus
CFB (centre for biotechnology)	F-MOC derivatives of amino acids	Atul products
IMTECH	Improved yeast grain for alchohol production	VMSRF

Ranbaxy, the number one Indian company in the pharmaceutical market, is possibly the best prepared for the integration of biotechnology. It has developed a high-class in-house R&D division which, in earlier years, enabled the company to launch several products through reverse engineering. Ranbaxy attracted attention in the global market by developing a process for an advanced Cephalosporin and getting it patented in the US though Eli Lilly had patented several stages in the process of the drug. The success of Ranbaxy's product based on quality and price had led Eli Lilly to make an agreement with Ranbaxy for joint R&D and a joint venture. Confident of its strength in traditional organic chemistry, Ranbaxy publicly made known its determination to commit funds for research in biotechnology that could lead to innovations. Ranbaxy is preparing to launch its own diagnostic kits for blood grouping, pregnancy tests, AIDS, and stem cell based therapy.[32]

Lupin, which has the third largest market share in India, also holds 60 per cent of the global market for the anti-TB drug Ethambutol. "Their Ethambutol process is so efficient that even the original discoverer Lederle is buying the bulk drug from Lupin".[33] It spends about 6.5 per cent of its sales revenue on R&D against an industry average of 2 per cent.[34] It has developed some products from technology transferred from Indian research institutes. Lupin's biotech division has launched an indigenous diagnostic kit for AIDS and is working on diagnostic kits for TB and hepatitis. Lupin will also be marketing similar kits made by the Italian firm Sorin.

Creating new chemical entities

Another type of product innovation for which the cost of commercialization is relatively low is new chemical entities. Among those that seek to create new chemical entities, there are not only big firms renowned for their technological capabilities like Dr Reddy's Labs, but also a handful of lesser-known technological innovators. For instance, a relatively little-known enterprise named Malladi Drugs and Pharmaceuticals is stated to be one of only two major producers in the world of Ephedrine, the other being Knolls Ltd in Germany.[35] Established only in 1980 by a research-minded chemical engineer, Malladi owes its success to its R&D capability, that had been systematically developed since its founding. Currently, with the help of the National Research Development Corporation, it is engaged in the developmental and clinical studies of a drug that could dissolve blood clots in about one-tenth of the time taken by the two foreign drugs that are currently in use. If clinical trials are successful and if the multinationals do not come up earlier with a blockbuster, Malladi Drugs might become the first Indian pharmaceutical company to have an important life-saving innovation with a market of about $700 million.

Creating products for developing countries

Kopran, the fifteenth-ranking company in the Indian market, is the largest producer of the antibiotic Amoxycillin trihydrate in Asia. It achieved this position through development and improvement of its final product. Though its turnover in 1994 was $57 million, it has only recently invested about $2.8 million in a research facility. The main objective of its R&D unit will be the creation of new molecules of therapeutic value for tropical and water-borne diseases, for which a large market exists in the Third World.[36]

Diversifying into non-healthcare biotechnology

Cadilla laboratories, among the top 20 pharmaceutical firms, has recently diversified into biotechnology. But the biotechnology application is not for the health sector but in tissue culture (with Dutch collaboration) and aquaculture. Its R&D centre, however, intends to engage in basic research in biotechnology and immunosuppressants.[37]

Technically competent R&D boutiques

These refer to a few dedicated biotechnology firms, often created by public laboratory researchers to do contract research or contract production for other firms. They have shown themselves to be competent and knowledgeable in a few specific areas of science and cater to niche markets. Two interesting examples known to us are Avra Labs and Bangalore Genei.[38] Avra Labs was created by A.V. Rama Rao, former director of the Indian Institute of Chemical Technology, with the financial support of the Daichi group and a renowned American scientist. The company has received contracts from American companies active in biotechnology such as Monsanto, Cytomid, and Chantel. Bangalore Genei was formed by T. Babu, who had been an associate professor at the Tata Institute of Fundamental Research. It produces speciality chemicals for Indian and foreign firms in a sophisticated R&D centre.

CONCLUSIONS ON THE INTEGRATION OF BIOTECHNOLOGY IN THE PHARMACEUTICAL SECTOR

In this chapter it was shown that in terms of either scientific knowledge or technological competence, there is no dearth of usable talent in India. The government has contributed substantially to the creation of scientific competence by investing in the setting up of a core group of research institutions. However, in spite of the existence of scientific competence, integration of biotechnology in the pharmaceutical industry is very marginal. Furthermore, the analysis of the different technology strategies of the Indian firms reveals that the extent of integration of biotechnology in a pharmaceutical firm (with few exceptions) depends on two factors: (1) its market share and profitability; and (2) its network with foreign firms. Firms among the top 30 have diversified into biotechnology through production of diagnostics or non-healthcare projects yielding quick returns, like tissue culture. A handful of dedicated biotechnology firms have been created by researchers, sustaining themselves substantially through their contracts with foreign firms. Thus, even though for a firm in the Indian pharmaceutical industry technological competence is essential both for medium-term and long-term survival, neither the market structure nor the market competition have been significantly affected by the integration of biotechnology, which in itself has been quite feeble.

Three reasons may be proposed to explain the above phenomenon of slow progress in the integration of biotechnology despite the availability of scientific talent at a cost lower than in advanced countries: the nature of the technology, inadequate financial resources, and lack of networks connecting the various types of agents needed to commercialize the new technology.

Indian firms over the years had invested in gaining knowledge of the chemical technology of creating bulk drugs, and the top tier firms had "learnt greatly by doing", improving upon the process technology, bringing down their prices, without investing in "formal R&D centres." These firms were confronted with biotechnology, a set of techniques that were new, different, and much more complex to integrate because of the increased multidisciplinary nature of the team required to create a product. In this context, given the costs of integrating biotechnology and the uncertainty involved in the commercialization process, many firms tended to shy away from diverting large funds to R&D in biotechnology even when they could see that they could not go on forever replicating MNC products that were off patents.

This led then to the second problem confronting a less developed country like India, where financial markets are more institutional and risk-averse. Very few firms can command the financial resources necessary to invest in R&D. The government has not done much to ameliorate this problem, restricting its attention to the two ends of the spectrum of the commercialization process. It has invested in the creation of scientific competence and it regulates the final market to benefit the consumer. There has been no grand programme as in Japan or France of promoting research consortia or university–firm collaborations. Good-quality scientific competence is created by a small number of elite institutions staffed by persons of high quality and dedication. The phenomenon of strategic alliances between firms of various sizes and competencies for pre-competitive R&D or commercialization of innovations, which so marks the biotechnology sectors in developed countries, is thus far absent here. The only firms that can do R&D and integrate the new technology, besides the top firms, are those that can get help from abroad. In the latter category we find Indian firms distributing foreign products, conducting contract research or producing with foreign technology and machines. Thus, without the requisite financial resources, alternatives to sharing risk and costs through financial markets, government programmes, or strategic alliances for R&D, integration of biotechnology in the Indian pharmaceutical industry cannot gather momentum.

The implications of the above are not serious in the short run, because anyway the foreign multinationals will sell the radical innovations developed in their country, in India, at a price that the Indian consumer can afford. But in the long run, it will represent an under-utilization of scientific talent due to lack of sufficient incentives. If creative means can be found to establish stable and productive networks between firms, researchers, and financial markets, to share the risks and costs of creating innovations, the Indian pharmaceutical industry will go further in strengthening its industrial competence.

NOTES

[1] Institut National de la Recherche Agronomique (INRA) Grenoble, France.

[2] International Affairs Research Group, New Delhi, India.

[3] "For the first time scientists have been released from the slow and uncertain techniques of trying to improve on nature by breeding mutant
strains, and instead have at their fingertips techniques which enable
them to do this with a surprising degree of certitude," M. Sharp (1989)
"Biotechnology in Britain and France: The Evolution of Policy", in *Strategies for New Technology: Case Studies from France and Britain*, edited
by M. Sharp and P. Holmes (London: Philip Alan) pp. 119–159.

[4] *Table* Top ten biotechnology drugs on the market from "A Survey
of Biotechnology and Genetics", *The Economist*, 25 February 1995,
pp. 1–18

Product	Developer	Marketer	Net sales, 1993 $m
Neupogen	Amgen	Amgen	719
Epogen	Amgen	Amgen	587
Intron A	Biogen	Schering-Plough	572
Humulin	Genentech	Eli Lilly	560
Procrit	Amgen	Ortho Biotech	500
Engerix B	Genentech	SmithKline Beecham	480
RecombinNAK HB	Chiron	Merck	245
Activase	Genentech	Genentech	236
Protropin	Genentech	Genentech	217
Roferon-A	Genentech	Hoffman-La Roche	172
Total sales of top ten			**4,288**
Total industry sales			**7,700**

[5] Turcq, D. (1995) "India and China: Asia's Non-identical Twins", *McKinsey
Quarterly*, no. 2.

[6] Centre for Monitoring Indian Economy, Economic Intelligence Service
(January 1996) "Drugs and Pharmaceuticals", *India's Industrial Sector*,
Bombay.

[7] According to Turq, it is "1/20 to 1/30 of US prices".

[8] Centre for Monitoring the Indian Economy (April 1996), "The Indian
Corporate Sector", New Delhi, A–27.

[9] Office of Technology Assessment (OTA), (1991) *Biotechnology in a Global
Economy*, US Congress Office of Technology Assessment, Washington,
DC, US Government Printing Office.

[10] Grabowski, H. and Vernon, J. (1994) "Innovation and Structural Change
in Pharmaceuticals and Biotechnology", *Industrial and Corporate Change*,
3 (2) pp. 435–449. Pisano, G.P. (1991) "The Governance of Innovation:
Vertical Integration and Collaborative Arrangements in the Biotechnology Industry", *Research Policy*, 20, pp. 237–249.

[11] Bull A.T., G. Holt and M.D. Lilly (1982) *Biotechnology: International*

Trends and Perspectives, OECD, Paris; Office of Technology Assessment (OTA) (1991) *Biotechnology in a Global Economy*, US Congress Office of Technology Assessment, Washington, DC, US Government Printing Office; Orsenigo, L., (1989), *"The emergence of biotechnology"*, London, Printer Publishers.

[12] *European Biotech 96 Volatility and Value* (1996) Ernst & Young's Third Annual Report on the European Biotechnology Industry. *Biotech 96 Pursuing Sustainability* (1996) Ernst & Young's Tenth Annual Report on the Biotechnology Industry; Joly, D. and Ramani, S.V. (1996) 'Technology Creation in the Biotechnology Sectors: The French Connection', *International Journal of Technology Management, Special issue on Access to Technological and Financial Resources for SME Innovation*, 12 (7/8) pp. 830–848.

[13] Cueni, T. "Pharmaceutical Innovation: Can Europe Compete?" reproduced by Pfizer Forum Europe, as an advertisement in *The Economist*, 25 February 1995. Cueni is Executive Director of Pharmaceutical Partners for Better Healthcare, which describes itself as a group representing 40 major research-based pharmaceutical companies worldwide.

[14] Probert, J. (1994) "Japanese Pharmaceutical Firms: Players in the European Market?" in Helmut Schutte, *The Global Competitiveness of the Asian Firm*, New York: St Martin's Press, p. 263.

[15] Ahmad, H. (1988) *Technological Development in Drugs and Pharmaceutical Industry in India*, Navrang, New Delhi.

[16] Singh, S. (1985) *Multinational Corporations and Indian Drug Industry*, Criterion Publications, New Delhi, p. 127.

[17] The Japanese, bowing to Western pressure, changed their patent law in 1976. Till the early 1980s Japan banned foreign firms from applying alone for the first stage of regulatory approval and required that the clinical testing for a drug should be carried out on Japanese citizens (Probert, pp. 238, 240).

[18] Redwood, H. (1994) *New Horizons in India*, Oldwicks Press Ltd, Suffolk, England, pp. 15–22.

[19] Kolte, S.B. (1977) "Prices and Profits in the Pharmaceutical Industry", PhD thesis, Poona University, 1977.

[20] Centre for Monitoring the Indian Economy (January 1996); Economic Intelligence Service, Bombay, *India's Industrial Sector*.

[21] Ibid.

[22] In the course of interviewing the firms in the directory a number of firms stated to the author that they plan to enter into biotechnology but have not done so as yet.

[23] Sasson, A. (1993) *Biotechnologies in Developing Countries: Present and Future*, vol. I, UNESCO publication.

[24] Opinions expressed by government officials in interviews.

[25] Adler, P.S. (1989) "Technology Strategy: A Guide to the Literature", *Research in Technological Innovation, Management and Policy*, vol. 4, 25–151.

[26] Carvalho, B. (1996) "A New Prescription for Prosperity", *Business World*, 6–19 March, pp. 70–71.

[27] Dibner, M.D., Sollod, C.J., and Sizemore, T.D. (1996) "India, despite

Limitations, Strives for Proficiency in Modern Biotech R&D", *Genetic Engineering News*, 16 (4) 15 February.

28 Shivanand, K. (1994) "Leaders in Technology", *Business India*, 4–17, July, pp. 52–60.

29 Speech by representative of Sol Pharmaceuticals Ltd at the 9th National Conference on In-house R&D in Industry, New Delhi, 28–29 November 1985.

30 "Potent Beyond Expiry Date", *Economic Times*, 2 October 1995.

31 "Dr Reddy's Laboratories", *Business India*, 12–25 September 1994, p. 68.

32 Shivanand, K., "Leaders in Technology", *Business India*, 4–17 July 1994, pp. 52–60.

33 Ibid.

34 (1995) "The Smart Investor", *Business Standard*, 5 November.

35 (February 1995) "Small Firms with Big Ideas", *Business World*, pp. 141–142.

36 (September 1995), "Banking on the Nameless", *Global*, New Delhi, pp. 38–40.

37 (1995) "Parting Ways", *Business India*, 19 June–2 July.

38 Hari, P. (1996) "A New Crucible of Capitalism", *Business World*, 6–19 March.

Index

90 0387677 0

SEVEN DAY LOAN

This book is to be returned on
or before the date stamped below

UNIVERSITY OF PLYMOUTH

PLYMOUTH LIBRARY

Tel: (01752) 232323
This book is subject to recall if required by another reader
Books may be renewed by phone
CHARGES WILL BE MADE FOR OVERDUE BOOKS